Kansas City vs. Oakland

SPORT AND SOCIETY

Series Editors
Aram Goudsouzian
Jaime Schultz

Founding Editors
Benjamin G. Rader
Randy Roberts

*A list of books in the series appears
at the end of this book.*

KANSAS CITY VS. OAKLAND

THE
BITTER SPORTS RIVALRY THAT DEFINED AN ERA

MATTHEW C. EHRLICH

UNIVERSITY OF
ILLINOIS PRESS
Urbana, Chicago, and Springfield

Library of Congress Cataloging-in-Publication Data
Names: Ehrlich, Matthew C., 1962– author.
Title: Kansas City vs. Oakland : the bitter sports
    rivalry that defined an era / Matthew C. Ehrlich.
Other titles: Kansas City versus Oakland
Description: [Urbana] : University of Illinois Press,
    [2019] | Series: Sport and society | Includes
    bibliographical references and index.
Identifiers: LCCN 2019000620| ISBN 9780252042652
    (hardcover : alk. paper) | ISBN 9780252084492
    (pbk. : alk. paper)
Subjects: LCSH: Kansas City Chiefs (Football
    team)—History—20th century. | Oakland Raiders
    (Football team)—History—20th century. | Kansas
    City Royals (Baseball team)—History—20th
    century. | Oakland Athletics (Baseball team)—
    History—20th century. | Sports rivalries—United
    States—History—20th century. | Sports—Social
    aspects—United States.
Classification: LCC GV956.K35 E47 2019 |
    DDC 796.04/40973—dc23
    LC record available at https://lccn.loc.gov
    /2019000620
Ebook ISBN 9780252051500

Contents

Acknowledgments

THANKS TO THE STAFFS of the following research facilities: the History, Philosophy, and Newspaper Library and the Rare Book and Manuscript Library, University of Illinois at Urbana-Champaign; Missouri Valley Special Collections, Kansas City Public Library; the Oakland History Room, Oakland Public Library; the Newspapers and Microforms Library and Institute of Governmental Studies Library, University of California, Berkeley; the Giamatti Research Center, National Baseball Hall of Fame, Cooperstown, New York; the Milstein Microform Reading Room, New York Public Library; and the Paley Center for Media, New York.

Daniel Nasset steadfastly supported this book from the start, and I thank him and the rest of the staff at the University of Illinois Press, including Marika Christofides, Tad Ringo, and Kevin Cunningham. Thanks as well to Aram Goudsouzian and Jaime Schultz for accepting the book for the press's Sport and Society series. Jerald Podair, Victoria Johnson, Travis Vogan, and an anonymous reader provided valuable feedback. Brittany Bradley at the Oakland Museum of California and Matthew Lutts at the Associated Press assisted with images. Dennis McClendon at Chicago CartoGraphics prepared the maps. Walt Evans copyedited the final manuscript.

My late father, George Ehrlich, was an urban historian in his own right, and I am pleased to cite his work here. My late mother, Mila Jean Smith Ehrlich, was a lifelong Kansas Citian and proud of her hometown. This book is dedicated to her memory.

Kansas City vs. Oakland

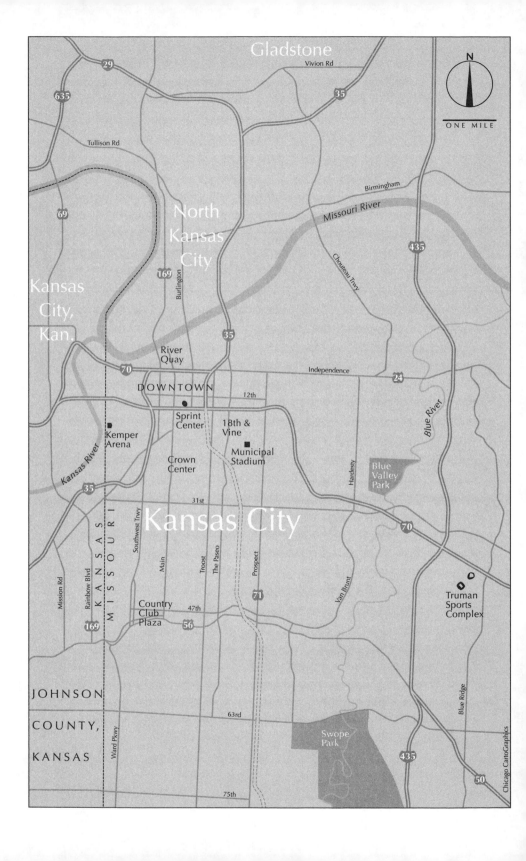

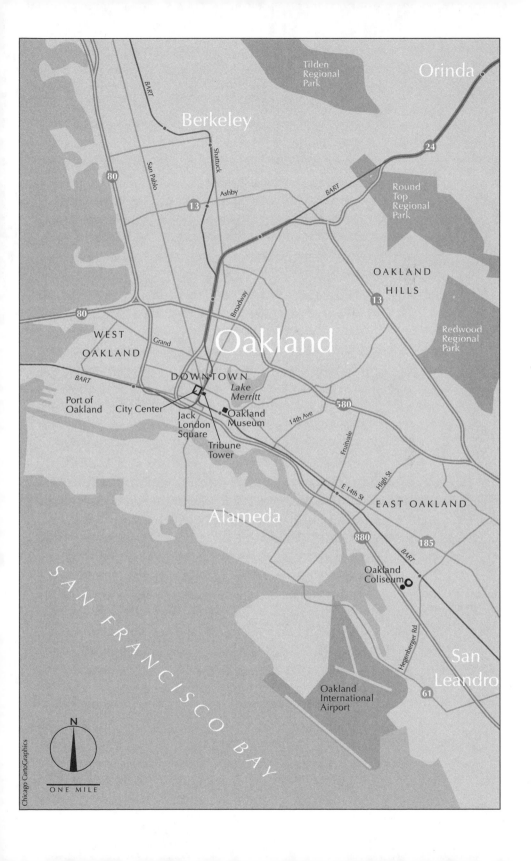

Introduction

"SOMEHOW IT ALWAYS SEEMS to come down to Kansas City and Oakland, as if God only follows those two football teams."[1]

So wrote sportswriter Wells Twombly about the Kansas City Chiefs–Oakland Raiders game of November 1, 1970. He was not being completely serious, of course. Twombly, a columnist for the *San Francisco Examiner,* was one of a new and irreverent breed of writers who had come of age during the 1960s and who delighted in seeing through the sanctity and self-seriousness of big-league sports. "Games are not life-and-death struggles; they're entertainment," he declared.[2] But as entertainment, nothing could quite compare to what would happen when the Raiders met the Chiefs in Kansas City's Municipal Stadium that autumn day. And for the two teams' home cities, the game took place amid much bigger struggles—even life-and-death ones.

The Kansas City Chiefs were the defending champions of professional football, having defeated the Minnesota Vikings the previous January in Super Bowl IV. The Chiefs had made it to the Super Bowl despite not even having won their own division during the regular season. The division championship belonged to the Oakland Raiders, who had beaten the Chiefs twice during the 1969 season. But in its final year of independent existence, the American Football League instituted a wild-card playoff, allowing the Chiefs into the postseason where Kansas City downed Oakland 17–7 for the AFL title. While the Chiefs went to New Orleans to beat the National Football League champion Minnesota

Vikings, the Raiders stayed home, bitterly disappointed. "I don't like Kansas City," said the Raiders' Jim Otto. "We never have liked them."[3]

The feeling was mutual, directed not only from the Chiefs toward the Raiders but also from the city of Kansas City toward the city of Oakland. Three years earlier, following a lengthy courtship, Oakland had lured away Kansas City's major league baseball team, the A's (short for Athletics). Owner Charlie Finley had been trying to escape Kansas City ever since he had bought the A's. At one point, he had even threatened to move the team to a cow pasture in rural Missouri. When baseball's American League finally permitted Finley to transfer the A's to Oakland, the sentiment in Kansas City was summed up in a wisecrack attributed both to *Kansas City Star* sports editor Joe McGuff and to U.S. senator Stuart Symington of Missouri: "Oakland is the luckiest city since Hiroshima."[4]

As it happened, Oakland by 1970 had reason to feel fortunate. The A's had been consistent losers in Kansas City, but as soon as they moved to California with a young and talented group of players obtained by Finley, they began to win. Their eighty-nine victories in 1970 had been the most by the franchise in nearly forty years. In September they had called up twenty-one-year-old pitcher Vida Blue from the minor leagues; he promptly threw a no-hitter for the A's. As for the Raiders, they had been professional football's winningest team over the previous three years, driven by franchise head Al Davis and the team motto "Pride and Poise." Even with the AFL championship loss to the Chiefs, the Raiders had beaten Kansas City in seven out of their last nine meetings. According to the *Sporting News*, they were football's "hottest franchise" heading into the 1970 season.[5]

The Raiders and A's played their home games in what one Oakland civic leader proudly called "the greatest sports complex in the world."[6] The Oakland–Alameda County Coliseum Complex had opened in 1966 and featured a stadium for football and baseball plus an arena for hockey and basketball. The arena already hosted the Seals of the National Hockey League, and soon the Warriors of the National Basketball Association would move there as well. The city also boasted a new terminal at what was dubbed the Oakland International Airport; new shipping container facilities on the east side of San Francisco Bay that were rapidly transforming Oakland into one of the world's busiest ports; and a new combined art, science, and history museum that had been described as "the most brilliant concept of an urban museum in America."[7] For the local Chamber of Commerce, which was closely aligned with the *Oakland Tribune*, such projects promised to distinguish Oakland as "the West's most imaginative city of the '70s."[8]

There were heady times in Kansas City too. When the Chiefs had flown home after the Super Bowl, they had landed at the new Kansas City International Airport being built northwest of downtown. It was intended to become "the dominating air terminal of Mid-America."[9] The Chiefs then rode by motorcade past as many as 175,000 people to a rally at the city's Liberty Memorial, which was next door to another major construction project. Crown Center—created by Kansas City's Hallmark Cards—would encompass hotels, apartments, offices, and shops. The *Kansas City Times* (which was the *Kansas City Star*'s morning paper) pronounced it a "model urban community" and "national showcase" in the making.[10] But for the Chiefs as they held the Super Bowl trophy aloft before their cheering fans, the most important project of all was taking shape miles away on Kansas City's far east side. A sports complex with separate football and baseball stadiums would become home to the Chiefs and the city's new major league baseball team, the Royals. The football stadium would seat more than 78,000 people, a vast increase over the capacity of the Chiefs' current home, and season tickets in the new, unfinished facility would sell out rapidly.[11]

The Super Bowl victory had vindicated Chiefs owner Lamar Hunt and coach Hank Stram. Hunt had founded the American Football League in 1960 to challenge the National Football League. In the first Super Bowl in 1967, the NFL champion Green Bay Packers had easily beaten the AFL champion Chiefs, and Packers coach Vince Lombardi had told the sports media that Kansas City was not as good as NFL teams. Now, in 1970, the two leagues had merged—a merger that Hunt had helped engineer—and Hunt owned the reigning world champions. Stram, meanwhile, was being hailed as a visionary for dismantling the Vikings. He proclaimed that the Chiefs exemplified the "football of the 1970s" and that Minnesota represented a "1960s league."[12] And Stram and Hunt were not the only Kansas City sports figures receiving national attention. Kansas City's own Ewing Kauffman owned the baseball Royals that had been awarded to the city as an expansion team to compensate for losing the

A's. *Sports Illustrated* praised Kauffman as being "refreshingly different" from Charlie Finley. Kauffman pledged that Kansas City would "never again lose major league baseball," and in 1969 when he was introduced before the first Royals home game, the fans had given him a lengthy standing ovation.[13]

If Kansas City and Oakland both had much to be proud of and seemingly much to look forward to, both also faced grave concerns, some rooted in their national images. For Oakland, the problem always had been that it was not San Francisco. "The situation is almost laughable," wrote Wells Twombly. "San Francisco is a painted beauty, cooing and beckoning seductively. Oakland is a blue-collar worker with stubble on its chin, beer on its breath and a hard hat on its head."[14] When *Holiday* magazine profiled the Bay Area in 1970, it called San Francisco the "American city that fascinates nearly everyone for all the obvious reasons," whereas Oakland was "desultory and drab" in comparison. (Inevitably, the magazine also quoted Gertrude Stein's epitaph for the city where she had grown up: "There's no there there.")[15] Similarly, *Newsweek* quoted Oakland's official city song ("She has pride / She has hope / And, oh, what a view! / Oakland, we're for you!"), while sardonically noting that "the new song was recorded by a firm called Fantasy, Inc."[16]

For Kansas City, a longtime agricultural hub located squarely in the middle of the country, the worry was that it was still viewed as a "cow town." A *New York Times* profile would refer to the city's reputation as "Hicktown, U.S.A., the butt of a thousand bad jokes" involving "corn-fed girls and good ole boys." Although the *Times* allowed that contemporary Kansas City was not quite that backward, it largely remained "a bucolic bore" with a populace most notable for its "deep-seated inferiority complex, its Babbitt-like desire to be accepted, its paranoia about its wallflower reputation." (Inevitably, the paper also quoted Rodgers and Hammerstein's song from *Oklahoma!* about how a seven-story "skyscraper" showed that "everything's up to date in Kansas City—they've gone about as far as they can go!")[17]

The two cities' problems extended well beyond their provincial images. Despite its blue-collar roots and booming port facilities, Oakland suffered from double-digit unemployment. It had lost thousands of manufacturing jobs to its suburbs, and the Port of Oakland's embrace of containerization meant that fewer workers were needed to load and unload cargo. The Port's charter also required it to reinvest income into its own facilities, angering those who felt that it should invest more into the city of Oakland and hire more local workers, especially from the African American community, where unemployment was many times higher than among whites.[18] In Kansas City, three lengthy construction strikes had crippled the building industry. The most recent strike had lasted 196 days from the spring into the fall of 1970, costing the area economy some three million dollars each day. All work stopped at the new airport and Crown Center and the dual stadium sports complex. *Fortune* magazine published photos of the halted construction under the headline, "In Kansas City They Couldn't Go As Far As They Wanted."[19]

Both cities also were experiencing racial strife. Following the 1965 Watts uprising in Los Angeles, the federal government had generated a list of "high tension" cities including Oakland where similar disturbances might erupt. Although Oakland never did experience a full-fledged riot, longstanding tensions between the police and the African American community helped give rise to the Black Panthers in 1966. The Panthers' platform, which was published in each edition of their newspaper, demanded "an immediate end to POLICE BRUTALITY and MURDER of black people." Following the October 1970 killing in Oakland of an African American man who police said had attacked them—a killing that had received only brief mention on an inside page of the *Oakland Tribune*—the Panthers declared in their own newspaper that they were "no longer surprised when a brother is murdered by the pigs and have it called justifiable homicide," and they called for "armed wrath" in response.[20]

Kansas City had not been included on the government "high tension" list, but after the 1968 assassination of Martin Luther King, disturbances in the city's African American neighborhoods had killed six people, at least four at the hands of police. In October 1970, Kansas City police said that an African American man had rushed them with a club in a vacant building near Municipal Stadium; they shot him four times and killed him (the killing had received minimal notice in the *Kansas City Star*). When the county prosecutor's office quickly ruled the shooting justifiable, many people in the African American community protested and began their own investigation. "We have to do the door-to-door work, talk to all of the people involved, and find witnesses," a community spokesperson told the *Kansas City Call,* the city's African American newspaper. "Everything that a police department would do to apprehend murderers in its community, we find ourselves having to do." Less than two weeks later, not far from the site of the original shooting, a police storefront center intended to improve police-community relations was bombed. Two officers were wounded, prompting the local police association to call for less attention to "police brutality" and more attention to "hoodlum brutality."[21]

Protest and violence and rage seemed to pervade the news everywhere in the days leading up to the November 1 Chiefs-Raiders game. In suburban Chicago, eleven African American players on the Elmhurst College football team boycotted practice, saying that their coaches had discriminated against them. In Cairo, Illinois, following years of racial unrest, African Americans with rifles and army fatigues attacked police headquarters. In Irvine, California, an arson fire heavily damaged a bank; "Death to the Pigs" had been spray-painted on the walls. In San Jose at the south end of San Francisco Bay, antiwar demonstrators threw eggs, rocks, and bottles at the car of President Richard Nixon, who had been campaigning for Republican congressional candidates. Nixon branded the demonstrators as "radical, antidemocratic elements," and Governor Ronald Reagan called them a "disgrace to California, to the human race. . . . They want victory for the enemy." U.S. senator George Murphy was running for reelection in California and tried to link his Democratic opponent to the San Jose incident with a newspaper ad topped by one giant word: "ANARCHY."[22]

So not all was happy in Oakland or Kansas City or the nation as a whole as the Raiders and Chiefs prepared to play. The two teams were coping with their own worries, as neither had performed fully to expectations. For the first time in recent memory, they would play with neither being in first place. Bay Area sportswriter Glenn Dickey wrote that it could "be all over" for the Raiders if they lost to the Chiefs because of the difficulty of Oakland's remaining schedule. Similarly, *Kansas City Star* sports editor Joe McGuff observed that a "loss Sunday would put the Chiefs in a desperate position," and he predicted a "classic confrontation" between the two teams.[23]

The game kicked off in Municipal Stadium, an aging facility shared by the Chiefs and the Royals in the heart of Kansas City's African American community. With baseball season over, temporary stands had been erected across the outfield, and both teams' benches sat side by side in front of the bleachers filled by the Chiefs' most rabid rooters, the "Wolfpack." More than 51,000 fans had crammed into the stadium (occupying "every place but the light towers," as Glenn Dickey put it), and the game was televised nationally on NBC.[24]

The teams fought to a 7–7 standstill at halftime. Oakland then took the lead in the third quarter on a touchdown pass from Daryle Lamonica to Raymond Chester. Kansas City answered by moving into Raiders territory, but the Chiefs—who would be hampered by penalties all day—saw their drive stall with a holding call and had to settle for a Jan Stenerud field goal to cut Oakland's lead to 14–10 heading into the final quarter. The stage was set for a climax that sportswriters would variously call worthy of *The Twilight Zone,* the Marx Brothers, and the Brothers Grimm.[25]

It began with Kansas City moving ahead of Oakland 17–14 on a Len Dawson touchdown pass to Otis Taylor. Oakland argued that Taylor had committed pass interference on the play. It was not the first time the Raiders had complained about Taylor. In the AFL championship game that Kansas City had won the previous January, Taylor had caught a long third-down pass from Dawson to move the Chiefs out of trouble near their own goal line. The Raiders believed—and video replay seemed to show—that Taylor had caught the ball out of bounds, which should have ruled the pass incomplete. Later during that same Kansas City drive, Oakland had been called for pass interference against Taylor, setting up the Chiefs' go-ahead score. The Raiders said that Taylor had been the one guilty of interference.[26]

Now, nearly a year later, Kansas City was once again leading Oakland, and after getting the ball back, the Chiefs had a chance to run out the clock. Facing a third-and-twelve at the Oakland forty-eight with little more than a minute left to play, Len Dawson called a bootleg run. As a thirty-five-year-old quarterback coming off a serious knee injury, he rarely ran with the ball (when asked afterward to recall the last time he had called such a play, he replied, "Oh, about 1963 or '64").[27] But now Dawson faked a handoff to his left, ran to his right, and found no Raiders in front of him. He fell to the ground after a nineteen-yard gain to the Oakland twenty-nine, apparently having secured a first down and

Kansas City's Otis Taylor catches a pass during the January 1970 AFL championship game in Oakland while being defended by the Raiders' Nemiah Wilson. (AP Photo)

a Chiefs win. Kansas City was about to move ahead of Oakland into a tie for first place.

And then suddenly—hurtling into home viewers' TV screens and Len Dawson's back—came six-foot-eight, 280-pound Ben Davidson.

By 1970 Davidson was a celebrity in his own right, embodying the unique blend of benevolence and malevolence that was central to the Raiders' image. On the one hand, he was what the *Oakland Tribune* called a "happy humanitarian" who helped hospitals, charities, and youth clubs. (Even Len Dawson would acknowledge that Davidson was "a heck of a nice guy.") He was a commercial spokesperson as well; a teammate recalled driving across the Bay Bridge and being startled to see Davidson's face on a billboard promoting drinking milk.[28] On the other hand, the Oakland defensive end with the handlebar mustache had been "accused of doing everything but tying quarterbacks across railroad tracks." He had gained notoriety for a late hit on New York Jets quarterback Joe Namath, who had said of Davidson, "Nothing that lives is lower than that." Davidson professed not to care what others thought: "I even enjoy the hate mail I get."[29]

Now he was diving helmet-first into the prone Len Dawson, later claiming that he had not been sure if the Kansas City quarterback was actually down or not. An official immediately threw a penalty flag, but just as Davidson got to his feet, he came face to face with the Chiefs' Otis Taylor. Oakland radio announcer Bill King related what happened next in a call that would be immortalized by NFL Films: "Here's Ben Davidson being jumped on by one of the Chiefs. Two more Chiefs come in. There's a big pileup. Davidson and Taylor are going at it. There are at least eight Chiefs—here come all the Raiders! *Holy Toledo!* It's a free-for-all!"[30]

It took the officials several minutes to restore order, and then they marked off the fifteen-yard penalty called against Davidson, moving the ball to the Oakland fourteen. Raiders linebacker Dan Conners, who had lost his helmet and been bloodied in the brawl, vociferously argued that because Otis Taylor had been ejected for fighting, Kansas City should be penalized just as Oakland had been. After another lengthy delay, referee Bob Finley ruled that offsetting "continuing action" fouls had occurred, nullifying the entire play. In effect, Len Dawson's first-down, victory-clinching run had never happened. The Chiefs protested mightily, but to no avail. Then more confusion ensued as no one on the

Oakland's Ben Davidson hitting the quarterback—in this instance, Miami's Bob Griese—during a 1970 game in Oakland. (Ron Riesterer, untitled. Gelatin silver, 10 x 8 in. The Oakland Tribune Collection, the Oakland Museum of California, gift of ANG Newspapers.)

field remembered where the original line of scrimmage had been. A call went up to the NBC booth for guidance, and finally the ball was placed on the Oakland forty-nine, one yard behind where it should have been. Kansas City ended up having to punt.[31]

Oakland quickly drove back into Kansas City territory. When a Raider failed to get out of bounds with the ball, it looked as though the clock might run out, but a Chiefs injury forced a timeout. George Blanda—age forty-three—lined up for a long field goal attempt. He had come off the bench the previous week to replace the injured Daryle Lamonica as quarterback and lead Oakland to victory. Now, against Kansas City, his forty-eight-yard field goal tied the game. The Chiefs' six-foot-ten Morris Stroud just missed knocking down the ball before it cleared the crossbar, but Joe McGuff would write in the *Kansas City Star* that even if Stroud had successfully blocked the kick, "the Chiefs probably would have been called for goal tending in view of the way their day was going."[32]

With three seconds left to play and Oakland set to kick off, the Chiefs and their fans melted down completely. Kansas City was called for two fifteen-yard unsportsmanlike conduct penalties that moved the ball all the way forward to the Chiefs thirty. The Raiders attempted an on-side kick, but the Chiefs recovered, ending the game with a 17–17 tie. Boos, curses, and debris rained down from the stands. One fan attacked someone from the Raiders sideline while another fan tackled official Art Holst. (Holst, who was unhurt, later said that his assailant had been a local bank president who would thank him for not pressing charges.) More sober-minded Kansas City spectators formed a protective corridor to allow the Raiders and officials to leave the field with a police escort. Chiefs coach Hank Stram stormed after the officials into their dressing room and let fly with what one witness described as "a flood of phonetics—some indiscernible, most unprintable." Bob Finley chased him away: "Don't you call me a crook! Get out of here!"[33]

The game was a media sensation. "After Sunday's spectacular show on national TV, the Raiders and the Chiefs are the hottest topic going today from coast to coast," the *Oakland Tribune*'s Ed Levitt wrote the next day. Sportswriters weighed in on Otis Taylor and Ben Davidson, with one Los Angeles columnist saying that "Davidson's piling-on was so vicious, so irresponsible, so dangerous and so unnecessary" that "those who respect fair play should be sending Taylor a medal." (No one in

Kansas City blamed Taylor for costing the Chiefs a victory; he received a rousing ovation when he was introduced at a community event later that week.)[34]

Chiefs fans deluged the *Kansas City Star* with calls and letters complaining about the officials. The newspaper published the address of the NFL's New York office so that fans could direct their wrath there.[35] Many fans and sportswriters questioned the "continuing action" rule invoked in the fourth quarter, with some saying that it seemed to reward cheap shots. It turned out that Bob Finley's crew had interpreted the rule correctly, but the *Star*'s Joe McGuff charged that they had "delayed so long and were so indecisive that they raised questions as to their competence." McGuff also could not resist noting that the referee shared the same last name as Charlie Finley, the A's owner who had left Kansas City for Oakland.[36]

As for the Raiders, even though the tie had moved them into first place, they were not totally happy about everything that had occurred during the game and its aftermath. "Wait 'till we get them out at Oakland," one of them had yelled as the Chiefs' fans hurled abuse at them. In the *Oakland Tribune,* Ed Levitt predicted that the next Chiefs-Raiders game would be "too big for the Oakland Coliseum—or even Alcatraz or Treasure Island. . . . Could you imagine what would happen if the Oakland-KC rematch were open now to the highest bidding promoter?"[37] Indeed, once again the following month it would all come down to Kansas City and Oakland, two cities whose sports teams could be counted on to produce a spectacle—divine or not.

* * *

This book broadly addresses the Oakland–Kansas City sports rivalry as it played out during one of the most turbulent periods in U.S. history, the mid-1960s thorough the mid-1970s. The two cities sought major league teams to show the rest of the world that they were no longer minor league in stature. Their efforts to attract big-league franchises pitted the two cities against each other. After they succeeded in landing those franchises, the cities' football and baseball teams regularly fought each other on the field: sometimes literally, as was the case during the Raiders-Chiefs tie game of 1970.

By 1977 Kansas City and Oakland would be much changed from what they had been only a decade previously. Their sports teams had brought them widespread attention and athletic glory, just as they had craved. They also had done much to try to improve themselves by building not only new sports facilities but also new cultural, retail, and transportation centers. But those triumphs came at a cost amid wrenching clashes over race and labor relations, pitched battles over urban renewal, and heated controversies over the lot of professional athletes.

There have been sports rivalries involving larger and more celebrated cities such as New York versus Boston or Los Angeles versus San Francisco.[38] For that matter, both Oakland and Kansas City experienced notable sports rivalries beyond the one they had with each other. For example, the Kansas City Royals played hard-fought series against the New York Yankees in the late 1970s and early 1980s, and the 1970s Oakland Raiders faced stiff challenges in overcoming the Miami Dolphins and especially the Pittsburgh Steelers to reach the Super Bowl.[39]

However, the Kansas City–Oakland rivalry is unique in that it encompassed both football and baseball while also involving two smaller cities that had had no major league franchises prior to the mid-1950s. For such cities—acutely concerned with how others saw them—the cachet attached to professional sports assumed added significance. Thus this book tells parallel stories: that of the clashes between the cities' sports teams, and that of the struggles of the cities themselves to show that they had become "big league" through sports and other major civic initiatives.

Regarding the cities' sports teams, much has already been written about the individual players and franchises from the 1960s and 1970s, especially the Oakland A's and Oakland Raiders given their outsized personalities and multiple championships.[40] The rivalry between Oakland and Kansas City has not received as much attention, even though the battles between football's Raiders and Chiefs were ferocious. "The games with the Raiders were not games," Chiefs quarterback Len Dawson recalled. "Games are fun. These were wars." Typically the stakes were high. "[With] Kansas City and Oakland, it seemed like it was always a big game," one sportswriter has said. "It was always the NBC game late on Sunday afternoons that all of America was saying, 'We've got to watch this, 'cause it's really fun!'"[41] In baseball the rivalry between the A's and the Kansas City Royals has been largely forgotten, but as sportswriter Filip Bondy notes, it "offered its own special bite" stemming from the animosity that Kansas Citians felt toward A's owner Charlie Finley after he moved the A's to Oakland.[42]

That animosity in turn points toward the two cities' struggles in being perceived as metropolises of the first rank. "In the United States, a major-league team is a prerequisite for big-city status," historian Jon Teaford writes in summarizing a longstanding conviction shared by city boosters. "Baseball, football, and basketball are not simply games; they are elements necessary to a city's rise to greatness."[43] That conviction has been especially prevalent among cities that never before had a big-league team. Journalist Calvin Trillin once observed that "concerning matters of civic personality, the United States is divided neatly into two parts." The first, he said, "is the part that had major-league baseball before the Second World War. The second part is all the rest." Cities of the second part were susceptible to what Trillin described as "dome-ism," or the hunger to obtain and develop civic status symbols comparable to Houston's Astrodome: "a big-league baseball franchise, of course, and a big-league stadium and a big-league symphony and an airport so big-league that it could be called 'international.'"[44] Trillin was writing specifically of his native Kansas City, but his words also could apply to Oakland; both communities aspired to greatness even as they grappled with the myriad of social and economic challenges that steadily mounted in U.S. cities in the decades following the war.

What follows, then, is a tale both about big games and the quest for would-be "domes." It tells of celebrated athletes confronting one another on the field while confronting strong-willed and idiosyncratic coaches, managers, and team owners off the field during a time of vast change in professional sports. It also tells of cities fighting over major league franchises while facing increasing challenges from citizens who held very different views of what civic priorities should be. Although the focus is on Oakland and Kansas City, the book relates a many-sided contest over money, respect, prestige, and power that helps illuminate broader debates over urban identity and professional sports that emerged during the postwar era and that have endured to the present day.

For example, Kansas City's and Oakland's efforts to obtain major league franchises exemplify what historian Glen Gendzel has described as "competitive boosterism: the active participation of local elites in luring trade, industry, and investment to their own cities from elsewhere, in a zero-sum Darwinian contest." Civic boosterism is almost as old as the United States itself, but in the post–World War II era, cities commonly practiced a growth-oriented strategy that included seeking big-league teams and building the facilities to attract and keep them.[45] Such was the case in Oakland and Kansas City. There as elsewhere, cities justified pursuing sports franchises on the premise that the franchises would produce significant economic benefits for their home communities.

Beyond economic gain, civic boosters also have embraced sports as a means toward improving a city's self-image and its image to others. According to Jon Teaford, "No matter whether a city was aging and declining or young and emerging, a winning sports team was a surefire remedy for feelings of urban inferiority."[46] Hometown newspapers including the *Kansas City Star* and the *Oakland Tribune* helped lead the campaigns to attract major league teams, even when those teams offered little immediate promise of becoming winners. "Like a city's business and political leaders, the press wants to be in the big time," political scientist Michael Danielson has written. Local media also promote the widely held idea that big-league sports can bring together a city's people. In Danielson's words, "Sports provides one of the rare opportunities for people to emphasize their communal ties."[47] One history of Kansas City concludes by suggesting that "many of the city's most positive steps toward unity and pride might not have occurred without the presence of" the Chiefs and Royals. A community of fans can even extend beyond the geographic boundaries of a city or region, as has been the case with the Oakland Raiders' international fan base known as "Raider Nation."[48]

However, many critics have questioned the extent to which big-league sports franchises actually produce economic benefits or genuine community for cities.[49] Charles Euchner argues that the true beneficiaries are not the cities themselves, but wealthy franchise owners who seek the most lucrative stadium deals and incentive packages possible: "By simply exploring options for playing in other cities—by playing the field, so to speak—teams have gotten all matter of largess."[50] George Lipsitz asserts that professional sports offers only the "illusion of inclusion and connection with others," and he rejects claims that pursuing a "'big-league' image" helps metropolitan areas: "It is true that individual corporations find it easier to recruit top-flight executives when they can offer them the use of tax-subsidized luxury boxes at sporting events, but nothing indicates that this is a wise investment for the entire area, that it means more to fiscal health of the region than adequate housing, medical care, or schools."[51]

In sum, according to the critics, a major league sports franchise can pack a stadium with cheering fans from disparate walks of life, but it cannot erase the differences and inequities among the fans or the broader citizenry, and it cannot mask that the whole enterprise is aimed more toward making rich people richer than it is toward generating prosperity for all. Thus one study has listed Kansas City as one of several cities that built new sports facilities but did not reap the widespread economic benefits that had been expected.[52] In another study, Maria Veri charges that "the promise of professional football for Oakland's economic development not only never materialized, but drove the city into greater racial and economic disparities"—and Veri wrote that study before the Oakland Raiders announced in 2017 that they were abandoning the city for the second time in franchise history, this time for a more profitable deal in Las Vegas.[53]

Examining the Kansas City–Oakland rivalry of the 1960s and 1970s helps put contemporary debates over the costs and benefits of big-league sports into historical context while also highlighting the contradictions in the connections between cities and sports teams. After the Oakland A's won the 1972 World Series, writer John Krich suggested that "when a team plays for a city, it plays for the *idea* of a team and the *idea* of a city."[54] The A's were a notoriously fractious collection of players who brawled among themselves and chafed under their owner; the team drew only meager crowds to the Oakland Coliseum. Oakland itself experienced bitter divisions over class and race, and the city in 1972 faced an uncertain future. Nonetheless the World Series championship sparked wild celebrations among the players and the people of Oakland. The idea of a unified, ascendant team representing a unified, ascendant city was at least for a time reaffirmed.

The sports histories of Oakland and Kansas City point to other such examples. The Raiders and the Chiefs originally belonged to the upstart American Football League, which recruited players from African American colleges that the rival National Football League had tended to overlook. Those athletes confronted discrimination in the cities in which they pursued their professional careers, including in Kansas City and

Oakland. In baseball, members of the A's and Royals along with players on other major league teams faced draconian restrictions on where they could choose to play. Athletes in general became more politically aware during this era regarding both social issues and their own positions as cogs in a vast money-making business; some athletes produced tell-all books revealing what pro sports were really like and what players had to endure. Franchise owners uprooted teams when expedient, just as Charlie Finley did with the A's. When Lamar Hunt's Dallas Texans drew poorly in Hunt's hometown, he moved the team to Kansas City to become the Chiefs. Al Davis grew increasingly restless in Oakland before finally pulling the Raiders out of town, and even Ewing Kauffman second-guessed himself about buying the Royals. In both Kansas City and Oakland, there was sharp questioning concerning the money spent on pro sports in comparison with other social needs.

These sorts of rifts and controversies did not negate the widespread joy when the A's won two more World Series, the Chiefs and Raiders each won Super Bowls, and the Royals ended years of baseball futility in Kansas City by winning their first division title. Still, the rifts and controversies remind us that the "idea of a team" and "idea of a city" are always contested: within cities and professional sports alike, there are always resentments, grievances, and competing agendas at play, and there are always winners and losers off the field as well as on. That is particularly true during historically fraught times when the cities involved see major league sports as "a critical talisman" of urban status,[55] when the teams and athletes involved believe that they have not received the respect or compensation they deserve, and when some of the citizens involved reject a vision of "big-league" success that they feel disadvantages and disempowers them. All of those conditions were in play in Oakland and Kansas City during the 1960s and 1970s.

The book will tell the story of the rivalry between the two cities roughly in chronological order, but it will alternate between baseball and football while also alternating between what was happening with the sports teams and what was happening in the cities themselves. Chapter 1 looks at how Kansas City and Oakland obtained major league franchises by poaching them from elsewhere, part of a nationwide trend that began in the 1950s and accelerated in the 1960s. The sports editor of the *Kansas City Star* helped lead that city's successful effort in 1954 to lure baseball's Athletics from Philadelphia. The team faced significant trials in the following years, first under owner Arnold Johnson and then under Charlie Finley. In 1963 football's Dallas Texans headed to Kansas City, where they initially experienced lackluster support. Oakland already had landed its own AFL franchise that foundered until Al Davis assumed leadership. The *Oakland Tribune* shepherded the drive to build the Oakland Coliseum as a home for the city's pro teams. In 1967 Kansas City passed a bond issue to build its own stadium complex, only to lose the A's to Oakland.

Chapter 2 examines the heyday of the Chiefs-Raiders American Football League rivalry. Their face-offs during the 1968 and 1969 seasons took place amid racial revolt that saw the ascent of the Black Panthers and the riots following Martin Luther King's death. It also was a time of increased activism among African American athletes, including those in the AFL, as players struggled to adjust to life in Kansas City and Oakland. Media coverage of the social ferment ranged from reactionary in the *Oakland Tribune* to more progressive in *Sports Illustrated*'s landmark 1968 series on the black athlete. Paralleling the struggles of Oakland and Kansas City to improve their public images, the AFL battled perceptions that it was an inferior league. Those perceptions were countered by the Chiefs' win in Super Bowl IV.

Chapter 3 relates the turnaround in the fortunes of the A's after they moved to Oakland, culminating in their 1972 World Series title. They won despite weak attendance and frequent disquiet under Charlie Finley. At the same time, the Kansas City Royals quickly established themselves as a model expansion franchise under Ewing Kauffman and general manager Cedric Tallis, but it was apparent that they had far to go to match the A's' success. Labor unrest engulfed both baseball and the two cities during this period, with baseball players walking off the job not long after lengthy strikes had halted work among construction workers in Kansas City and dockworkers in Oakland. Even as the growing power of the Major League Baseball Players Association began to transform baseball radically, organized labor elsewhere faced an increasingly harsh climate.

Chapter 4 tells of the slow but steady decline of the Chiefs after they lost a heartbreaking overtime playoff game to Miami in 1971 and moved to their new stadium the following year. The Chiefs still could beat the

Raiders at home (with Oakland fullback Marv Hubbard becoming an especially reviled villain in Kansas City), but coach Hank Stram was finally fired. The Raiders dominated the American Football Conference West but routinely lost during the playoffs, and they were branded as not being able to win the big game. The two football teams' frustrations coincided with confrontations over Kansas City's and Oakland's investments in professional sports: citizen groups filed legal challenges over Kansas City's new sports complex and its planned new hockey and basketball arena, and the Black Panthers used their newspaper to present a comprehensive critique of Oakland's ruling elite, including the people who built and profited from the Coliseum.

By 1973 intense competition had emerged between the A's and the Royals, which is the focus of chapter 5. The A's won two more world championships, but they still fought among themselves and especially with Charlie Finley, who drew widespread condemnation for his conduct during the 1973 World Series. The Royals had developed a strong core of players through trades and their farm system but could not beat the A's when it counted the most, and the team experienced turmoil of its own with coaches, managers, and general managers being demoted or fired. Kansas City's and Oakland's decisions to build new sports facilities outside their central business districts contributed to the decline of the two cities' downtowns, which the municipalities tried to counter through an array of new civic projects—a reflection of the "dome-ism" of which Calvin Trillin would write. In turn those new projects provoked controversy of their own.

Chapter 6 examines the culmination of the Oakland–Kansas City sports rivalry. The chapter's title, "Triumph and Tragedy" (borrowed from an NFL Films production), calls attention to the dramatic highs and lows that would be experienced by the two cities and the professional athletes who played there. In Kansas City, the Royals finally overtook the A's to win their first division title in 1976, the same year that the city reveled in the attention generated by hosting the Republican National Convention. In Oakland, the Raiders finally overcame their playoff woes to win their first Super Bowl in 1977, the same year that the city (where blacks had begun to outnumber whites) elected its first African American mayor. But the two cities were scarred by the violence inflicted by organized crime and self-styled revolutionaries, as businesses were dynamited and an African American school superintendent was assassinated. Players on the cities' sports teams were enmeshed in charges of racism and thuggery, and some members of the Raiders and Chiefs sustained profound injuries that would not become fully apparent until years later.

Finally, the conclusion summarizes what happened after the heyday of the Oakland–Kansas City rivalry to the cities and their sports teams. It also considers the implications of yesterday's rivalry for today's era of city-sports relations.

We begin, though, by returning to what might deceptively seem a simpler and more innocent era—when Kansas City and Oakland were still "minor league."

1

Striving for the Big Leagues

STRICTLY SPEAKING, KANSAS CITY had hosted major league baseball multiple times prior to the 1950s. Each stint in the "big time" had been brief and without distinction, if not without drama. One such team, the Kansas City Cowboys of the National League, lasted only as long as the 1886 season. They played their home games on a grassless field and amassed a dismal 30-91 record before disbanding. According to baseball historian Lloyd Johnson, "Several gun incidents, on the field and off, convinced the Eastern baseball establishment that Kansas City was too rough for their ball players."[1]

The gunplay was symbolic of the city's turbulent history. "Most of the forces that have disturbed this nation have surged into Kansas City, and very often have met there opposing forces driving in from another quarter," one chronicle of the city noted.[2] Its central location made it a prime distributor of agricultural products (especially meat and wheat) from the West to the East and of manufactured goods in the opposite direction. But it also stood on the dividing line between the North and the South, making it a Civil War flash point while bequeathing to it a complicated race relations legacy that the city still would be grappling with more than a century later. In addition, Kansas City represented a battlefield between gentility and vice. It had created stylish residential and retail districts through developer J. C. Nichols as well as a picturesque boulevard system. It also had spawned boss Tom Pendergast, whose Democratic machine bilked the city out of millions and contributed to its scandalous image during the 1930s.

By the mid-1950s, Pendergast was long gone and *Coronet* magazine was hailing the citizenry for having "turned lawless, graft-ridden, bankrupt Kansas City into a model metropolis."[3] The *Kansas City Star*—which had opposed Pendergast—was one of the nation's most influential newspapers, "the voice of [a] wide swath of Middle America, stretching from the Mississippi to the Rocky Mountains."[4] Its editor Roy Roberts was a Republican kingmaker who had helped launch the political career of Dwight Eisenhower. Yet not everything was well with the *Star* and its morning paper, the *Times*. The federal government had launched an antitrust investigation of the *Star* in 1952, possibly spurred by President Harry Truman's dislike (Truman had gotten his political start in Kansas City through Pendergast). The investigation into the paper's monopolistic practices led to an indictment, trial, and guilty verdict, and the *Star* was forced to divest itself of its radio and television stations.[5] Kansas City had its own worries. For years the stockyards at the confluence of the Kansas and Missouri Rivers had made the city a literal "cow town," but a 1951 flood had devastated the yards and other industries. The city also faced a spike in crime, a decline in convention business, and an outdated airport. Those problems received national press attention, the *Coronet* article notwithstanding. As historian George Ehrlich writes, "Everything was not up to date in Kansas City, and the point was repeatedly driven home."[6]

Amid that emerging sense of drift and dissatisfaction, *Star* sports editor Ernie Mehl received a news tip in March 1953: baseball's Boston Braves were moving to Milwaukee, the first major league team move in fifty years. The *Milwaukee Journal* and other city boosters had successfully lobbied the franchise, which had been drawing poorly in Boston, to move to a new ballpark that the city had just built. Kansas City and Milwaukee had been longtime rivals in the minor league American Association, prompting Mehl to wonder whether his hometown might boost its fortunes by successfully following Milwaukee's path to the big leagues.[7]

Since its abortive major league forays in the previous century, Kansas City had hosted some wonderful baseball teams and players. The Kansas City Blues were one of the top farm clubs of the New York Yankees, featuring future stars including Phil Rizzuto and Mickey Mantle. However, the Blues were completely subordinate to the needs of their parent team. Players could be summoned to New York at a moment's notice, producing frustration and resentment among Blues fans. (As one fan declared, "I for one am sick and tired of these raids the Yankees make on the Blues every year.")[8] Kansas City was also home to the Monarchs, the greatest franchise in the history of the so-called "Negro leagues." The Blues and Monarchs shared the same home field—what later became known as Municipal Stadium—and at times the two teams drew mixed crowds of whites and African Americans, with the Monarchs occasionally staging exhibitions against white players and beating them. Still, race relations in Kansas City were such that one white baseball fan recalled never attending Monarchs games: "But for that invisible but granite wall of racism and unthinking indifference, we would have seen Ernie Banks, Kansas City's own Satchel Paige, and others, including the legendary 'Buck' O'Neil, the Monarchs' manager. What knuckleheads we were."[9]

Now it seemed possible that Kansas City might obtain its own major league franchise, provided that (like Milwaukee) it could persuade an existing team to move; expansion was not then on the horizon. Ernie Mehl took the lead in June 1953 with a series of columns in the *Kansas City Star* touting the benefits of big-league ball. Soon the editorial pages of the *Star* and *Times* took up the cause. "A big league team would put Kansas City's name on the front page of all newspaper sports editions in the country and every day of the week for half the year," the *Times* wrote. "Such advertising is tremendously important in practical business terms." The *Star* pointed to the passionate reception that the baseball Braves were receiving in their new home, saying that if a major league team could arouse such a response in "ultra-conservative old Milwaukee," one could only imagine what might happen in "already lusty and enthusiastic Kansas City."[10] Baseball fans from across the region petitioned city hall to back the effort. "Let's get that major league club in here and quit taking the back seat," one fan said.[11]

Even if Kansas City boosters saw their hometown as superior to "ultra-conservative" Milwaukee, they were highly unlikely to land a team as good as the Braves, who had had a strong group of players when they moved from Boston, along with a prodigiously talented young outfielder named Hank Aaron, who would soon make his major league debut. The Braves became immediate winners in Milwaukee and set attendance records there. In contrast, Kansas City had to set its sights on the bottom feeders of the big leagues. The city missed its first target—the woebegone St. Louis Browns—when the American League voted in 1953 to move that team to Baltimore to become the Orioles. By the day after the vote, the *Star*'s Ernie Mehl already had shifted attention to another struggling American League franchise, the Philadelphia Athletics (or "A's" for short). Mehl told his readers that "there is a strong belief that the Athletics shortly will be compelled to move," but he added that "there is only one possible solution to a realization of the goal here and that is to work with the New York Yankees."[12]

Indeed, for Kansas City to get the Philadelphia team, the Yankees almost certainly would have to back the move. They dominated the American League on the field, and as one New York sportswriter observed, they also seemed to have a "strange stranglehold" over league operations.[13] Moreover they owned not only the Blues but also the Blues' ballpark. Although there were efforts in Kansas City to buy the park from the Yankees, in December 1953 Chicago entrepreneur Arnold Johnson bought both the Blues' stadium and New York's Yankee Stadium.

Johnson, it turned out, already had close business ties to Yankees co-owners Del Webb and Dan Topping. The Yankee Stadium deal was designed to provide tax breaks for everyone involved, with Johnson promptly leasing the stadium back to the Yankees' owners. Yet now that Johnson also owned the Kansas City ballpark, Ernie Mehl asked him about seeking a major league team to go with it. At first Johnson demurred, but with the backing of a coalition of Kansas City civic and business leaders, he decided by the summer of 1954 to pursue the Philadelphia A's. There was an implicit condition, though: voters needed to approve a bond issue that would raise money for Kansas City to buy the ballpark from Johnson and expand it to big-league specifications. The *Times* lobbied for the bonds in a front-page editorial ("the progress and the growth of the city hinge on the result"), and on the day of the vote Mehl wrote, "Today Kansas City either goes or does not go major league." The bonds passed easily.[14]

Arnold Johnson's efforts to buy the A's and move them to Kansas City encountered obstacles. Some American League team owners outside New York greatly distrusted Johnson's ties to the Yankees. They also were skeptical of Kansas City being big enough to support major league baseball—one account holds that the skeptics "believed the city's boosters were counting corn stalks and heifers in their population claims."[15]

Philadelphians mounted a campaign to keep the A's, and after it already had been announced that the team would head west (moving the *Star* to proclaim in another front-page editorial that it was "one of those genuinely great days in the history of a city"), Kansas Citians were shocked to hear that Philadelphia business interests would apparently buy the A's instead. In the end, though, Johnson made his offer attractive enough to sway the team's owners, and with the backing of the Yankees, the American League finally approved the move to Kansas City in November 1954.[16]

The Philadelphia Athletics had been wildly successful at times during their long history under owner-manager Connie Mack, but they were in shambles when Arnold Johnson bought them from Mack's sons Roy and Earle. (Apart from being inept owners, the two sons loathed each other.) The sorry state of the team did not discourage Kansas City. It quickly renovated and expanded its ballpark during the winter of 1955. Few people seemed concerned that the project was overseen by a construction company owned by the Yankees' Del Webb. When the A's arrived in Kansas City for their April home opener, they paraded through a downtown crowd of at least 150,000, and then they drew nearly 1.4 million spectators during the 1955 season, second in the league only to the Yankees. A promotional film called Kansas Citians "the most rabid baseball fans in the country" and boasted that the A's had been "transplanted from Philadelphia to grow strong and sturdy in the rich, fertile soil of the mighty Midwest."[17]

Soon enough, disenchantment set in. After finishing sixth in the eight-team league during their first season in Kansas City, the A's sank to last in 1956, losing 102 games. They would not rise above seventh for the next three seasons after that as attendance declined from its early peak. And while the Milwaukee Braves won back-to-back National League pennants and beat the New York Yankees in the 1957 World Series, the Kansas City A's began trading many of their best players to the Yankees—Bobby Shantz, Clete Boyer, Ryne Duren, Ralph Terry, Art Ditmar, Hector Lopez, and most notoriously, Roger Maris. The Maris deal in December 1959 provoked Chicago White Sox president Bill Veeck to condemn what he called the "unholy alliance" between the A's and Yankees. Veeck would criticize the American League for having moved franchises to Kansas City and Baltimore instead of to such larger, booming cities as Los Angeles and San Francisco. In fact Veeck charged that the Yankees' Del Webb had orchestrated the A's' move to Kansas City with the ultimate goal of "getting control of a franchise which he could eventually move to Los Angeles himself."[18] As it happened, the National League staked claim first on the West Coast in 1958, with the Brooklyn Dodgers moving to Los Angeles and the New York Giants moving to San Francisco. Other cities across the country were following the examples of Milwaukee and Kansas City in aggressively pursuing big-league sports.[19]

Arnold Johnson shrugged off criticism of himself and the A's' deals with New York. He said that he was just trying to help his team: "Every time a top player is traded certain risks are involved. We are willing to take these risks."[20] Roger Maris—who had not wanted to leave Kansas City—would win back-to-back Most Valuable Player awards in New York while breaking Babe Ruth's single-season home run record. Meanwhile, the team that had sent him to the Yankees headed to spring training in Florida in 1960. "This could be our year," Arnold Johnson proclaimed just before leaving an A's intra-squad game on March 9. He got in his car, drove six blocks, and collapsed against the steering wheel, sounding the horn for ten minutes until a woman called police to complain about the noise. A few hours later, he died in the hospital.[21]

History would judge Johnson harshly. Baseball scholar John Peterson says that although the much-maligned Yankees trades were not wholly one-sided in that they brought the A's a few decent players in return, Johnson did little to rebuild the team's farm system.[22] Another writer, Jeff Katz, asserts that Johnson maintained the Kansas City A's as a de facto Yankees farm team, just as the Kansas City Blues had been: "While it is impossible to prove collusion, the pattern was made abundantly clear, and the case is strong." Katz also argues that the *Star*'s Ernie Mehl was "the water carrier for the Yankees' lies."[23] Perhaps that assessment is unduly harsh, but Mehl had said bluntly that working with New York was the only way to get a major league franchise. He also was loyal to the last to the A's' late owner. "That Johnson had gone into this purely for financial gain, as some said, was ridiculous," Mehl wrote the day after Johnson's death. "We knew him to be honorable."[24]

Even so, Mehl now strove to find local ownership for the A's, presumably to avoid the charges of carpetbagging and collusion that had been levied against Johnson while also lessening the threat that another city would take the A's from Kansas City. "I am bitter when I read in those Eastern papers that this city is dead, because that means that we who live and work here are dead," the sports editor told a business luncheon. "That's not so, and we have a chance to prove it."[25] If attendance for 1960 fell below 850,000, the A's could cancel their stadium lease and leave town, and there was already interest in New Jersey, Dallas, Houston, and Minneapolis–St. Paul in obtaining the team. A ticket drive boosted attendance enough to maintain the lease (even though the A's finished last again), and for a time it looked as though local ownership might materialize as well. In December 1960, the American League provisionally approved a Kansas City group's bid to buy the team, despite reservations about the group's financing. Then Charles Finley—who like Arnold Johnson was from Chicago—pledged to top whatever bid the local group might make. The league approved the sale of the A's to Finley the week before Christmas.[26]

Joe McGuff, then the A's beat writer for the *Star,* lamented that there had not been enough financial support to secure home ownership. Yet he labored to be optimistic: "For better or worse, Charles O. Finley and Kansas City have been joined together in the bonds of major league baseball. It is a tenuous union, but there is a possibility that in time it will grow stronger."[27] There was in fact a brief honeymoon. Finley was a tireless, ebullient promoter who could be charming when the mood struck him. He declared that the A's would never abandon Kansas City ("brother, I mean to tell you, I'm here to stay!"), and he staged a public burning of what he said was the escape clause allowing him to leave if attendance declined. He also promised that there would be no more trades with the hated Yankees—and he burned a bus that he said represented the shuttle that had carried players from Kansas City to New York. Appropriately enough, *Sports Illustrated* in June 1961 called Finley a "ball of fire"; the magazine also claimed that he was "the kindliest owner in baseball." He had specially adapted a box seat to accommodate Kansas City's rotund and sonorous mayor, H. Roe Bartle. When the Yankees came to town with their star pitcher Whitey Ford, Bartle happily heckled him: "I remember you when you were a Kansas City Blue, Whitey! You're still bluuuuuuue!" As for Finley, the mayor's praise was unstinting: "He holds the heart of the city in the palm of his hand."[28]

Not everyone was a believer, particularly not Ernie Mehl and the *Kansas City Star*. They increasingly viewed Finley as a mendacious huckster prone to pettiness and vindictiveness. It developed that Finley had not actually burned the escape clause; it had been just a prop, and the clause remained in effect. In June just after the *Sports Illustrated* article appeared, Finley fired A's manager Joe Gordon; shortly thereafter, a syndicated sports columnist related how Gordon in his last days on the job had given umpires a lineup card inscribed "Approved by C.O.F." to mock the owner's controlling ways.[29] Two months later, Mehl learned that Finley was seeking to move the A's to Dallas. The sports editor, who was also a lay minister, lit into Finley with a column full of brimstone: "Had the ownership made a deliberate attempt to sabotage a baseball organization, it could not have succeeded as well. . . . There never has been a baseball operation such as this, nothing so bizarre, so impossibly incongruous." Mehl said that Finley's interference had made it virtually impossible for anyone to manage the A's and had demoralized the team: "And the real losers are the fans—the most loyal and patient in baseball, who have suffered now through seven seasons with hopes never realized, promises broken."[30]

Finley retorted that it was purely coincidental that he happened to be in Dallas toting a briefcase with materials regarding the city's viability as a baseball market. He added that the criticism of him had wounded him: "It makes me sick enough to want to take the ball club out of Kansas City."[31] And he staged an "Ernie Mehl Appreciation Day" before an A's home doubleheader. A truck festooned with red, white, and blue bunting drove around the field with a "1961 poison pen award" banner and a caricature of Mehl. The ballpark organist played "Who's Afraid of the Big Bad Wolf?" and fireworks went off as a sparse crowd watched in puzzled silence.[32] While baseball commissioner Ford Frick issued a public apology to Mehl, Finley stepped up his attack by pulling all advertising for the A's from the *Star*. He charged that under Arnold Johnson, the team had paid the travel expenses of Mehl and Joe McGuff, which Finley branded as "payola." The A's also had paid Mehl to edit the A's yearbook and McGuff to keep statistics for the team. Mehl countered that there had been nothing wrong with the yearbook or statistics arrangements and that neither he nor McGuff was receiving travel expenses from the A's.[33]

Eventually things were patched up enough that Mehl was invited to throw out the first pitch at the A's' 1962 home opener, with Finley acting as catcher; by then Finley also had signed an agreement deleting the attendance escape clause.[34] But the tone of the "tenuous union" between Finley and Kansas City had been set: there would be periodic blow-ups followed by temporary reconciliations amid continual dalliances with other city suitors. Impetus toward the final breakup would come with the arrival of a second big-league franchise in the city.

If Ernie Mehl and the *Star* had toiled mightily to bring the A's to town, Lamar Hunt and the Kansas City Chiefs "kinda came out of the blue," according to Joe McGuff.[35] Hunt was the son of Texas billionaire H. L. Hunt. The elder Hunt had made enemies through his extravagant lifestyle and vociferous right-wing views; his mild-mannered son offended no one. "Even the pro-Communist writers like him," said H. L. of his son's relationships with the press after the young man had become famous. Still, when twenty-seven-year-old Lamar Hunt announced in 1959 that he was forming the American Football League, at least one reporter felt sorry for him: "Here was this poor little rich boy, son of one of the world's richest men, standing up there like he was making a speech in catechism class. He spoke almost in a whisper, without any force or authority."[36]

The reporter's reaction foreshadowed the difficulties that Hunt and the AFL would face in garnering respect and successfully competing with the established National Football League. Hunt's original goal had been to obtain an NFL team for Dallas. After he failed to get an existing franchise to move or to persuade the NFL to expand, he decided to start a league of his own that would include his own team, the Dallas Texans. The NFL promptly announced that it would expand after all, placing the new Dallas Cowboys in direct competition with the Texans. Hunt quietly persevered: "I just know that it is very important that I succeed."[37] The Texans did succeed in winning the 1962 AFL title in an exciting overtime game that generated favorable publicity for the new league, but they struggled at the gate. It became clear to Hunt that the NFL Cowboys would command more loyalty than the Texans; he also had to worry about the future viability of the AFL, which needed strong franchises that fans supported. So despite Hunt's devotion to Dallas (he had been raised there, had gone to college there, and would always make his home there), he decided that he would have to move his team.[38]

Lamar Hunt (standing, left) in an awkward moment for the fledgling American Football League in 1959. Hunt is telling the press that the AFL's planned Minnesota franchise will not jump to the National Football League. After the Minnesota franchise did in fact jump to the NFL, the AFL would be forced to locate in Oakland instead. (AP Photo/Gene Herrick)

New Orleans was Hunt's first choice for a new site, but when Tulane Stadium was not available, he looked elsewhere. Kansas City had been investigating getting its own AFL team. It had inquired about the Oakland Raiders, who had been doing poorly both on and off the field, but the Raiders stayed put. In light of their experiences with Arnold Johnson and now with Charlie Finley, Kansas Citians wanted local ownership of a pro football franchise. "It would not be an easy or inexpensive thing," said Ernie Mehl in November 1962, "but we would have the pride of having a team that we owned ourselves, and one that would stay here indefinitely, as long as we supported it."[39] Although Lamar Hunt was not from Kansas City, Mayor H. Roe Bartle invited him to town after hearing of his intent to move the Texans. To indulge Hunt's desire for secrecy and Bartle's own taste for drama, the mayor introduced Hunt to everyone as "Mr. Lamar" and Texans general manager Jack Steadman as a mysterious investigator known only as "Jack X." ("I had some business associates and friends suggest certain persons Mr. X should investigate," Bartle later said.) Hunt confirmed in the spring of 1963 that the Texans would head north, and the *Kansas City Times* hailed the move as enhancing "Kansas City's 'big league' label" by providing "solid economic benefits" to "a well-balanced and growing American city."[40]

Some people questioned the means used to land the football team. Mayor Bartle and the city council approved a contract charging the team only one dollar in rent for each of the first two years of a seven-year stadium lease. Two council members voted against the contract. They argued that taxpayers should not subsidize a professional sports franchise, particularly when it belonged to a new league whose prospects seemed murky at best. "Mr. Hunt did not come to Kansas City with his hand out," countered Bartle. "He was approached by the mayor on bended knee."[41]

The city's "bended knee" gesture provoked a speedy reaction from Charlie Finley. He asked Mayor Bartle and the city council for a similar deal for the A's, saying that he had spent $400,000 of his own money on stadium improvements. Bartle was about to leave office after a sometimes bumpy tenure as mayor. His leadership had been questioned; according to one history of Kansas City, although Bartle was "an accomplished speaker and better than average public relations man, he had little experience or ability to run a large city."[42] Nevertheless, he was determined to maintain Kansas City's hard-won big-league status, consistent with his public relations instincts. With what the mayor said was the backing of the local Chamber of Commerce, the city council voted to give Finley what he wanted: a revised stadium lease charging a dollar a year rent for two years. That vote occurred immediately before the new mayor Ilus Davis and a new city council took office. In turn Davis and the new council promptly shelved the revised lease. They said—and Bartle later acknowledged—that the lease had been illegally executed.[43]

The already-strained relationship between the city and Finley was pushed to the breaking point. "I want to say now that this new city council is not going to push Charlie Finley around and give him a rotten deal," he fumed. He had spent the previous baseball season still trying to move the A's to Dallas. Now he contacted Atlanta sports editor Furman Bisher about possibly moving the A's there. Atlanta had wholeheartedly embraced the pursuit of major league sports as a strategy for raising its national profile. After Bisher and Atlanta's mayor gave Finley a tour of potential stadium sites, Finley returned to Kansas City determined to transplant his team south. In May 1963, a picture of him sitting next to Lamar Hunt appeared on the front page of the *Kansas City Times* with the caption, "They Have Faith in Their Teams." It was later revealed that Finley had urged Hunt to move his football team to Atlanta along with Finley's A's and ditch Kansas City altogether, with Finley telling Hunt, "This is a horseshit town, and no one will ever do any good here." Finley abandoned the Atlanta idea when he learned that other American League baseball owners would not support it, but by then he had eyes for another new suitor—this one in California.[44]

* * *

In the 1860s, Bret Harte published a short story about a fictional earthquake that destroyed San Francisco but left Oakland intact, demonstrating that "there are some things the earth cannot swallow." The quip came to be cited as one of the more infamous putdowns of Oakland, although it could just as easily be seen as a tribute to the city's indestructability. When in 1906 a real-life earthquake and fire ruined San Francisco, Oakland was largely spared, and the city became a haven for tens of thousands of refugees from across the Bay—not that it necessarily provided any lasting boost to Oakland's standing in the eyes of its neighbor.[45]

The reality, as historian Beth Bagwell has noted, was that power and prestige became concentrated on the west side of the Bay: "The banks, the stock exchange, and the U.S. Mint were in San Francisco, as well as the attorneys and courts and the headquarters offices of corporations." But the "cotton or lumber or wheat or canned peaches that the tycoons bought and sold" most likely came via Oakland.[46] The city's blue-collar roots were established early in its history. The first transcontinental railroad made Oakland its western terminus, and the railroad spawned industries ranging from mills and canneries to shipyards and automobile plants. World War II brought more industry to town and a huge influx of defense workers, including African Americans from the South. Then the war ended and many of the jobs disappeared. By the 1950s and 1960s, according to Bagwell, "Oakland became the example everyone thought of to illustrate the urban problems of crime and blight."[47]

Such negative publicity rankled the *Oakland Tribune* and the family that published it. Joseph Knowland had bought the *Tribune* in 1915 after serving five terms as a Republican in the U.S. Congress; he built the Tribune Tower that became a downtown Oakland landmark. His son William served as the Republican leader in the U.S. Senate before a failed run for California governor in 1958 ended his career in electoral politics. The younger Knowland returned to Oakland to become editor of the *Tribune,* and then he became editor-publisher-president after his father died in 1966.[48]

"The influence of the Knowland family has run through every facet of city life," a study of Oakland would observe. The *Tribune* had "few equals in political influence among urban newspapers," ensuring that conservatives and pro-business interests maintained control of municipal government. Members of the city council and the school board largely selected their own successors, as described by the *New York Times* in 1966: "When a member is ready to retire he usually resigns before his term has expired. This gives the Council the opportunity to appoint a successor to fill out the term. The new member can then run for re-election as an 'incumbent.' Because of the apathy toward city politics, incumbents almost never lose."[49]

The city council also was almost exclusively white despite Oakland's growing African American population. That was in keeping with the *Tribune*'s editorial policy, which critics charged gave readers "a picture of a peaceful, all-white city that did not exist."[50] The newspaper banned the use of "ghetto" or "flatlands" in news stories, the latter being a term that identified African American neighborhoods in the city. Nor were those the only prohibited words: "homosexual" was prohibited in favor of "sex criminal," and "rape" could be used only in headlines, where it fit more easily than the preferred alternative "criminal assault." According to a reporter who worked for the *Tribune* in the early 1960s, the paper "stalwartly opposed all welfare legislation, all forms of federal aid (except those beneficial to newspapers, such as the second-class mailing subsidy), decried the affairs of organized labor, and seemed to suspect most Democrats of being un-American."[51]

Regardless, the Knowlands and the *Tribune* remained steadfast boosters of Oakland. When the city opened a new "international" air terminal in 1962, the newspaper mandated that *Tribune* staffers use it at all times, even though it offered only a fraction of the flights of the San Francisco airport. When a bond issue supporting a local community college was on the ballot, William Knowland's editorial board informed him that they unanimously opposed it. "The vote is one to five, and I win," Knowland replied. "We endorse the bonds."[52] And when the *New York Times* called Oakland "a dull, shabby city suffering from commercial and cultural blight" in the same 1966 article detailing how the city's council members were selected, Knowland sprang to his hometown's defense (much as the *Kansas City Star*'s Ernie Mehl had bristled over the unnamed "Eastern papers" that he said had disrespected his city). "Most of us were shocked that a paper with the reputation for objectivity and integrity should have permitted itself to be used as the medium for this type of biased and misleading reporting," Knowland wrote in a letter to the *Times*. "It is a libel against the community of Oakland." In his signature, he identified himself not as editor-publisher of the *Oakland Tribune*, but instead as president of the Oakland Chamber of Commerce.[53]

Unsurprisingly, the *Tribune* fervently backed Oakland's efforts to land major league sports. The city had long hosted the Oakland Oaks, a minor league baseball team that sports historian Paul Brekke-Miesner would call "the athletic heart and soul of the city for three generations." The Oaks had belonged to the Pacific Coast League, which shortly after World War II had unsuccessfully petitioned to be designated a separate major league.[54] Now with San Francisco and Los Angeles having joined the big time via the Giants and Dodgers, Oakland wanted to follow suit.

First, though, the city would get an American Football League charter franchise. That opportunity arose only because the AFL's planned Minneapolis franchise jumped to the National Football League. Just as the NFL's entry into Dallas would prompt Lamar Hunt to move his team to Kansas City, the NFL's move into Minneapolis prompted the AFL to find a different site for its franchise. Oakland emerged as the leading candidate (the owner of the AFL's Los Angeles Chargers wanted a second team in California), but the mayor of San Francisco, which already had an NFL team, questioned the move. In return the Oakland City Council blasted the mayor for what council members called his "attack" on their city. The AFL finally did vote in January 1960 to place the team in Oakland, with William Knowland promising that it would promote "civic interest, enthusiasm, and the spirit of moving forward."[55]

The new franchise immediately ran into trouble. The *Tribune* cosponsored a contest to name the team, but the winning entry—the "Oakland Señors"—drew so much ridicule that the team was quickly renamed the "Raiders."[56] Even with the new moniker, the Raiders were a sad-sack outfit. Upon traveling to Boston for a preseason game, the team had to use a youth sports field for practice until they were evicted for a Little League game. Training table meals, according to the Raiders' Jim Otto, consisted of "eighth-inch thick roast beef, make-believe mashed potatoes, and frozen green beans." There was no stadium in Oakland, and the University of California had refused the use of its stadium in Berkeley. Hence the Raiders played their home games in San Francisco's Kezar Stadium and Candlestick Park before crowds so small "they could have fit the fans in our locker room," as another Raider recalled. Before the end of the Raiders' first season in 1960, it was already rumored that they might move to a different city.[57]

The team's dire straits lent extra urgency to Oakland's building a stadium of its own. As part of the bid to land the Raiders, the city council had unanimously endorsed such a facility, but there was disagreement over where to locate it and how to pay for it. A proposal to build the stadium near downtown was rejected in favor of an East Oakland industrial site near the airport; it offered more space, better traffic access, and fewer land acquisition problems, and it also was said to be at the geographic center of the Bay Area's population. As for financing, a so-called lease purchase plan was devised. A nonprofit corporation would sell tax-exempt bonds to fund the stadium's construction. The corporation would then operate the completed stadium and collect rent from the city and Alameda County, with the rent used to pay off the bonds. The corporation's board of directors would include William Knowland and local industrialist Edgar Kaiser, and its head would be real estate developer Robert Nahas.[58]

The can-do Nahas represented the white conservative establishment that ran Oakland, although he objected to the "establishment" label. "In this age of dissent and demonstrations, we have often heard the term 'power structure' or 'the establishment' referred to scathingly as though it were a group of privileged characters sitting in a closed room amongst luxurious surroundings busy dividing up somebody else's property," he would tell a luncheon held in his honor. In reality it consisted of "selfless people who serve on commissions, boards or committees" and who "help in small ways or large ways to build a finer and better community." Still, the new stadium was carefully planned to avoid the need for voter approval. Back in 1946, voters had rejected a bond issue that would have built a new ballpark for the Oaks, and there was little confidence that a new ballot initiative would succeed now. The lease purchase plan did not require citizens to endorse it, and the plan also helped ensure that Nahas and other businesspeople would be in complete control of the project once construction began. As Nahas put it, "If I had to clear everything with the city council, I wouldn't touch it with a ten-foot pole."[59]

Matters did not always proceed as swiftly or smoothly as Nahas may have preferred. It took all of 1961 to obtain the land and develop architectural plans for the Oakland–Alameda County Coliseum Complex, which would include an arena in addition to a football-baseball stadium. Meanwhile the Raiders stumbled to a 2-12 record during the 1961 season, and co-owners Wayne Valley and Ed McGah threatened to move the franchise if it had to continue playing home games in San Francisco. Oakland built a temporary facility near Lake Merritt east of downtown called Frank Youell Field, which was named after a city council member and sports booster. It opened in time for the 1962 season, but it did not help the Raiders, who finished at 1-13 amid new rumors that they might move to Kansas City or elsewhere as the AFL continued to struggle to find stable, secure homes for its teams. The speculation surrounding Oakland ended only when Wayne Valley announced in November 1962 that the team would not be sold and that Mayor John Houlihan would lead a drive to sell 12,000 season tickets for 1963.[60]

By then the reliably pro-business Oakland City Council had voted to approve the plans for the new sports complex. "If we fail now, we'll never have a stadium, and we'll always be a doormat," Frank Youell had told the council before its vote. Afterward, Mayor Houlihan declared it to be "the day of the big breakthrough in the effort to get Oakland moving forward again."[61] Most eloquent was George Ross, the sports editor of the *Oakland Tribune* and the person who would be called the "Mother Superior" of Oakland's professional sports teams. "The City of Oakland took a bold and unhesitant step forward last night and pulled the entire Eastbay miles toward major league greatness," Ross told his readers. He foresaw World Series and pro football championships in Oakland's future thanks to the complex: "It generates momentum which can place us in the family of great cities of America. . . . If we lift our eyes we can see our fine home town, long scorned as the 'bedroom of the Bay Area,' a proud and honored place." Robert Nahas said that the sports complex might be ready by 1964.[62]

However, Nahas could not persuade California investment bankers to buy bonds to fund the project; the bonds had to be sold out of state. In an outraged editorial, the *Tribune* blamed "a concerted campaign inspired by certain San Francisco financial houses and newspapers not noted for their interest in Oakland progress."[63] The city and Alameda County still had to approve the contracts to begin construction, and the *Tribune* vigorously advocated for approval with a multipart series extolling the multitude of blessings that the Coliseum promised to bestow: it would help schools; it would promote trade; it would attract concerts and graduations; it would spark hotel construction and bring in horse shows and boost membership in the Boy Scouts.[64] A small group of public officials and taxpayers in Alameda County did question why citizens would not be able to vote on the project, but that opposition faded, and in April 1963, the contracts were approved.[65] Then legal challenges were filed against the financing plan and leasing terms for not fully complying with state law. Favorable court rulings and tweaks to the lease finally allowed groundbreaking to take place in May 1964. "Like a new-born sun," the *Tribune* gushed, the Coliseum would radiate "continuous, life-provoking warmth."[66]

* * *

One of the Coliseum's biggest advantages (as the *Tribune* also had been careful to point out) was that it offered a potential home for a major league baseball team.[67] Baseball was critical to the new complex's success, for the Raiders would play there only a few days a year in comparison with the eighty-plus days that a baseball team would be in residence. Thus did Oakland and Charlie Finley emerge on each other's radar. In the summer of 1963, Finley remained at odds with Kansas City over the A's' stadium lease, and with Atlanta no longer an option, he turned to Oakland as a possible new site for his team—or rather he turned to San Francisco, considering there was not yet a finished stadium in Oakland able to host the A's. However, San Francisco Giants owner Horace Stoneham refused to allow Finley to use Candlestick Park as a temporary home until the Coliseum was completed. Then Oakland offered to rebuild Frank Youell Field to accommodate baseball. It was widely believed that the American League wanted a team in Oakland; the league recently had placed an expansion team (the Angels) in the Los Angeles area, and adding a Bay Area team would make for a natural rivalry. But league president Joe Cronin said that the league was not convinced that Finley was justified in leaving Kansas City.[68]

The battle between Finley and Kansas City dragged on into the winter of 1963–1964 and turned farcical. When city officials informed Finley that his Municipal Stadium lease would automatically renew on January 1 if the A's were still occupying offices there, Finley moved the offices to a team employee's garage. He declared that the A's would play their home games in a cow pasture, and he toured potential sites with reporters. (One such pasture near Peculiar, Missouri led to jokes about the "Peculiar A's.") Negotiations over a new Kansas City lease degenerated into Finley yelling at the city council: "Do you want my coat? Do you want my shirt?"[69] Finley then announced that the A's would move to Louisville, saying that they might change their name to the Kentucky Colonels so that they could keep the "KC" on their caps. *Kansas City Star* sports editor Ernie Mehl warned that the good of baseball was at stake: "It is being threatened. It is being challenged. It is being defied." The other American League owners vetoed the move and threatened to expel Finley if he did not come to terms with Kansas City. Undeterred,

Finley pivoted back toward Oakland and struck a tentative deal to play there. *Oakland Tribune* sports editor George Ross made it clear that the city had invited Finley and that it was telling Major League Baseball, "We're courting."[70]

In the end, American League owners rejected the Oakland move just as they had the Louisville move, and in February 1964 Finley finally signed a new, non-cancellable four-year lease to stay in Kansas City, protesting that he had been the victim of "one of the greatest injustices in baseball history." Oakland turned to Cleveland to try to persuade the major league team there to move, but when that effort failed, the city seemed content to wait until the completed Coliseum was ready to host either a new expansion team or Finley's A's once his new lease in Kansas City expired.[71] Crucially for the long-term future of the A's, Finley had begun spending considerable sums to sign players—not the castoffs from the Yankees and other teams who had weighed down the A's to that point, but instead young, blue-chip talent identified by A's executive Hank Peters and team scouts. Infielders Bert Campaneris and Dick Green, catcher Dave Duncan, and pitcher John "Blue Moon" Odom already were on the big-league roster by 1964. Over the next three years, the A's would acquire pitchers Jim "Catfish" Hunter, Rollie Fingers, and Vida Blue; third baseman Sal Bando; catcher–first baseman Gene Tenace; and outfielders Joe Rudi, Rick Monday, and Reggie Jackson. Most of those players would make their major league debuts in Kansas City, but almost none would develop fully until after the A's moved to Oakland.[72]

Instead of winning baseball, Finley gave Kansas City glitz and gimmicks. He outfitted the A's in what he called "Kelly green," "Fort Knox gold," and "wedding gown white" uniforms. He installed a pop-up mechanical rabbit named "Harvey" to deliver baseballs to the home plate umpire in Municipal Stadium and a compressed air jet to blow dirt off home plate. He put sheep and a shepherd on the grassy hill beyond the right field fence. He changed the team mascot to a live mule named "Charlie O" and toured the country with the mule. He moved the fences in and out and built a "Pennant Porch" to replicate the dimensions of Yankee Stadium until Major League Baseball ordered him to remove it. In September 1964, Finley spent $150,000 to bring the Beatles to town. (The Beatles forfeited a planned free day in New Orleans to play in

Charlie Finley with his then-wife Shirley in 1973 after he had moved his A's to Oakland. The team's mule mascot "Charlie O" is at far left. (Russ Reed, untitled. Gelatin silver, 10 x 8 in. The Oakland Tribune Collection, the Oakland Museum of California, gift of ANG Newspapers.)

Kansas City. When they were asked during a Kansas City news conference if there was any place they really wanted to see but could not, John Lennon immediately replied, "New Orleans.")[73] Finley hired and fired managers and radio announcers and micromanaged his players while the A's languished around the bottom of the league, with attendance following suit. One long-suffering fan called the franchise "a grimy, dirty machine, grotesquely inefficient and with a personality nobody liked." Another fan remembered pestering visiting teams for autographs, but never the A's, for they were "hapless, and we were embarrassed to be seen in the same city."[74]

By 1965 it seemed that big-league sports in Kansas City was in crisis—not just the A's, but also Lamar Hunt's AFL team. After being talked out of keeping the name "Texans," Hunt had renamed his team the Kansas City Chiefs, partly in tribute to Mayor Bartle, whose nickname was "the Chief."[75] The team heavily employed Native American imagery. Hunt designed an interlocking "KC" inside an arrowhead for the players' helmets. The old team logo featuring a six-shooter-wielding cowboy superimposed on a map of Texas gave way to a tomahawk-wielding Native American superimposed on a map of Missouri, Kansas, Iowa, Nebraska, Arkansas, and Oklahoma. A man wearing a headdress would ride a horse named Warpaint around Municipal Stadium after every Chiefs touchdown.[76]

For all of Hunt's efforts to rebrand his franchise, the Chiefs appeared cursed during their first years in their new home. Rookie Stone Johnson broke his neck in a 1963 preseason game and died a few days later. Offensive lineman Ed Budde got into a brawl in a midtown Kansas City tavern in March 1964 and ended up with a plate in his skull. The following December, on a street not far from where Budde had been hurt, a man slugged tight end Fred Arbanas, blinding him in one eye. (As sports historian Michael MacCambridge notes, Kansas City was then "sprinkled with a series of mean little bars and dimly lit nightclubs, some of them still under Mafia control.") Arbanas and Budde were able to continue their football careers, but late during the 1965 season, tragedy struck again: running back Mack Lee Hill died during seemingly routine knee surgery.[77]

Compounding the Chiefs' woes was a mediocre record and tepid attendance. They were unable to win more than half their games in any of their first three seasons in Kansas City. Even with a six-state territory, the team confronted indifference toward pro football and the American Football League. The *Kansas City Star*'s Bill Richardson recalled that he was assigned to cover the Chiefs only because other *Star* sportswriters did not want to give up covering college football for an "unknown pro team." Richardson also said that the Chiefs' ticket prices were significantly higher than those for college games, which hurt attendance.[78] In addition there was what the *Star*'s Joe McGuff described as "the Charles O. Finley syndrome"—Kansas Citians suspected that Lamar Hunt might skip town just as Finley had been trying to do. It did not help when

Chiefs head scout Don Klosterman was quoted in 1965 as saying that Kansas City was "a little like living in purgatory. It's not exactly heaven, but it isn't hell." Klosterman felt compelled to resign early the next year after the Associated Press took his remarks out of context and erroneously made it sound as though the Chiefs might move to Los Angeles.[79]

Fear of losing its teams propelled Kansas City toward building its own new sports complex. Discussion of such a complex dated back many years, but by 1965 it had assumed added urgency. One of the complex's most passionate proponents was Jackson County official Morris Dubiner. "We must not be left at the starting gate," Dubiner said. If the city and county failed to act, "we would slip back to minor league status or worse." The *Star*'s Ernie Mehl also was a forceful advocate: "We must keep up with the other cities. We must build a new stadium or lose major league football and baseball." Not everyone was swayed by such arguments, just as not everyone had been convinced that the Chiefs and A's deserved generous stadium leases. City counselor Herbert Hoffman warned that the competition to obtain and retain major league teams by building expensive new facilities was getting out of hand and that it was allowing team owners to take unfair advantage of cities: "We've got to stop this insanity before it goes any further."[80]

Hoffman's warning went unheeded; events were moving too quickly. By April 1966, Atlanta's vigorous boosterism had paid off with a major league baseball team. The Braves had left Milwaukee—the city that had inspired Kansas City to seek its own big league team—after just thirteen seasons, lured to Atlanta by a much richer broadcasting contract as well as a new stadium that was rushed to completion with the specific goal of landing just such a franchise. (Atlanta Mayor Ivan Allen Jr. later boasted that the stadium had been built "on ground we didn't own with money we didn't have for clubs we had not yet signed.")[81] The following September, the new Oakland Coliseum opened. The delays in groundbreaking had added to costs, forcing the construction team to economize. The entire complex was built for $30 million. Its centerpiece, a stadium seating up to 53,000, could politely be described as utilitarian. Less politely, San Francisco sportswriter Wells Twombly would describe it as looking "as if the Great Concrete God threw up in a parking lot." *Oakland Tribune* sports editor George Ross did not care. "Congratulations, Oakland. You're beautiful," he wrote upon the

Coliseum's opening. "You've moved with grace and class and quiet pride this September Sunday when all America smiles a warm greeting as you curtsy in debut into the family of major league sister cities."[82]

The Coliseum already had secured the Raiders as tenants. The football team had executed a remarkable turnaround under new coach and general manager Al Davis. He had upgraded facilities and personnel while giving the Raiders new, distinctive silver and black uniforms, and they promptly ascended from their 1-13 mark in 1962 to a 10-4 mark in 1963. After a losing record in 1964, the Raiders began a run of sixteen consecutive winning seasons, establishing themselves as one of the most successful professional football franchises ever. Davis coined the team motto "Pride and Poise" early in his tenure and urged Oakland to support the team: "You've got to grow with us." The city embraced the Raiders' blue-collar image that was fostered by Davis. "I hope that Oakland always retains the 'hungry boy on the wrong side of the track' attitude and avoids becoming the dilettante and sophisticate like some people I know," said Robert Nahas at a Raider Appreciation Dinner. The implication, of course, was that the "dilettante and sophisticate" lounged on the opposite side of the Bay.[83]

But the Coliseum still needed a baseball tenant—and in Kansas City, Charlie Finley had been conspicuously silent regarding the talk of a new stadium being built there. In contrast, Lamar Hunt and the Chiefs were much more receptive. They worked with the new Greater Kansas City Sports Commission in selling 22,000 Chiefs season tickets for 1966. (Ernie Mehl, newly retired as *Star* sports editor, chaired the commission.) They also worked with the new Jackson County Sports Complex Authority in planning a complex. The original idea was to build a dome modeled on the Houston Astrodome, whose construction had landed Houston an expansion big-league baseball team. When the Astrodome opened in 1965, it had been labeled the "Eighth Wonder of the World." Kansas City's own dome was to have been located downtown, following the desires of city business leaders. But some Jackson County interests opposed the downtown site as serving Kansas City at the rest of the county's expense. Businesses that would be displaced threatened to move across the state line to Kansas. Traffic and parking concerns and anticipated high construction and energy costs also worked against the downtown dome proposal.[84]

Thus a different site was selected for the new facility. It would be on the far eastern edge of the city and located more centrally within the county as a whole; it also would sit near the intersection of two major freeways. And if the city could not have an actual dome—something that, after all, at least one other city already had—then Kansas City would have something nobody else had: a dual stadium complex with a rolling roof to cover either stadium in inclement weather. There would be separate stadiums for football and baseball in accordance with the wishes of Lamar Hunt and Chiefs general manager Jack Steadman, who believed that multipurpose facilities (the "cookie cutter" stadiums like the Oakland Coliseum that other cities were then building) worked poorly for football.[85]

Unlike in Oakland, Kansas City's new sports complex required voter approval of a bond issue, and the unique dual stadium, rolling roof concept was a powerful selling point. According to historian Robert Lewis, voters had another motivation to support the complex: "They were going to prove, by God, that Kansas City was big league, and if anybody was bush, it was [Charlie] Finley."[86] Yet there still was hope that passing the bonds might persuade Finley and the A's to remain in town. Joe McGuff, who had succeeded Ernie Mehl as *Star* sports editor, wrote that some people opposed the bond issue on the grounds that fans had not been filling Municipal Stadium for the A's and so a new baseball stadium could not be justified. In response McGuff pointed to the surge in attendance in such cities as St. Louis and New York, where new stadiums had just opened. And, McGuff noted, San Diego, Pittsburgh, and Philadelphia were building their own new facilities to try to land big-league teams or keep the ones that they already had. McGuff argued that approving the bond issue "would solidly establish Kansas City and Jackson County as one of the growing, progressive areas in the country," a stance echoed by the *Star* in front-page editorials. The June 1967 ballot question on the sports complex required a two-thirds majority vote for approval; it passed with 68.9 percent voting yes.[87]

The day after the vote, McGuff hailed the result, but he admitted that Charlie Finley's continued refusal to commit to the new complex was "disappointing." It was especially so in that the sports commission had had some success in selling season tickets for the A's and that the young team had recently shown some potential. They had won seventy-four games during 1966—hardly an earthshaking number, but still their most wins ever in Kansas City, and enough to make the A's the subject of a *Sports Illustrated* cover story during spring training the next year. By the time of the bond issue vote, though, the team was back in the doldrums and manager Al Dark was calling the A's "snake-bitten."[88] Then in August Finley publicly accused his players of getting drunk on a team flight, and he suspended pitcher Lew Krausse. In quick succession, the players issued their own public statement protesting Finley's actions; Finley fired, rehired, and then refired Al Dark over the manager's support for his players; A's player Ken Harrelson blasted Finley in the press; and Finley released Harrelson. Kansas City fans responded by hanging Finley in effigy and displaying signs such as one that said, "Go, Go, *Finkley*—Stay A's."[89]

By the fall of 1967, it appeared increasingly likely that Finley would go, but increasingly unlikely that the A's would stay. Finley had refused to sell the A's to anyone in Kansas City, and with his stadium lease there about to expire, he had shopped his team to Milwaukee (which was seeking a replacement for the Braves) as well as to New Orleans and Seattle. Oakland returned to the top of his wish list—unlike New Orleans and Seattle, it had a stadium ready; and unlike Milwaukee, Oakland would allow him to retain sole ownership. In October Finley officially announced his intent to move the A's to Oakland, saying that the Coliseum offered "the finest facilities for major sports anywhere in the world" and that the city's climate was "second to none in the country." Taking no chances with Finley's wanderlust, Oakland would sign him to a twenty-year stadium lease.[90] The American League team owners planned to meet later in October to vote whether to approve the move, and the outcome was uncertain.

Anticipating that Finley would try to leave, Joe McGuff and Ernie Mehl had spent much of the 1967 baseball season quietly lobbying other team owners. McGuff recalled that Boston Red Sox owner Tom Yawkey told him that an owner should be able to do what he pleased with his team. "I told [Yawkey] I agreed with that if the owner was on the level, if he was trying to operate a good ball club," McGuff said. "But in Kansas City, we had an owner who was trying to sabotage the club in order to get it out of town."[91] When the owners convened at a Chicago hotel to decide the A's' fate, McGuff and Mehl traveled there with a Kansas City

delegation that included Mayor Ilus Davis, U.S. senator Stuart Symington of Missouri, and Dutton Brookfield of the Jackson County Sports
Complex Authority. The Oakland delegation included Robert Nahas
and William Knowland. After a lengthy and contentious meeting, the
owners announced their verdict: Finley's A's would be allowed to start
play in Oakland in 1968, and Kansas City and Seattle would receive
expansion franchises "as soon as practicable," but no later than 1971.[92]

Upon hearing the news, Stuart Symington asked a league lawyer just
what "as soon as practicable" meant. When the lawyer expressed uncer-
tainty, Symington stormed out of the room, followed by Mayor Davis.
Downstairs in the hotel lobby, Joe McGuff and Ernie Mehl encountered
Tom Yawkey. "I guess you got what you wanted," Yawkey told them. "No,
Tom, we didn't get what we wanted!" the sportswriters said. They did
not want Kansas City to be without big-league baseball for a prolonged
period, and they feared that *as soon as practicable* might easily turn into
never. Yawkey told the two men that he would see what he could do,
and McGuff and Mehl soon learned that the owners had reconvened,
although without a quorum. There was the implicit threat that Kansas
City would sue, or worse, that Senator Symington would initiate antitrust action in Congress against Major League Baseball. The state of
Wisconsin had filed an antitrust suit unsuccessfully trying to keep the
Braves from moving to Atlanta, and the owners were wary about inviting a new and potentially more dangerous action against them. At 1:15
in the morning, the league issued a new announcement: Kansas City
and Seattle's new teams were guaranteed to begin play in 1969.[93]

News of the A's' impending arrival thrilled Oakland. The front page
of the *Tribune*'s sports section was emblazoned with a drawing of an
Athletics pennant. "Do you realize we have on our hands the greatest
sports complex in the world?" an elated Robert Nahas told the paper. The
Tribune in turn praised him as the "patient and brilliant man who, more
than any other single person, brought about Oakland's emergence into
major league prominence which rivals and surpasses that of San Francisco." The *Star*'s Joe McGuff told his readers that Kansas City had "paid
a heavy price to rid itself of Finley. It has given up a team that has several
potential stars." Yet "a new team with local ownership will at least offer
the fans a chance to root for a team that belongs to Kansas City"—not,
it was implied, to New York (home of the Yankees), to Chicago (home
of Arnold Johnson and Charlie Finley), or to any other rival city.[94]

McGuff did not tell readers about the role that he and Mehl had played in the proceedings in Chicago. Nor, at least not according to the available evidence, did McGuff or Stuart Symington say publicly that Oakland was "the luckiest city since Hiroshima" (although it seems likely that one or the other said it in private).[95] Yet Symington did have choice words regarding Finley in a speech to the U.S. Senate: "At long last the people of Kansas City and the Midwest have rid themselves of one of the most disreputable characters ever to enter the American sports scene. . . . Our only regret is that Mr. Finley has now been foisted on our good friend, former Senator Bill Knowland." Senator George Murphy of California delivered a decidedly more upbeat Senate speech that made the A's' move sound almost like Manifest Destiny: "In the 19th century, Kansas City was the jumping-off place for Americans heading west. Thousands of pioneers rendezvoused in Missouri before setting out on the trail for California and the other states west of the Mississippi. I am happy to report that the movement continues to this day."[96]

Charlie Finley arrived in Oakland on October 26, 1967 and was greeted by a sign-waving crowd of about four hundred well-wishers. "In Kansas City, we played practically all our games before groups of this size," he told the crowd. Ron Bergman, at the start of what would be an eventful run as the A's beat writer for the *Oakland Tribune*, reported that Finley hoped to see a substantial boost in broadcast revenue in Oakland over what he had been receiving in Kansas City, similar to the boost that the Braves had seen when they moved from Milwaukee to Atlanta. Finley also rejected warnings by San Francisco Giants owner Horace Stoneham that the Bay Area was not big enough for both the Giants and the A's: "I wouldn't have fought for five years to come to Oakland if I did not think the area could support two teams."[97]

All in all, the A's owner made a good first impression; Bergman noted that by "his second day in Oakland, Finley still hadn't antagonized anyone." Finley remained exultant when he ran into Joe McGuff in late November at the baseball winter meetings in Mexico City. "Oakland is heaven after Kansas City," Finley told McGuff. "Wait two years and then let's see what you'll say," McGuff retorted.[98] In fact, plenty of antagonism was in store for Finley and the A's, and Oakland and Kansas City were in for no small share of both heaven and hell.

2 Chiefs vs. Raiders, Part I

"WE HAVE BEEN ASKED OVER and over again what we think about the Kansas City Athletics moving to Oakland. Well, to be honest with you, we're not thinking of the Athletics as a baseball team but more in the vein of what economic profit it will bring to the black man in the East Bay."

Sam Skinner was sports editor of the *Sun-Reporter*, an African American newspaper in the Bay Area. His October 1967 comments in the paper highlighted Oakland's serious unemployment problem among African Americans. An accompanying *Sun-Reporter* editorial highlighted another reality—there had been no African Americans in the Oakland group that had gone to Chicago to lobby baseball owners to allow the A's to move west. "If publisher and former Senator William F. Knowland [was] on the delegation, surely one soul brother should have made up part of the delegation," the paper said.[1]

The late 1960s would bring high excitement to both Oakland and Kansas City as they reveled in their big-league status and the notice that their football teams brought them. The Raiders and Chiefs overcame their early woes to emerge as powerhouses, and a fierce rivalry developed between them as they struggled for preeminence in the American Football League. But they and the AFL still were saddled with the "Mickey Mouse" image thrust upon them by partisans of the National Football League.[2] The African American star athletes on their rosters confronted the same discrimination that African American citizens of the two cities had long faced. Increasingly—as suggested by the *Sun-*

Reporter's coverage of the A's' move—many citizens and athletes challenged the slights and injustices that they experienced both in the cities and in the sports world.

* * *

Kansas City and Oakland had had vibrant African American communities for many years. During the 1930s when Tom Pendergast ruled Kansas City, the 18th and Vine neighborhood east of downtown hosted nightspots featuring such jazz and blues legends as Count Basie, Big Joe Turner, and a young Charlie Parker. It also hosted the Street Hotel, where the Kansas City Monarchs were resident celebrities. "You were actually thrown right in the limelight in that time, and that part of town was really jumping," the Monarchs' Buck O'Neil recalled.[3] In the West Oakland flatlands where multiple railroad lines converged, Pullman porters enjoyed similar status. Oakland native and future mayor Ron Dellums described the porters as the "astronauts" of the African American community in that they "ventured out into the broader world and then came back to tell stories about who they saw, who they met, what they heard, what they learned." World War II brought thousands of defense jobs to West Oakland and thousands of African Americans from the South to fill the jobs, and 7th Street became a robust retail and entertainment district catering to the new arrivals.[4]

Yet both cities had been hostile toward their African American residents. During the 1920s, at least two thousand Oaklanders were members of the Ku Klux Klan, which sought "to remove the Jews, Catholics and Negroes from public life in California." After the war, unemployment soared in West Oakland because of a decline in the shipbuilding and passenger railroad businesses, and the neighborhood was torn apart by the building of the Cypress Freeway (which would collapse during a 1989 earthquake) and rapid-transit lines.[5] Kansas City had its own large KKK population in the 1920s when future NAACP leader Roy Wilkins lived there. He said that the city was "thoroughly segregated" and "a Jim Crow town right down to its bootstraps." Segregation persisted after the war, and many Kansas City–area residential districts had covenants prohibiting African Americans from living there.[6]

That was the environment the Dallas Texans encountered when Lamar Hunt moved the team to Kansas City in 1963 to become the Chiefs. Like other American Football League teams, the Texans had sought to be competitive by seeking players from African American colleges that the National Football League often had ignored. As one AFL player later put it, "The league couldn't afford to have a racist bone in its body." Just before moving to Kansas City, the Texans had made Grambling defensive lineman Buck Buchanan the number-one overall pick in the AFL draft. "I was the first player from a small black school drafted in the first round," Buchanan would recall. "That's one of the reasons I came to the American Football League." In its early years, the AFL also needed money to outbid the NFL for college players, and Lamar Hunt was rich. The same year that Hunt's team obtained Buchanan, it also obtained other future mainstays of the team: offensive linemen Ed Budde and Dave Hill, punter Jerrel Wilson, and linebacker Bobby Bell, the latter of whom signed what a Chiefs official later said was the biggest contract a pro football player had ever received up to that time.[7]

None of the team's players—new or old, black or white—was particularly happy about leaving Dallas for Kansas City. Defensive lineman Jerry Mays and other players had strong family ties to Dallas. (Mays would briefly retire after the 1963 season in Kansas City to return to Dallas, before being persuaded to return to the team.) Quarterback Len Dawson recalled that some people seemed to believe that Kansas City had "horses and cattle running in the middle of the main street in the city." Such misconceptions may not have been dispelled by the literature that the players received publicizing homes in Prairie Village, Kansas. "We said to ourselves, 'Prairie Village!'" remembered wide receiver Chris Burford. "What kind of place is that?"[8]

Prairie Village was actually a very nice place, a suburb of Kansas City, Missouri, that developer J. C. Nichols had founded in the 1940s. After the war, it and other suburbs just over the state line in Johnson County, Kansas, had seen their populations boom. But like many other Nichols developments and Johnson County suburbs, Prairie Village was closed to African American homeowners. Bobby Bell hailed from Minnesota and had thought that as an African American, he would be treated the same in the Kansas City area as he had been back home. Instead it took him five years—until 1968—to find someone willing to sell him a home in Johnson County's Overland Park. Soon after he bought the house, he received a flier about a neighborhood meeting: "Turns out it was to protest me and my family moving in."[9]

Oakland also had covenants and segregation that had restricted African Americans to living in West Oakland and a narrow area immediately to the north. After the war, the growing African American population began to find homes elsewhere in the city as whites left. According to one resident, by the 1960s "you had this mass migration from West Oakland to East Oakland. The whites were giving it up out there."[10] But next door to East Oakland, the suburb of San Leandro disallowed African Americans from buying homes, and relatively few African Americans lived in Oakland's tonier neighborhoods in the hills overlooking the flatlands. Clem Daniels played for the Raiders during the 1960s while Wayne Valley co-owned the team; Valley also had developed the Sequoyah Country Club in the Oakland Hills. As late as 1985, according to Daniels, the country club still had no African American members. Daniels said that Valley offered to admit him, calling him "one of the 'good' ones," but he refused.[11]

Regardless of the owner's racial attitudes, Daniels noted that Raiders coach and general manager Al Davis treated African Americans respectfully: "Davis felt that he had athletes who could think, and it was like a shock to many of us." Davis also recruited receiver Art Powell to the Raiders despite Powell's having a misfit reputation as well as a white wife. "Davis looked at Powell and his wife and saw while the skin didn't match, Art could catch the ball," the Raiders' Ben Davidson said.[12] Similarly, Kansas City Chiefs owner Lamar Hunt and coach Hank Stram were noted for their fairness toward African Americans. "We don't particularly care where [a player] is from, what color he is, what nationality, what anything," said Stram. "We're only concerned about helping our football team win football games."[13]

That did not mean the Chiefs and Raiders were entirely free from racial divisions. For a time, there was a tacit understanding that white players sat in the front of the Chiefs' charter plane and African American players sat in the back. (Bobby Bell ended the practice when he sat up front and nobody challenged him.) Both the Raiders and Chiefs adhered to football's unspoken rule that white players roomed with other whites on the road while African Americans roomed with other African Americans. And both teams experienced ugly racial incidents in training camp during the mid-1960s. In the Chiefs camp, fights between a white player and an African American player led to a broken nose and a broken jaw; Hank Stram cut both men from the team. In

New Raiders head coach Al Davis (center) reviews plays in 1963 with players Clem Daniels (left) and Tom Flores (right). Many years later, Flores would himself become Oakland's head coach. (Ron Riesterer, untitled. Gelatin silver, 8 x 10 in. The Oakland Tribune Collection, the Oakland Museum of California, gift of ANG Newspapers.)

the Raiders camp, a confrontation between teammates escalated to the point of African American players facing off against white players while one player reportedly waved a gun. Al Davis called a team meeting: "If you're doing shit like this, not only are you off the Raiders; I'll get your ass out of football."[14]

African Americans on the two teams were not content simply to watch their coaches take action. The Chiefs' Curtis McClinton, who had found it difficult to find housing in Kansas City, organized an investors group to build an integrated apartment complex in a predominantly white neighborhood. (The city council's refusal to allow construction spurred a push for a citywide fair housing ordinance, although community resistance prevented such an ordinance from being approved until after Martin Luther King's assassination in 1968.)[15] In Oakland, the Raiders' Clem Daniels helped raise scholarship money for African American high school students and organize boycotts of businesses with discriminatory practices. When Daniels and Art Powell learned from sports journalist Sam Skinner that a scheduled Raiders exhibition game in Mobile, Alabama would be played to a segregated crowd, the players pressured Al Davis and the AFL into moving the game to a different site.[16]

The biggest confrontation over race occurred before the AFL All-Star Game scheduled for New Orleans in January 1965. When African American players arrived in the city, white cab drivers and Bourbon Street clubs refused to serve them; they also were subjected to racist taunts. The players announced that they would not play in New Orleans, and the game was moved to Houston. Wire service stories such as one published in the *Kansas City Times* quoted New Orleans's mayor as saying that the athletes had done "themselves and their race a disservice through precipitous action." In contrast, the *Pittsburgh Courier,* an African American newspaper, said of the players that "never has such universal admiration for a large group been so widespread."[17] *Sports Illustrated*—which was taking steps toward more nuanced coverage of African American athletes—published a firsthand account from AFL All-Star Ron Mix, who was white. Mix said that he had tried to talk the players out of the boycott, but they had stood firm. "We must act as our conscience dictates," said the Raiders' Art Powell, a stance seconded by his Oakland teammate Clem Daniels and by the Chiefs' Abner Haynes.[18]

Even though the boycott succeeded, Haynes would say that he suffered repercussions. He received a letter from Chiefs general manager Jack Steadman saying that his actions had not been in the team's best interests. Haynes was soon traded to Denver, but he had no regrets: "I'm more concerned with being a good dad and my sons not hearing 20 or 30 years later how I chickened out and didn't have [any] backbone. It was time for some men to stand up and be counted."[19]

The Chiefs quickly replaced Haynes with new African American stars, but they too encountered discrimination as well as naïveté among whites concerning race relations. "African Americans really weren't allowed on the Country Club Plaza," wide receiver Otis Taylor recalled of the posh Kansas City shopping district when he arrived in town in 1965.

"There was a saying in the black community: 'You get your ass off the Plaza before six'" (although Taylor noted that some establishments made exceptions to serve Chiefs players). When running back Mike Garrett enrolled in a local college class on teaching at-risk children, he was irritated to hear a fellow student say that it was "a lucky thing that Kansas City doesn't have a ghetto."[20]

Whatever Taylor and Garrett may have experienced personally, their decisions to sign with the Chiefs helped bring the American Football League closer to parity with the National Football League. Following its early travails with franchises being forced to move or teetering on collapse, the AFL had inked a lucrative television deal with NBC in 1964; that deal and a revenue sharing arrangement among teams ensured the league's financial stability and helped it ramp up its battle with the NFL. Both leagues had wanted Otis Taylor, and the NFL had hidden him in a Dallas motel in hopes of preventing him from signing with the AFL. In a celebrated incident, the Chiefs' Lloyd Wells (pro football's first full-time African American scout) had spirited Taylor through the motel room window in the middle of the night and taken him to Kansas City. As for Mike Garrett—a Los Angeles native and Heisman Trophy winner for the University of Southern California—he had been expected to sign with the NFL's Los Angeles Rams, but a contract estimated at $500,000 swayed him toward the Chiefs. The climax of the AFL-NFL war came in 1966 after the NFL breached an unwritten agreement by inducing an AFL player to jump to the other league. The Oakland Raiders' Al Davis, who had just been named AFL commissioner, promptly targeted several NFL stars that the AFL could poach for itself.[21]

Unbeknownst to Davis, Tex Schramm of the NFL Dallas Cowboys already had approached Lamar Hunt to begin secret negotiations toward a merger; teams in both leagues had been losing money over the bidding war for players. An AFL-NFL peace agreement was announced in June 1966. A merger would not occur for four years, but in January 1967 the two league champions would meet in what would become the first Super Bowl (a name coined by Hunt), and a common draft of college players would begin later that year.[22]

Official peace between the leagues did not mean that the NFL respected the AFL any more than it had previously, nor did it assuage the resentment that many in the AFL felt toward the senior league.

During the merger negotiations, Lamar Hunt and the AFL had success-fully resisted an NFL demand that the Raiders leave Oakland so that the NFL San Francisco 49ers could have the Bay Area to themselves. Nonetheless, Al Davis felt that the merger was grossly unfair toward his league. The AFL had made Davis its commissioner specifically to do battle with the NFL, even though Davis's reputation for secrecy and ruthlessness had made him few friends outside Oakland. (*Sports Illus-trated* had commented in 1965 that it was "not at all certain where Al Davis would finish in a popularity contest among sharks, the mumps, the income tax and himself.") Now he left the commissioner's position, to remain eternally bitter over the AFL-NFL peace terms. "At least they let us keep our homes and our families," he would say. "They took away all my medals and broke my sword."[23]

Davis returned to the Raiders as managing general partner. He al-ready had fought fiercely to elevate his team and bring it respect. In that cause, Davis had been closely allied with George Ross, sports editor of the *Oakland Tribune*. Ross had enthusiastically backed the Raiders even during their dreadful early years, in keeping with the *Tribune*'s unceasing boosterism of Oakland as well as with the newspaper's own aspirations for big-time status. "My view was this," he later said. "If we're ever gonna be a major league paper and not just a satellite, it was gonna be by nursing a sick baby." Ross and *Tribune* sportswriter Scotty Stirling sat in on Al Davis's 1963 job interview with the Raiders owners; during a phone conversation afterward, Ross encouraged Davis to take the job. Davis made Stirling the Raiders' public relations director the following year, and Stirling assumed general manager duties while Davis served as AFL commissioner. Ross continued to enjoy ready access to Davis even as the *Tribune* sports editor also headed the Raiders Booster Club for a time.[24]

In Kansas City, the Chiefs had experienced their own struggles for legitimacy and fan support during their first seasons, and they developed their own strategy for raising their profile and ensuring positive media coverage. They persuaded local station KMBC-TV to hire quarterback Len Dawson as a sportscaster in 1966. "The Chiefs wanted one of their guys on one of those stations so that they weren't getting badmouthed and hopefully to sell some tickets," Dawson would say. With the same motivation, the team also persuaded rival station WDAF-TV to make wide receiver Chris Burford its own sportscaster. Tension eventually developed between the teammates and on-air competitors, although Burford denied rumors that it led to a fistfight: "I'd never hit a little guy like him anyway."[25]

The "little guy" jibe hinted at the negative perceptions that Dawson already had battled. When the quarterback had joined the Dallas Texans before the 1962 season, Lamar Hunt had viewed him as "skinny and soft looking." For the previous five years, Dawson had languished in the NFL as a little-used reserve. Like several other players who could not find playing time in the older league, he had found haven in the AFL, contributing to the belief among the league's detractors that its players were not good enough to make it in the superior NFL. Texans coach Hank Stram helped Dawson restore his skills and become the team's starting quarterback. By then Lamar Hunt believed in him enough that he traded the team's previous quarterback to Oakland for a first-round draft pick (who would turn out to be Buck Buchanan). Although Dawson led the Texans to the 1962 AFL title, he was not always so successful during the next three seasons in the team's new home in Kansas City, and many fans called for him to be replaced. They also criticized Stram for failing to win more games with the talent his team had.[26]

Still, things finally seemed to be looking up for the Chiefs in 1966. A season ticket drive had been a great success, and the Chiefs also had begun successfully promoting membership in the Wolfpack, the group of fans who sat in the Municipal Stadium bleachers directly behind the team benches and who came to the games armed with cowbells, air horns, and vitriol. The Chiefs amassed an 11-2-1 record and won their division with stellar performances from Otis Taylor and Mike Garrett. After they beat the Buffalo Bills 31–7 for the AFL title, they flew home to be greeted by more than 12,000 fans celebrating what sports editor Joe McGuff called "the greatest achievement in Kansas City sports history."[27]

As the Chiefs prepared to play the NFL's Green Bay Packers in the inaugural championship game between the two leagues, Kansas City's most controversial player seized the spotlight. Cornerback Fred Williamson had come to the Chiefs from the Raiders in a 1965 trade. Williamson ripped Al Davis after the trade and offered advice to his new team: "Don't psych me. Don't try to understand me. Don't even like me if you don't want." In fact, some of his new teammates—especially some white teammates—did not like him. Williamson was an African American athlete with a gift of gab rivaling that of his contemporary, Muhammad Ali. The cornerback was a fount of news for sportswriters who reported on his business interests (including car sales, a Mexican restaurant, and an architectural firm), his six-foot-tall Swedish wife, his villa in Spain, and especially his penchant for taunting opponents. *Life* magazine's January 1967 Super Bowl preview told of what Williamson called his "Hammer Tackle," which he described as "a blow delivered with great velocity perpendicular to the earth's latitudes." He promised to use it on the Packers' Boyd Dowler: "I feel sorry for the guy."[28]

Williamson's boasts did not endear him to his coach Hank Stram; they also did not impress those sportswriters who continued to look down on the AFL. "The probability is that the Packers, vastly more experienced in clutch games than the Chiefs, will win by three or four touchdowns," wrote *Sports Illustrated*'s Tex Maule prior to the Super Bowl. Kansas City played well early, but Green Bay dominated the second half to win 35–10. To the Packers' delight, Williamson was knocked unconscious and carried off on a stretcher late in the game. Afterward, the media pressed Packers coach Vince Lombardi for his impression of the Chiefs: "I think the Kansas City team is a real tough football team, but it doesn't compare with the National Football League teams. That's what you want me to say; I said it." The game seemingly had done little to counter the "Mickey Mouse League" image of the AFL or the "cow town" image of Kansas City. In the somber Chiefs locker room after the game, Chris Burford donned one of the cowboy hats that a Kansas City clothing store had given the team. "Where are you going to go from here?" a reporter asked him. "Back to the cornfields," Burford retorted.[29]

The following August, the Chiefs exacted a measure of revenge. The Chicago Bears—one of the NFL's charter franchises—came to Kansas City for an exhibition game before a standing-room-only crowd. By halftime the Chiefs already led 39–10; they gleefully continued running up the score to the very end, winning 66–24. "For 220 days the Chiefs had lived with the searing memory of that [Super Bowl] loss and Lombardi's taunting remarks," Joe McGuff wrote. "The Chiefs had a point to prove. They proved it and proved it and proved it." The Kansas City cheerleaders did not necessarily have anything to prove, but it seemed symbolic when one of them accidentally poked venerable Bears coach George Halas in the face with a pompon.[30]

As it turned out, that preseason game would be Kansas City's highlight for the year. The 1967 regular season would belong to Oakland as Al Davis's team came fully into its own. Davis and the Raiders' Ron Wolf had shrewdly drafted such players as wide receiver Fred Biletnikoff and offensive lineman Gene Upshaw, with Upshaw picked specifically to block the Chiefs' Buck Buchanan. Davis also did not hesitate to jettison players who had passed their prime. He traded Art Powell to Buffalo for quarterback Daryle Lamonica, who would be named the 1967 AFL Most Valuable Player. And the Raiders obtained other players whom rival teams no longer wanted: running back Hewritt Dixon, tight end Billy Cannon, kicker-quarterback George Blanda, wide receiver Warren Wells (who had been waived by the Chiefs), defensive backs Willie Brown and Dave Grayson (the latter of whom had been obtained from the Chiefs in the Fred Williamson trade), and defensive linemen Tom Keating, Ike Lassiter, and Ben Davidson. The Raiders thus developed a gritty underdog image appropriate for a league and a city hungry to prove themselves. They were dubbed the "Foreign Legion of pro football," and Oakland's defense gained renown as the "Eleven Angry Men."[31]

Al Davis's compulsion to control all aspects of the Raiders created conflicts with co-owner Wayne Valley and the team's new coach, John Rauch. Valley was irritated by constant references to Davis as a "genius" in the *Oakland Tribune* and elsewhere. ("Ask 'The Genius,'" Valley would say when reporters asked him questions concerning the team's performance.) When Davis seemed to be trying to take over a practice in Rauch's presence, the coach scolded him in front of the team, and Davis left the field. Regardless, the Raiders rolled to a 13-1 record in 1967 and trounced the Houston Oilers 40–7 in the AFL title game. The *New York Times*—which not long before had dismissed Oakland as "a dull, shabby city"—gave the new champions their due: "The team across the big bay, the San Francisco 49ers, have never won a title. . . . And now the Raiders from 'Li'l ol' Oakland,' as [Al] Davis likes to say, [have] surpassed their more sophisticated neighbors."[32]

Unfortunately for the Raiders, they still had to go to Miami to play Green Bay in the Super Bowl. *Sports Illustrated*'s Maule gave them no more respect than he had granted Kansas City the previous year: "The Packers, to put it bluntly, are capable of beating Oakland's Raiders by four touchdowns, if not by more." The final result was not quite that bad, but Green Bay still won 33–14 in Vince Lombardi's last game as Packers coach. "The press down there was brutal," said Raiders assistant coach Ollie Spencer. "Every day for two weeks it was Packers, Packers, Packers, and we didn't do a very good job of handling it." Green Bay's Henry Jordan did have encouraging words about the AFL: "They're getting better. If they improve as much each year, they'll be on a par with us soon."[33] The AFL's vindication would come sooner than most expected, but meanwhile Oakland and Kansas City had more serious matters to confront.

* * *

The key concern that Sam Skinner pointed toward in October 1967—jobs for African Americans in Oakland—had been the subject of protest for years. Civil rights groups had picketed the *Oakland Tribune* in December 1964 over the newspaper's hiring record (they said that fewer than thirty of the paper's 1,250 employees were African American). The *Tribune* normally had all but ignored the city's African American population, but now the paper charged that the picketers were a "threat to the entire community" and that similar demonstrations targeting other Oakland businesses undermined the local economy.[34]

Another longstanding concern among Oakland's African Americans was ill treatment by the police. The most celebrated response came from the Black Panthers, founded in Oakland in 1966 by Huey Newton and Bobby Seale. The Panthers' platform included calls for "full employment for our people," "education that teaches us our true history," and reparations for slavery, among other points. But the demand for "an immediate end to POLICE BRUTALITY and MURDER of black people" received particular attention, accompanied as it was by the assertion that "all black people should arm themselves for self-defense." The Panthers dramatized that call in May 1967 by marching into the California State Assembly with guns to protest a bill that would have outlawed public carrying of loaded firearms. An *Oakland Tribune* editorial dismissed the action as a childish stunt, consistent with the paper's harsh treatment of the Panthers generally; yet the *Tribune*'s frequent coverage of the Panthers gave them invaluable publicity. After Newton was arrested for the fatal shooting of an Oakland police officer in 1967, the Panthers' newspaper campaigned to free him from jail, and media reports of Newton's trial and conviction made "Free Huey" a national rallying cry among the political left.[35]

Kansas City had experienced its own battles over race. Community activists had fought against segregated schools, stores, and parks, and in 1964 the African American political organization Freedom, Inc. helped push through narrow voter approval of a measure banning discrimination in public facilities. Activists also marched on police headquarters in 1966 to protest police treatment of African Americans. In addition, the city had its own chapter of the Black Panthers. After a white off-duty police officer was killed during a robbery, the Panther newspaper published an account provided by the Kansas City chapter: "The people of Kansas City are in an ecstatic state today following the execution of a pig [who] was shot by three black brothers." Chapter chair Pete O'Neal was soon arrested for transporting a gun across state lines, and while out on bond, he fled to Africa.[36]

Particularly dramatic and tragic confrontations erupted in the spring of 1968. Just after the assassination of Martin Luther King, the Panthers' Eldridge Cleaver led an attempted ambush of police in West Oakland; it resulted in the police fatally shooting seventeen-year-old Bobby Hutton of the Panthers as he tried to surrender. The killing spurred formation of a "Blacks for Justice Committee" that boycotted a downtown Oakland store where many African Americans shopped. The goal was to pressure the city to reform the police department. The *Oakland Tribune*'s response was even more vitriolic than it had been regarding the picketing of the newspaper's offices. The paper published a front-page editorial calling the boycott "extortion which no decent citizen will yield to and retain his self-respect." The *Tribune* also led a "Citizens Pledged Against Coercion" campaign, and it printed a full-page ad with a gloved hand pointing a gun directly at the reader. The caption read, "What would you do in a case like this?" A white *Tribune* editor and an African American reporter resigned in protest, saying that the ad could incite violence.[37]

Oakland did avoid a full-scale riot in response to Martin Luther King's assassination; Kansas City was not so fortunate. The day of King's funeral, public schools in neighboring Kansas City, Kansas closed, but the schools in Kansas City, Missouri chose to remain open. African American students walked out of class in protest and joined an increasingly angry march to downtown's city hall. Police launched tear gas to disperse the crowd, and later they also fired tear gas into a church basement where African American youths had gathered for a dance that had been intended to relieve tensions. Two nights of mayhem followed, the worst of it in the vicinity of 31st and Prospect on the city's east side (the "ghetto" that Mike Garrett's Kansas City classmate did not know existed). Six African American males were shot to death and many businesses were burned or looted. The *Kansas City Star* was not so incendiary in its coverage as the *Oakland Tribune,* but historian G. S. Griffin would later note that it and other mainstream local media had routinely downplayed the racism and joblessness that had helped spark the riot.[38] In contrast, the city's African American paper, the *Call,* gave voice to residents who sharply questioned the police's role in escalating the violence. "The relationship between the Negro community and the Police department, already at the straining point, is now on the brink of breakage," wrote the *Call.*[39]

Curtis McClinton, Buck Buchanan, and Otis Taylor of the Chiefs were inadvertently caught up in the first day of the riot. They had been scheduled that day to speak to four local high schools whose student bodies were almost entirely black, and the athletes ended up marching with the students to city hall while urging the marchers to remain peaceful. McClinton said that after violence erupted, he was struck in the chest by a pellet bullet. Undeterred, he moderated a televised forum allowing local African Americans to air their grievances.[40] Fred Williamson also had accompanied the group of Chiefs to the schools, although he was no longer with the team. Earlier in 1968, he had overturned his car while driving with two young women in Kansas City; after a picture of the accident appeared in the *Star,* the Chiefs released him. Just after the April riot, Williamson dropped his usual bravado in a message aired and published in the local media: "I am appealing as a fellow Negro, a brother. . . . We have to fight on an economical and social level. We cannot fight in the streets with guns and weapons. We cannot win this way."[41]

Williamson and his former teammates had gone to the schools to talk about what became known as the Black Economic Union (Curtis McClinton would head its Kansas City chapter). Former NFL player

Jim Brown founded the union, which was intended to create economic opportunities for African Americans. "I want to see black people pooling their monies, their skills, their brains and their political power to better themselves," Brown told Alex Haley in an interview published in *Playboy* in 1968. Brown added that he did not care how white America viewed him: "I'm a *man*, a *black* man, in a culture where black manhood has been kicked around and threatened for generations. So that's why I don't feel I need to take too much advice about how I'm supposed to think and act."[42] Brown's words reflected the pride and awareness that had continued to grow among African American athletes following the 1965 AFL All-Star Game boycott. Sociologist Harry Edwards would help organize protests that included John Carlos and Tommie Smith's Black Power salute on the medal stand during the 1968 Olympics. In his book *The Revolt of the Black Athlete,* Edwards wrote that "'your colored boy' in athletics is rapidly becoming a man, and he is determined to be respected and treated as such—by any means necessary."[43]

Edwards also noted how white sportswriters had typically ignored "the dehumanizing, demoralizing aspects of the black athlete's experiences."[44] Partly in response to such concerns, *Sports Illustrated* in 1968 ran a series titled "The Black Athlete: A Shameful History." Prior to its publication, *SI* managing editor André Laguerre had purposefully kept the series secret from his superiors to prevent potential interference. "The Black Athlete" drew more than a thousand letters from readers, the majority of them positive, and historian Michael MacCambridge would say that the series "provided a more nuanced, fully dimensional view of black America than almost any mainstream publication of its time."[45]

"The Black Athlete" related how the Chiefs' Mike Garrett felt like a "marginal man" who as a star athlete felt "cut off from the Negro world I came from. The Negroes of Boyle Heights in Los Angeles would say to me, 'You have left us,' and the white world says to me, 'We don't want you yet in our world.'" The series also told of a star athlete at Kansas City's Lincoln High School, which was next door to Municipal Stadium; it was one of the city's virtually all-black schools. The young man could barely read or write—and yet he still anticipated college scholarship offers to play sports. Football's segregation was highlighted via the Raiders' Clem Daniels: "Out comes the rooming list on the road and all the blacks are paired, except on this club where we had eleven blacks, so one was given a single room." The magazine pointed as well toward the proclivity to allow African Americans to play only certain football positions. "We ain't got the brains to play center, 'cause we can't count, but we can follow that flanker's ass all the way down the field, *yuck, yuck,*" a defensive back said sarcastically.[46]

Finally, the series revealed how even the most enlightened white athletes could have blind spots. Many years later, Chris Burford would be praised as a mentor by Otis Taylor, and Abner Haynes would be so moved by Burford's friendship and support that in 2010 Haynes would nominate Burford for successful induction into the African American Ethnic Sports Hall of Fame. But back in 1968, Burford had told *Sports Illustrated* that African Americans were "moody" and that "if you get in a game on a day when a majority of them are moody, then you can be in trouble." Hence, he said, it was best to have no more than "seven to ten" of them on a team.[47]

* * *

By 1968 the Kansas City Chiefs would soon be starting eight African Americans on defense alone. They included five future Hall of Famers: Buck Buchanan, Bobby Bell, Curley Culp, Emmitt Thomas, and Willie Lanier, the latter of whom became pro football's first African American starting middle linebacker. (Middle linebacker was one of the positions that African Americans allegedly were not bright enough to play. Lanier was completing a business administration degree when the Chiefs drafted him, and he threatened to sue the team unless he received an equitable contract.)[48] The Raiders also had added key African American players including running back Charlie Smith, George Atkinson (who joined a defensive backfield that would become known as the "Soul Patrol"), and Art Shell (who would line up next to Gene Upshaw in cementing a formidable offensive line).

Those players helped distinguish the Chiefs and the Raiders as the class of the AFL, along with the New York Jets and their star quarterback "Broadway Joe" Namath. Oakland and Kansas City were in the same division and played twice each season, with first place commonly at stake. By 1968 the rivalry between the two teams and cities had reached a fever pitch, particularly now that Charlie Finley had moved the baseball A's from Kansas City to Oakland.

The Raiders and the Chiefs both had their troubles heading into their first matchup of the year. Oakland had a 4-1 record behind an explosive offense. Yet Raiders coach John Rauch still felt undermined by Al Davis, and co-owner Wayne Valley derisively called Rauch "Charlie McCarthy" after a famous ventriloquist's dummy. Kansas City was 5-1 thanks largely to its defense, but its offense had struggled, and fans continued to take out their frustrations on coach Hank Stram and quarterback Len Dawson. ("Even at home my wife and kids tell me what I should have done," Dawson said.) Kansas City's two starting wide receivers would miss the Oakland game with injuries, so the Chiefs' chances did not seem propitious.[49]

Kansas City coach Hank Stram was known—and often criticized—for his newfangled offensive schemes. For this game, though, he installed what he called a "high-button shoes offense" with three running backs and two tight ends. Stram's allusion to antique footwear pointed out that it was a decidedly old-fashioned, 1940s-vintage formation that pro teams rarely used anymore. It caught the Raiders off guard, and the Chiefs ran the football at will, winning 24–10 before an ecstatic capacity crowd in Kansas City. When asked afterward about the Chiefs' offensive strategy, Raiders coach John Rauch smiled grimly: "I don't care to say anything, because Stram might be saying he invented it."[50]

Just two weeks later, the two teams met again in Oakland. This time the Raiders trounced the Chiefs and their vaunted defense, winning 38–21. Coach Rauch pronounced it "the finest game a Raider team has played since I've been here," while Hank Stram took the long view: "From here to the end [of the year] it is going to be a fight."[51]

Neither team lost again during the regular season, although Oakland experienced a close call in a game against the New York Jets that produced one of the most infamous incidents in pro football history. The Jets led with little more than a minute to play when NBC abruptly cut away from its telecast of the game in the eastern part of the country for the scheduled broadcast of the movie *Heidi*. Thus many fans missed the Raiders taking the lead with a touchdown and then scoring again when the Jets fumbled the ensuing kickoff. Angry fans bombarded NBC with calls; when the switchboard broke down under the strain, some people called the emergency police number to complain. Although NBC abjectly apologized, one of its employees later said that the network secretly was delighted. The incident suggested that fans across the country had grown to care as much about the once-ragtag AFL as they had about the NFL.[52]

The Raiders and Chiefs both finished the regular season with 12-2 records and thus met for a third time in a playoff to determine the division winner. The Chiefs had been playing especially well and entered the game in Oakland as slight favorites. They were unhappy to find the Coliseum turf wet, with some suspecting that Al Davis had deliberately saturated it to slow the running attack that Kansas City had employed so effectively against Oakland earlier in the year. However, as the *Kansas City Star*'s Joe McGuff later wrote, "By the time the first quarter was over, it was apparent that the condition of the field was not going to be a factor." By then the Raiders already led 21–0 on the way to a rout more devastating than the one they had inflicted on the Chiefs a few weeks before in Oakland. Daryle Lamonica threw five touchdown passes in the 41–6 win, and Kansas City's Emmitt Thomas grew so frustrated toward the end that he slugged Oakland's Fred Biletnikoff in the eye. "What had been billed as an intriguing sudden-death playoff yesterday simply turned into a deadly carnage of the Chiefs," the *Oakland Tribune* reported happily. Hank Stram sat alone on the plane back to Kansas City mumbling repeatedly: "I just can't believe it."[53]

While the Chiefs struggled to comprehend the calamitous end to their season, the Raiders went to New York to play the Jets for the AFL championship. Oakland was heading toward a potential winning touchdown late in the game when Daryle Lamonica threw a pass that accidentally went backward, making it a free ball. The Jets recovered the ball to win the title and play in the Super Bowl against the Baltimore Colts. The AFL champions were heavy underdogs for the third straight year, but quarterback Joe Namath guaranteed a victory, and the Jets shocked Baltimore 16–7. For AFL players who had struggled so mightily for respect, it was a glorious win. "When we got back to the hotel after that game, I can remember the three guys I saw—Emmitt Thomas and Buck Buchanan and Willie Lanier, three of the Chiefs," Namath would recall. "They greeted us as we got off the bus. And we hugged."[54]

Soon after the 1968 season, John Rauch resigned as Raiders coach, believing that Al Davis was unfairly blaming him for losing to the Jets in the AFL title game. Rauch's replacement was Oakland assistant coach

John Madden, a stout and plainspoken man who proved to be an ideal leader for the Raiders. "I've always felt that the fewer rules a coach has, the fewer rules there are for players to break," Madden would say. "Maybe it was because I didn't particularly like a coat and tie, but I preferred my players to be comfortable when they traveled. I never agreed with coaches who thought that a coat and tie [or] rules against long hair, beards, or sideburns developed discipline."[55]

Madden did not say so explicitly, but he clearly seemed to be referring to Chiefs coach Hank Stram, who loved coats and ties and sartorial style while insisting that his team adhere to the same standards. Stram remembered that as a boy in Catholic school, "the nuns would kind of inspect the way we looked and if we were well-dressed and well-groomed they would call us to the front of the class and give us a gold star." In training camp before the 1969 season, Stram told his players that there would be no long hair or beards or sideburns. The Chiefs also would travel in matching blazers and slacks, and they would line up in numerical order for the playing of the national anthem before games. "My feeling is that a team should be a group of people who think and look alike," the coach said. "If they are to be successful, they must have unity, pride and discipline." Although Stram wanted his players' hair short, he himself indulged in hairpieces that became longer and thicker as the years went by.[56]

The 1969 preseason made it apparent how rabid the Raiders' and Chiefs' fan bases had become. Not many years before, the two teams had struggled at the gate during the regular season. Now exhibition games featuring nothing but rookie players drew more than 30,000 spectators in both Kansas City and Oakland. "So what's the difference, it's the Raiders," said one Oakland fan. "I'd pay five dollars to see them play a team of orangutans."[57]

Soon after the regular season began, Chiefs quarterback Len Dawson injured his knee. After his backup also was injured, the Chiefs were forced to start third-string quarterback Mike Livingston. Nevertheless, they kept winning until Dawson was able to return. Kansas City's record stood at 9-1 and Oakland stood at 8-1-1 heading into the teams' first matchup of the year. If the Raiders needed any extra motivation, the AFL provided it with a news release praising the Chiefs as "exuding omnipotence." Before a record crowd in Kansas City, the Raiders beat the Chiefs 27–24. Len Dawson threw five interceptions, two of which were returned for touchdowns. Raiders defensive back Dave Grayson was especially pleased afterward. He had had a "troublemaker" reputation in Kansas City before being traded to Oakland, and now he had returned to beat his former team: "It couldn't have happened in a nicer place."[58]

The teams met again in Oakland in the regular-season finale. Oakland was now 11-1-1 and Kansas City was 11-2, and the winner of the game would also win the division. Mindful of the Chiefs' multiple turnovers in their previous matchup with the Raiders, Hank Stram chose to employ a highly conservative offense and shun the passing game almost entirely. It did not work: for the fourth straight time, Oakland beat the Chiefs, with the final score 10–6. An *Oakland Tribune* sportswriter mockingly suggested that Stram should receive the game ball. Kansas City fans boiled over in frustration, and even some of the Chiefs players criticized Stram. "If this had been the final game of the season, I think it would have destroyed the Chiefs," one player later said.[59]

Luckily for Kansas City, it was not the final game. For one season only, the AFL—which would merge into the NFL the next year—instituted a four-team playoff whereby each division winner played the other division's second-place team. (The change was made partly to allow NBC to televise an extra week of playoff games, similar to the multiweek NFL playoffs that CBS already was airing.) As a result, Oakland stayed home to crush Houston while the Chiefs went to New York to play the world-champion Jets. A dramatic goal-line stand by the Chiefs defense prevented the Jets from taking the lead in the fourth quarter, and then a long pass from Len Dawson to Otis Taylor set up the touchdown that won the game for Kansas City.[60]

So it came down once more to the Raiders and Chiefs playing in Oakland, their sixth meeting in the past two years. This time the AFL championship and a Super Bowl trip were at stake. While Oakland exuded confidence, the Chiefs' defense taunted the team's offense during practice for its recent anemic performance. "We can move the damn ball against anybody," Len Dawson promised the team. However, Oakland was favored to win. In addition to a capacity Coliseum crowd, the game was expected to draw fifty million TV viewers.[61]

The teams battled to a 7–7 tie at halftime. In the third quarter, Oakland drove deep into Chiefs territory three times but could not score—twice

George Blanda missed field goals, and then the Chiefs intercepted a Blanda pass. (Blanda had taken over as quarterback after Daryle Lamonica injured his hand.) The interception left Kansas City near its own goal line, but on third down, Len Dawson hit Otis Taylor with a long pass that the Raiders would forever say was out of bounds. Then came a defensive pass interference call that the Raiders would forever say should have been called on Taylor instead.[62] Kansas City scored to take a 14–7 lead.

The final quarter was a mess for both teams' offenses. Lamonica returned as quarterback but could not grip the ball properly; Kansas City also put great pressure on him. Twice he threw interceptions, only for the Chiefs to fumble the ball right back to the Raiders. Then Lamonica was intercepted once more, and Emmitt Thomas's long return set up a Jan Stenerud field goal that secured a 17–7 victory and a championship for Kansas City. While leaving the Coliseum, the Chiefs had the satisfaction of seeing the Raiders trudge by with their luggage. Oakland had been all packed for a Super Bowl trip that now would never come.[63]

It was the Raiders' turn for second-guessing and self-recrimination. "We should have beaten them," said center Jim Otto. "We had so many opportunities." Fred Biletnikoff complained that Daryle Lamonica had not thrown to him enough. Most controversial were George Blanda's quotes in the *New York Post*: "Daryle was hurt. He should never have come back in there. I might have moved the club after a while." Blanda immediately distanced himself from the quotes, saying that he had been talking off the record and had been taken out of context. Like Len Dawson, Blanda was a one-time NFL player who had found refuge in the AFL. He was now forty-two years old and his professional future seemed dim. "I just hope that all this mess over what I didn't say doesn't hurt my chances of [staying] with the team," he said.[64]

Len Dawson soon would be the focus of a much more serious controversy. The Chiefs had gone to New Orleans to play the Minnesota Vikings in the Super Bowl, and Kansas City was a thirteen-point underdog, indicating that the AFL still was not being taken seriously. Five days before the game, NBC reported that Dawson was expected to be called before a federal grand jury to testify about sports gambling. The report triggered a media frenzy around Dawson, who said that he had done nothing wrong. Hank Stram and the Chiefs did their best to shield their quarterback from the turmoil, but the *New York Times* observed that Dawson now would be under extra scrutiny: "If he is intercepted or if he fumbles, the suspicions of the cynics will be nourished. . . . To avoid criticism, he must produce an almost flawless game and that is difficult for the best of quarterbacks under the best of circumstances."[65]

Hank Stram did make one fateful accommodation to the media before the Super Bowl. Ed and Steve Sabol ran NFL Films, which already had established a reputation for turning pro football games into high drama through striking cinematography and stirring music. They asked Stram if they could put a microphone on him during the game, and the coach agreed (though only after negotiating financial compensation, according to Steve Sabol). NFL Films had made a propitious choice, for whereas Minnesota coach Bud Grant was taciturn—"I can't afford the luxury of emotions," he would say—Stram was a natural performer. "Hank was our Errol Flynn," said Steve Sabol. "He was the first swashbuckler, the first coach who really understood, more than any other coach, that football was also entertainment."[66]

The game came to be remembered through the Sabols' film. It showed that the Chiefs had many heroes: Jan Stenerud, who kicked three field goals to give Kansas City a 9–0 lead; Mike Garrett, who scored the Chiefs' first touchdown to make the score 16–0 at halftime; Otis Taylor, who took a short pass into the end zone with a brilliant run in the second half; the Chiefs defense, which shut down the Vikings almost all day; and Len Dawson, who in fact produced an almost flawless game in being named the Super Bowl's Most Valuable Player as the Chiefs won 23–7.

Yet from the start, the film's narration left no doubt who the star was: "Hank Stram, the coach of the Kansas City Chiefs, stands apart as an original thinker. In 1969 his progressive theories made Kansas City the most entertaining team in all of football." And Stram was the most entertaining coach. The microphone captured his putdowns of the Vikings ("They look like they're flat as hell"), his criticisms of the referees ("How in the world can all six of you miss a play like that?"), and his exhortations to his team ("Just keep matriculating the ball down the field, boys!"), all of which NFL Films accompanied with chipper musical variations on the song "Everything's Up to Date in Kansas City." Most famously there was "65 Toss Power Trap," Stram's play call that produced Mike Garrett's touchdown. Stram cackled joyously after the

Hank Stram is carried from the field at the end of the Chiefs' Super Bowl victory over the Vikings in New Orleans in January 1970. (AP Photo)

play while affectionately referring to his players as "rats" and himself as "The Mentor." Garrett, who had a sometimes contentious relationship with his coach, playfully ruffled Stram's hairpiece, which Stram reflexively smoothed back into place.[67]

Kansas Citians, of course, watched the game live on television and listened to it on the radio. Streets were deserted; police calls were a fraction of what they normally were; electrical usage (presumably to power all the radios and TVs) was up dramatically. Less than two years before, the city had been scarred by riots in the African American community. Now black and white fans alike turned out en masse to welcome the Chiefs home for a victory parade and rally. Bill Grigsby, the Chiefs' ebullient radio announcer, proclaimed it "the greatest day in the history of Kansas City," while Len Dawson called the city—which recently had lost the A's and for a time looked as though it might lose the Chiefs—"the greatest football and sports town in the world." The *Kansas City Star* summarized the civic mood in a headline: "Victory Makes a Cow Town Walk Tall." For all the excitement over their world championship, several of the Chiefs suggested that the team's biggest victory of the season had actually come before the Super Bowl. "To me, Oakland is tough," said Buck Buchanan. "[The Vikings] aren't as tough as Oakland."[68]

Hank Stram had been markedly more calm and contained after the game than he had been during it. The innovations that he had helped introduce to pro football (the "power I" formation, the "triple stack" defense) had been dramatically vindicated, as had the American Football League; the Vikings' much more conservative style modeled on NFL legend Vince Lombardi had seemed outmoded. "We have to win with grace and class," said Stram when reminded by reporters of Lombardi's unflattering comments about the Chiefs after Super Bowl I. "Even though that wasn't expressed the last time we played in the Super Bowl, we are not going to deviate from our beliefs." A *Kansas City Star* sportswriter wrote of the coach's eyes: "They told you that only a man who has known disappointment appreciates triumph."[69]

Stram had no way of knowing it, but things would never be so sweet for him or his Chiefs again.

3

A's vs. Royals, Part I

THE POLITICAL ACTIVISM and interest in social change that some professional football players displayed during the 1960s did not extend to all athletes, especially not major league baseball players. "You *could* talk about the war in Vietnam, only you had to say, 'Look at those crazy kids marching in the street. Why don't they take a bath?'" pitcher Jim Bouton observed of his fellow players. Bouton felt fortunate to be earning $22,000 with the expansion Seattle Pilots in 1969, a time when baseball teams controlled their players down to making bed checks to make sure that the athletes were in their hotel rooms on the road. "Right now baseball is about twenty years behind the most puritanical of freshman girl dormitories," said Bouton's teammate Steve Hovley.[1]

Baseball was about to be dramatically transformed. For Oakland owner Charles Finley and Kansas City owner Ewing Kauffman, some innovations were long overdue. Finley and Kauffman were both self-made men who sought to shake up baseball while turning their teams into winners. Finley's A's had a substantial head start over Kauffman's expansion Royals in building a top-notch roster, and despite tepid fan support in Oakland, the A's became world champions. Yet some off-the-field changes would alarm baseball owners. Their workforce—the players—grew increasingly unhappy with one-sided salary negotiations and the strictures of the reserve clause that kept them from playing where they wanted. In 1972 they staged the first mass walkout in major league history, and their successful strike signaled a momentous shift in the power balance between owners and players. Labor actions elsewhere in the country would not be so successful. Strikes against the construction industry in Kansas City and against the Port of Oakland threatened endeavors key to the two cities' big-league aspirations. The resulting repercussions would portend a precipitous decline among organized labor nationwide.

* * *

When the *Chicago Tribune* interviewed Charlie Finley in December 1967, it found him "as coltish as a boy spotting a new toy under the Christmas tree." Finley's toy was his new baseball home in Oakland. "I have everything going for me," he said, including a ballpark that was much bigger and newer than the one he had left behind in Kansas City, plus a broadcasting contract that was far more lucrative. As with other media profiles of the A's owner, the newspaper wrote of Finley's rags-to-riches background. Twenty years previously, he had spent Christmas in a sanitarium during a long and arduous recovery from tuberculosis. While there he conceived the plan that would make him wealthy: selling group disability insurance to doctors. He went on to fulfill his dream of owning a major league baseball team, and now he was finally free from his travails in Kansas City. "My goal is to draw 1.5 million fans our first year in Oakland," said Finley. "We'll have all the promotions I introduced in K.C. Maybe I'll even have a hippie night."[2]

Finley's attendance goal did not seem outlandish; the San Francisco Giants had attracted well more than a million fans in each of their first ten seasons across the bay. Moreover, Oakland had a rich baseball tradition. Apart from hosting the Oakland Oaks of the Pacific Coast League, the city also had been remarkably fertile ground for young athletic talent. In the early 1950s, a single high school—McClymonds in West Oakland—produced Frank Robinson, Curt Flood, and Vada Pinson, all of whom would enjoy stellar major league careers; during the same period, the school also produced Bill Russell, who became the linchpin of a Boston Celtics team that would win eleven National Basketball Association titles.[3]

Now Oakland had major league baseball, and *Oakland Tribune* sports editor George Ross predicted that not only would the A's soon become as beloved as the football Raiders, but also that they would "rank with the [Giants'] Willie Mays, Juan Marichal, [and] maybe even with Joe

DiMaggio"—the latter of whom Finley had named as A's executive vice president. On opening night in April 1968, the team drew more than 50,000 to the Oakland Coliseum. Then abruptly the fans stopped coming, with barely 5,000 showing up for the second game. Ominously, the poor attendance continued even as the young A's started doing extraordinary things. In May twenty-two-year-old Jim "Catfish" Hunter pitched against Minnesota. (Charlie Finley had given Hunter his nickname for promotional purposes, concocting a tall tale about how the North Carolina youth had run away from home at age six to go fishing.) Hunter pitched the American League's first regular-season perfect game since 1922. Only 6,298 spectators saw it.[4]

There were multiple theories as to the paltry attendance, including the games being scheduled at night when it was chilly in Oakland. But some observers saw a more fundamental problem. "I honestly don't know why he came here," said one Oaklander of Finley. "There may not be enough interest in this area to support two teams." In fact attendance for the San Francisco Giants dropped sharply after the A's arrived in Oakland, which suggested that there were only so many baseball fans to go around in the Bay Area, exactly as Giants owner Horace Stoneham had warned before the A's' move. Almost immediately some San Francisco sportswriters began speculating that Finley might move the A's yet again, ignoring that Oakland had bound him to a twenty-year stadium lease.[5]

The festive mood that Finley had displayed at Christmas soon darkened. He did not abandon his promotional schemes, even though at least one Oakland fan professed dislike for them: "I know Finley means well, but this stuff might go better in San Francisco. I like plain baseball."[6] The A's owner always would be outspoken about baseball's need to enliven its product. Some of his ideas (multicolored uniforms, World Series night games, the designated hitter) eventually gained favor, while others (red, yellow, and blue bases, orange baseballs, a designated pinch-runner) never gained traction. But just as he had in Kansas City, Finley began micromanaging all aspects of the A's. He pronounced the Oakland Coliseum's vending operations as "rotten" after he said that he waited in line more than half an hour to buy hotdogs and a soft drink. He fired manager Bob Kennedy after just one season even though Kennedy in 1968 had guided the franchise to its first winning record in sixteen years.

After pitcher Jim Nash was quoted as saying that perhaps the team should leave Oakland owing to the weak attendance, Finley publicly upbraided his player and ordered his new manager Hank Bauer to hold a team meeting, presumably to squelch such complaints.[7]

In 1969 Oakland was placed in the new American League West division along with the league's two new teams, the Seattle Pilots and the Kansas City Royals; given that expansion franchises typically fared poorly at first, the A's figured to benefit at their expense. Even so, Royals owner Ewing Kauffman had high ambitions for his team. Kauffman was similar to Finley in many ways. He had overcome protracted illness, spending nearly a year as a boy bedridden in Kansas City with rheumatic fever and a heart defect. He then made his fortune by founding a drug company, Marion Laboratories, that he originally underwrote through his poker winnings. When *Fortune* magazine profiled him, it poked fun at the nouveau-riche extravagances that he and his wife Muriel enjoyed in their mansion in the wealthy Kansas City suburb of Mission Hills, Kansas; among those indulgences was an illuminated fountain that shot water twenty feet high. Even Kauffman's friend, baseball commissioner Bowie Kuhn, acknowledged that the Royals owner had a healthy ego: "His wife, Muriel, called him 'Mr. Wonderful' and there is not the slightest reason to think he demurred at that evaluation."[8]

Yet Kansas Citians loved Kauffman, whom they called "Mr. K." He spent millions to help the Royals stockpile young talent, and he also invested in innovative organizational programs. "Baseball people generally are too conservative," he said. "We need new ideas—scientific ideas on how to be a better hitter and things like that." Apart from instigating comprehensive computer analyses of pitching, hitting, and fielding data, Kauffman also created the Royals' Baseball Academy in Florida to turn young athletes with little baseball experience into major leaguers. But most important for local fans, Kauffman was actually from Kansas City. Charlie Finley had been an outsider in the city, just as he would also be an outsider in Oakland. In contrast, Kansas City baseball boosters Ernie Mehl and Earl Smith had specifically recruited Kauffman to show Major League Baseball that the city had the commitment and financial wherewithal to support an expansion franchise with local ownership.[9]

Kauffman also differed markedly from Charlie Finley, at least at first, in pledging not to interfere with the Royals' on-field operations. He

Royals owner Ewing Kauffman (left) and general manager Cedric Tallis in 1968, the year the franchise was founded. (Courtesy of Missouri State Archives)

hired Cedric Tallis to serve as executive vice president, declaring that Tallis "will run the show." The Royals set an all-time American League record for season-ticket sales. They also signed a broadcasting contract worth more than three million dollars—vastly superior to the ones that the Kansas City A's had had—and they hired twenty-six-year-old Denny Matthews to help call the games on radio, a position he still would hold five decades later. Just before the team's inaugural season, Tallis made one of the first of what would become a remarkably successful series of trades when he obtained Lou Piniella from Seattle. Piniella had four hits in the Royals' home opener that they won in extra innings, with the fans giving Kauffman a standing ovation before the game. According to Joe McGuff in the *Kansas City Star*, the wind partially blew down one of the American League team pennants that hung from the Municipal Stadium roof: "By the strangest sort of coincidence it was a green and gold pennant bearing the name 'Athletics.'"[10]

Although Lou Piniella went on to win Rookie of the Year, the Royals lost ninety-three games in 1969, but they still finished fourth in their six-team division. The Oakland A's finished second with an 88-74 record as some of the young players acquired by Charlie Finley reached their full potential. By now the A's owner was serving as his own general manager and setting his own roster. *Oakland Tribune* sportswriter Ron Bergman was no idolater of Finley, but he would come to see his eye for talent in almost mystical terms: "He could look into your soul and see whether you were a winner." Bob Oates of the *Los Angeles Times* would be even more effusive, calling Finley "the closest thing to a sports genius this nation has produced."[11] But the gifted athletes under Finley's command grew steadily more resentful over his treatment of them, particularly when it came to money.

The biggest star for the A's was outfielder Reggie Jackson. He had made his big-league debut during the team's final season in Kansas City but had not played well, feeling "like I was standing off to the side watching this overmatched hick, age twenty-one, try to act like a major leaguer." Jackson blossomed spectacularly in Oakland in 1969, and before the end of July, he had already hit forty home runs. He was profiled in *Time, Newsweek,* and *Ebony,* and *Sports Illustrated* speculated whether he might break Roger Maris's single-season home run record. *SI* also praised his poise: "The words he uses are carefully selected and almost always polysyllabic. Jackson never will be called a 'dumb jock.'" But Jackson also liked to boast. "It was as if all the power of the earth and the sky and the sands and the waters were in these hands," he said of his own feats with the bat. In addition, the young African American player developed what one biographer would call "the reputation of being combative and—in the racist parlance of the day—'uppity.'" He eventually wore down under the intense media attention in 1969 and hit just seven more home runs during the final two months of the season, later saying that he had become "a wreck."[12]

Still, Jackson felt that he deserved a healthy raise to his $20,000 salary. He asked for $75,000; Charlie Finley refused to go higher than $40,000. After holding out during 1970 spring training, Jackson finally signed for $45,000, but he would struggle all season. Finley threatened to send him to the minors: "If there's one individual who's hurting this ball club, it's him. I'm not knocking him, mind you."[13] Matters came to a head in a game in September against Kansas City. Although the Royals were not yet fully competitive with the A's, a rivalry already existed between the two teams (Kansas City fans had lustily booed Finley when he attended an A's-Royals game there earlier in the season), and dramatic things seemed to occur during their matchups. On Fan Appreciation Day at the Oakland Coliseum—when, true to form, fewer than 10,000 fans showed up—Reggie Jackson pinch-hit against the Royals. He hit a grand slam home run, and when he crossed home plate, he glared up at Finley's box seat and mouthed an obscenity. Finley professed delight at the public insult, but in private he forced Jackson to sign an apology, reducing his player to tears. The A's again finished second in 1970, and for the third straight year, Finley fired his manager. "There's only one man who manages this club, Charlie Finley," said catcher Dave Duncan. "And we'll never win so long as he manages."[14]

In comparison with Oakland, Kansas City's 1970 season was similarly desultory off the field while being much less successful on it. The Royals' original manager, Joe Gordon, had quit at the end of the previous season, saying that baseball players were changing: "It is tougher to control them." Gordon's replacement Charlie Metro lasted only a few months before being fired, his relationship with his players having deteriorated beyond repair. (Metro later blamed the situation on a bleeding ulcer that he exacerbated with too many scotch and waters.) New manager Bob Lemon established a better rapport with the team, and new center fielder Amos Otis showed star potential, but the Royals finished with a 65-97 record. "This was not a vintage year," wrote Kansas City sports editor Joe McGuff. He noted that the city had now suffered through fifteen straight losing baseball seasons dating back to the A's and that the Royals' attendance had plunged by more than 200,000 from 1969.[15]

McGuff did point to one external factor affecting fan turnout: a lengthy construction strike in Kansas City. "[It] is reasonable to assume the strike has cost the Royals at least 100,000 in attendance," he wrote.[16] In fact the strike would cost Kansas City and its sports teams much more than that while also foreshadowing a change in fortune for the U.S. labor movement.

* * *

Kansas City's labor history had often been contentious. In the 1910s, the International Workers of the World—the "Wobblies"—had made numerous organizing speeches in the city. Police arrested the speakers by the dozens. In 1918 a strike of female laundry workers led to a general strike that shut down the city for nearly a week.[17] Oakland and the Bay Area's own labor history had at times turned violent. In 1934 the dockworkers union struck West Coast ports. Police shot and killed two San Francisco strikers, provoking a general strike. Twelve years later, another general strike in Oakland saw a hundred thousand workers walk off the job. To counter anti-labor press coverage, the strikers shut down the *Oakland Tribune* and prevented other newspapers from being delivered in the city. Following the strike, a pro-labor slate was elected to the city council.[18]

By the late 1960s, conservative interests had firmly reestablished control over Oakland, with the *Tribune* and the Knowland family aggressively pushing a business-friendly agenda. That agenda would often be at odds with the African American community that felt excluded from the labor market, but it was not wholly at odds with the dockworkers union, whose strike had rocked the Bay Area in 1934. Back then, the union's leader Harry Bridges had been branded a communist, and Congress had tried multiple times to deport him to his native Australia. But Bridges remained, and in 1960 his International Longshoremen's and Warehousemen's Union (ILWU) approved a plan allowing ports to install facilities that loaded and unloaded cargo using shipping containers and cranes. In return the dockworkers received concessions concerning pay, work hours, and retirement benefits. "The much-reviled radical Harry Bridges became a labor statesman, praised by press and politicians, and waterfront workers, once considered the scum of the earth, became high-paid and envied workers," wrote labor historian Albert Vetere Lannon.[19]

Oakland benefited greatly in that it had room to accommodate the new mechanized container facilities, whereas San Francisco did not. Soon the city far exceeded San Francisco in annual port activity and income—an achievement that made the *Oakland Tribune* crow. "Today they say Oakland hustled while San Francisco slept," the paper would boast while also publishing a photo captioned, "Progress Passed Outmoded and Rotting San Francisco Piers." It was satisfying enough that Oakland had become truly big-league in international shipping; that it had done so at the expense of its haughty neighbor made the feat even sweeter.[20]

Other unions had done well for themselves, just as the ILWU had done. According to one history of U.S. labor, unions "seemed firmly integrated into a corporate welfare state" by the end of the 1960s through negotiated contracts that provided "stability for large enterprises and income gains for workers."[21] Building trade workers took advantage of a nationwide construction boom, including in Kansas City, where major projects included the new airport, the Crown Center development south of downtown, and the dual stadium sports complex. Contracts for the various trade unions expired at different times, allowing unions across the country to engage in "whipsawing," or staging consecutive strikes to drive up wages continuously. "If one [trade] got a raise for so much, the other would say, 'Well, we're better than they are, so we want double,'" an ironworker would remember.[22] The trades honored one another's picket lines, leading to regular construction shutdowns throughout the Kansas City metropolitan area.

Thus, in 1967, a plumbers' strike halted building for three months. In April 1969, ironworkers and painters struck, prompting the *Kansas City Star* to warn in a front-page editorial of a "community catastrophe" if a quick resolution was not reached. It was to no avail; that strike lasted four months.[23] In April 1970, cement finishers, bricklayers, lathers, and laborers walked off the job, and this time the shutdown dragged on into October. A carpenter's wife spoke of taking multiple odd jobs to bring in money while cutting corners elsewhere: "I've had to learn how to give our six-year-old girl her allergy shots myself, because we can't afford to go to a doctor." Advertising in the *Star* and on local television newscasts shriveled, store sales and summer employment nosedived, and some area public schools failed to open in the fall because of a lack of revenue. Bumper stickers appeared: "Save Our City—End the Strike." Noting that Kansas City led the country in work time lost because of strikes, Mayor Ilus Davis said glumly, "It's not always fun to be No. 1."[24]

The construction halt added to the troubles facing Kansas City's new sports complex. The general obligation bonds that voters had approved in June 1967 allocated $43 million toward the complex, but it soon became obvious that the sum would not be nearly enough to complete the project. That shortfall raised the ire of Charles Wheeler, then a judge on the Jackson County Court. (The court was the county's governing body; its three members were called judges.) "Oakland was able to build a football and baseball stadium for [only] $30 million," Wheeler told the Sports Complex Authority. At the same time, he chided Oakland for allowing Charlie Finley to pay artificially low stadium rent as part of the deal that lured the A's from Kansas City. "I have noted in other areas of the country an unhealthy relationship between owners and sports authorities to put something over on the public," said Wheeler. "I'd like to see Jackson County be the first area where the sports teams pay their own way." In June 1969, when construction bids for the sports complex came in much higher than anticipated, the complex's planned rolling roof was abandoned to cut costs, even though the roof had been a key selling point to voters. Revenue bonds would cover the remaining funding gap, with rent from the Chiefs and Royals paying off the bonds. But now work had stopped on the complex—the complex that had been touted as being essential to maintaining Kansas City's big-league status—and it was anyone's guess as to when the two teams actually would be able to play in it.[25]

The 1970 strike triggered a backlash against the trade unions, with the local chapter of the American Institute of Architects publishing a special issue of its magazine that derisively commemorated the "Annual Kansas City Construction Strike." The magazine urged the unions to "consider the staggering effect of their requests on the future of construction activity in Kansas City." It also republished several editorials from the *Star* and *Times* and other newspapers condemning the strike. When a settlement finally was reached in October, the *Times* struggled to sound an upbeat note: "The community now looks forward with firm expectancy to an era of peace in the construction industry." One national business magazine was not so conciliatory. In a piece headlined "The Building Trades Versus the People," *Fortune* charged that construction unions nationwide were devoted to "redistributing wealth by force" and posed "a grave and growing menace to the economic and social health of the U.S."[26]

In the Bay Area, the dockworkers union and its leadership would experience its own backlash. Many ILWU members believed that Harry Bridges had grown too complacent and conciliatory during his long tenure as union head, especially in the face of mechanization and containerization, which had greatly reduced the workforce needed to handle cargo. The union went on strike in July 1971, targeting Oakland and other West Coast ports. Although an injunction temporarily stopped the strike, no formal settlement was reached until the following February, when the union accepted terms that it had previously rejected. It did so under pressure; President Nixon had threatened federal interven- tion if the strike did not end. Then the national Pay Board, which had been created under Nixon as a temporary measure to fight inflation, reduced the wages and benefits increase to which the union had agreed. Bridges had warned that the ILWU would strike again if the Pay Board took such action, but in the end he and the union backed down. Soon afterward a contributor to the socialist magazine *New Politics* charged that "the defeatism of the Bridges leadership" had had a "profoundly demoralizing effect on the labor movement."[27]

Labor historian Albert Vetere Lannon has been kinder toward Bridges and the ILWU's acceptance of mechanization, noting that many union members benefited financially and that dock work became much safer than it had been previously.[28] But the Port of Oakland's employment policies and its lack of investment in the city of Oakland remained con- troversial. The *Black Panther* newspaper excoriated the Port for failing to "channel its immense wealth back into the hands of the Black and poor community." Meanwhile, the number of dockworkers plummeted. In 2003 a retired longtime ILWU member from Oakland reflected on how much had changed: "We used to bring the ship in, and to discharge it and reload it would take, like, nine days. Now they can do it in a day and a half. And with maybe twenty people where before they had two hundred people."[29]

As for the building-trade unions, the economic slowdown of the mid- 1970s would severely curtail new construction, driving up the industry's unemployment rate to 22 percent by 1975. The lack of jobs shifted power back toward those doing the hiring. "When times are tough, as they are now in construction, union men who haven't worked for months and months . . . put their [union] cards in their pockets or in their shoes, and they go to work nonunion," a building union official remarked. By 1978 *Harper's* magazine was reporting on what it called "The Last Days of the Labor Movement." The magazine noted that nonunion labor had taken over the majority of U.S. construction jobs as unions across the country increasingly fell victim to their own failures and to hostile media coverage. As a result, "The vaunted labor vote has vanished; the labor lobby has come down with pernicious anemia, and labor itself, this once mighty force in the society, has shrunk to the status of just another special-interest group."[30]

* * *

Back in 1970, the prospect of labor being enfeebled would have seemed unlikely, though not so unlikely as the prospect of baseball players one day earning millions of dollars a year. While unions elsewhere were enjoying their heyday, Major League Baseball had resisted any significant changes to the working relationship between clubs and ballplayers. The so-called reserve clause effectively allowed a team to do whatever it wanted with a player. Baseball also enjoyed an exemption from federal antitrust law and cultivated its public image as the national pastime, with players expected never to threaten the "good of the game" and always to remain grateful for the chance to play.[31]

Yet there were signs of restiveness within baseball. Jim Bouton's diary of the 1969 season, *Ball Four,* became a bestseller. It revealed the deep resentment that many ballplayers felt toward management while also highlighting their juvenile hijinks and their rampant popping of pep pills. When baseball commissioner Bowie Kuhn summoned Bouton to the commissioner's office to scold the player for purportedly undermining baseball despite all that the game had given him, Bouton retorted, "Baseball didn't *give* me anything. I *earned* it." Marvin Miller, executive director of the Major League Baseball Players Association, also attended the meeting with Kuhn. The MLBPA was the union that represented the players, and Miller was protecting Bouton from any sanctions that Kuhn might be tempted to impose. Miller also told Kuhn that it was high time that fans were disabused of a "phony, unrealistic" image of baseball.[32]

Much more was at stake than the fate of Bouton, who would soon leave the sport. Unhappy over having been traded against his will, St. Louis outfielder Curt Flood had enlisted the players union's backing in challenging baseball's reserve clause. (Flood's lawsuit eventually made it to the U.S. Supreme Court, which in 1972 ruled against him.) Flood would publish his own memoir that recounted his upbringing in West Oakland and the virulent racism he had experienced as an African American ballplayer. He acidly described the relationship between player and owner: "Whatever we had, we owed to the employer with

abject gratitude. . . . He was a feudal lord and we were his humble pe-
titioners." Flood was even more blunt during a television interview,
calling himself a "well-paid slave."[33]

Flood's suit and angry remarks aroused the ire of some sportswriters, much as *Ball Four* had done.[34] "I never knew he was so damned
unhappy," said Bob Broeg of the *St. Louis Post-Dispatch* about Flood
while also claiming that the ballplayer cared only for money. For his
part, Flood expressed astonishment at sportswriters who "become
incensed when a young man with a career expectancy of five years
undermines the Good of the Game by holding out" for higher wages.
Marvin Miller similarly questioned how such writers would respond
"had newspaper owners asked why grown men demanded payment to
watch games and *write* about them—and still expected decent salaries
and benefits."[35]

But others in the media were sympathetic toward Flood. The African
American press praised him for his courage while pointing out baseball
owners' abuses, as with Sam Lacy's commentary in the *Baltimore Afro-
American:* "Owners fire their hands at will. They move across state lines
into new [cities] whenever they have a whim to do so. They blacklist
people, and they hire the commissioner they want to tell them what
to do, constantly reminding him, however, not to forget who is paying him." Such mainstream publications as the *Sporting News* and the
New York Times similarly criticized baseball's reactionary tendencies.
"If [owners] are sometimes less than sensitive in their dealings with the
help, it's probably because they have grown so accustomed to regarding
the players as possessions that they forget the players are people," wrote
Red Smith in the *Times*.[36]

Sportswriters in general were becoming less reverential about the
national pastime and the people who profited from it, particularly such
people as Charlie Finley. "Nothing is too gross for the man if it attracts
attention," wrote Glenn Dickey of the *San Francisco Chronicle* about
Finley. But the writers' low views of the A's owner had nothing on the
low views of the A's themselves, as the *Oakland Tribune*'s Ron Bergman
came to know well. Upon the firing of yet another A's manager following
the 1970 season, Bergman quoted an anonymous player who spoke of
a "general hatred" among the team toward Finley.[37]

Finley's new manager would be Dick Williams, who said that he benefited from his players' dislike of the owner: "It's impossible for even

baseball players to truly hate two of their bosses at once. . . . I was the one who lucked out." In 1971 the A's quickly moved to the top of the American League West behind the pitching of twenty-two-year-old Vida Blue, who had served notice of his prowess the previous season by throwing a no-hitter during a brief call-up to the majors. By the All-Star break in July, Blue had a 17-3 record. He became the focus of media fascination just as Reggie Jackson had two years previously, only now the attention was even more frenzied. At first Blue seemed to accept it with equanimity. "A whippy young lefthander like Blue who combines such protean heat with such acute composure is almost an unnatural phenomenon—a Marilyn Monroe with inner security, a Keats with good lungs," *Sports Illustrated* enthused.[38]

Soon enough the composure faded and Blue became increasingly curt with the media. "I try to give the writers what they want, but they always want something new and I just haven't lived long enough to have done enough different things to please them all," he said. When Charlie Finley tried to pressure him into changing his name to "True Blue" for promotional purposes, he angrily refused. Worse, one of the A's' broadcast announcers tried to saddle the young African American pitcher with the nickname "Blue Boy," which Blue successfully resisted. At times he grew morose: "I waited all my young life for this and now that it's here I wish it would just go away." The A's coasted to the division title with a 101-60 record; it was the franchise's first championship of any kind in forty years. However, despite Blue's having become a major attraction around the league, the team still failed to draw consistently well at home. After Baltimore swept Oakland in the American League championship series, Finley and the A's had to fend off new rumors that they might move again, this time to Washington, D.C.[39]

The Kansas City Royals' 1971 season was sunny in comparison, even though they finished far behind the A's. Kansas City sportswriters were less caustic than some in the Bay Area. "You don't want to disembowel people and leave them bleeding in the streets," the *Star*'s Joe McGuff would say. (His opinion of Charles Finley never changed, though: "I just think there was something wrong with Charlie.")[40] Fans and media had plenty to cheer about as the Royals achieved the first-ever winning big-league baseball season in Kansas City with an 85-76 record.

Kansas City was led by three players whom Cedric Tallis had obtained through trades with teams in the National League, then generally regarded as superior to the American League. Reminiscent of one-time NFL players who had found refuge in the AFL, all three of the Royals' acquisitions had come to their new league and team feeling that they had something to prove. Veteran second baseman Cookie Rojas had arrived via St. Louis, where he had been frustrated over his lack of playing time. Shortstop Fred Patek—a proud and tightly wound young man—had come from Pittsburgh. At five-foot-four, Patek was the smallest player in the majors and hence was a frequent butt of jokes ("Mickey Mouse wears a Freddie Patek watch" was just one of them). Given the chance in Kansas City to start consistently for the first time, he led the American League in triples in 1971 and garnered significant support in Most Valuable Player voting.[41]

Kansas City's top star was Amos Otis, who had been obtained from the New York Mets. Although at first the Mets had regarded Otis highly, many in the organization had come to view him as "lackadaisical," a label that he never would entirely escape. His talent was such that his play often appeared effortless, and his occasional aloofness and prickliness gave him a reputation for having a bad attitude. ("I've never seen an attitude hit a fastball," he retorted.) Still, he had a droll sense of humor that he could turn on himself, and more important for the Royals, he brought them exceptional speed and defense along with a capable bat.[42]

The Royals approached 1972 brimming with hope. They finally were due to move into their new stadium, which was nearing completion following the construction strike delays. Ewing Kauffman predicted that the team could contend for the pennant if it obtained a power-hitting first baseman. Cedric Tallis—who had just been named major league Executive of the Year—obliged by trading for another National Leaguer, John Mayberry, who had been unhappy over how he had been used in Houston. The influential sportswriter Dick Young called the Royals "the upcoming power outfit of baseball."[43]

The A's too had reason to be optimistic. Charlie Finley retained Dick Williams for a second season as manager despite rumors that Williams would be fired like so many other A's managers before him. In addition Finley heeded Williams's wish for another starting pitcher by trading for Ken Holtzman. And Finley decked out his team in new stretch double-knit uniforms of white, green, and gold. "The colors are so vivid," he gushed. "These whites are polar bear whites. Polar bear whites are whiter than the wedding gown whites we used last year."[44]

Not everything was so bright or cheery for the two teams or for baseball generally. As spring approached, it increasingly became clear that Kansas City's new baseball stadium would not be ready by the start of the 1972 season as promised. The Royals' first scheduled game there was pushed back to July before Ewing Kauffman finally decided not to play at all in the new park until the following season. Meanwhile, Fred Patek went on the disabled list during spring training owing to nervous exhaustion. "I keep telling myself now that I've got to key down and relax," he said after returning to the lineup.[45]

In Oakland the big news was Vida Blue's holdout. Despite wearing down during the last part of the 1971 season, Blue had still finished with a 24-8 record and had won the league's Cy Young (for best pitcher) and Most Valuable Player awards. For his efforts, he had earned $14,750, a sum so paltry that it became a running joke. "I'd like to be the lawyer who negotiates your contract next year," President Nixon had told Blue during a White House reception. Blue also had done a TV commercial for Aqua Velva aftershave: "You've probably heard I'm the lowest-paid superstar in America. Well, I am. But next year, I'm gonna make a whole lot of money." He asked Charlie Finley for $115,000 for 1972; the owner countered with $50,000 and said that he would go no higher. "I pay a lot to sign a player and I do not expect him to hold me up for a veteran's salary the second he does something good," said Finley. "When players request ridiculous raises right away they never remember the big [signing] bonuses paid them." As the standoff dragged on, Blue announced that he would retire to pursue a public relations career. Some teammates suggested that he was being selfish. Finally, commissioner Bowie Kuhn intervened, and in May, Blue signed a package worth $63,000. It included cash bonuses on top of a base salary of $50,000, thus allowing Finley to claim that he had never budged from his initial offer. "Charlie Finley has soured my stomach for baseball," Blue said. "He treated me like a damn colored boy."[46]

While Blue was still holding out, major league players went on strike. Marvin Miller had long been appalled at the ballplayers' pay. When he took charge of the players union in 1966, the minimum salary had risen only $1,000 over the previous twenty years to $6,000. On top of that were the restrictions imposed by the reserve clause. Miller later called the players "the most exploited group of workers I had ever seen—more exploited than the grape pickers of Cesar Chavez." He helped negoti-

ate modest gains for the players in his first six years on the job. Prior
to the 1972 season, the union asked for an increase in the club owners'
contribution to the pension fund, with an existing surplus in the fund
helping to defray the increased cost. The owners, believing that they
had conceded far too much already, refused. (They already were angry
over Miller's suggestion that the owners devote money from a new $70
million television contract toward player salaries.) "We're not going to
give them another goddamned cent," said St. Louis Cardinals owner
Gussie Busch. "If they want to strike, let 'em!"[47]

Miller was highly reluctant to strike over what seemed to him a relatively minor issue: "You only get one chance at a first strike, and if you
don't win that one, you have lost the union." But the ballplayers had been
incensed by Busch's comments and were eager for a confrontation. Apart
from their natural competitiveness as athletes, they also shared a growing consciousness that their labor underpinned the whole enterprise of
sports and the quest for big-league success. Reggie Jackson—not long
removed from his confrontation with Charlie Finley over salary—was
particularly vocal in shoring up support among player representatives
for a walkout, which began on April 1 and lasted past the scheduled
start of the season.[48]

Many fans and sportswriters condemned the athletes. "The baseball
player belongs to a privileged, pampered class," wrote the *Oakland Tribune*'s Ed Levitt. "If the players think their pension plan is so bad, ask
them would they like to trade it for what the mailman or milkman or
policeman or fireman has." The strike also angered both Charlie Finley
and Ewing Kauffman. "As sure as God made little apples, the players are
going to kill the goose that laid the golden eggs," said Finley, whereas
Kauffman—already frustrated over the delays in the opening of his
team's new stadium—lamented what the strike and the Royals were
costing him: "It is good for Kansas City that we have a major league club.
At the same time, there are so many better ways I could have utilized
the money I have lost."[49]

The owners' collective resolve soon cracked, and they largely gave
the players what they had asked for, with the 1972 season beginning
on April 15. Ironically, it had been Charlie Finley who had helped or-
chestrate a settlement, claiming that he and the other owners had not
fully understood the pension issue at first. Joe McGuff of the *Kansas*

City Star did not consider himself to be especially sympathetic toward the players, but soon after the strike was settled, he suggested that the sport had just undergone a profound change. Marvin Miller, he said, was now "the dominant figure in major league baseball."[50]

After the season finally started, the A's were once more engulfed in turmoil. A rusty and unhappy Vida Blue pitched far below the standards that he had established the previous year. Reggie Jackson and first baseman Mike Epstein scuffled in the clubhouse over the allocation of free passes to a road game. Charlie Finley tried to counter his negative public image by hiring broadcast announcers who constantly sang his praises; when the *Oakland Tribune*'s Ron Bergman wrote a story poking fun at the broadcasters, the owner temporarily banned Bergman from traveling with the team. According to Finley, the sportswriter had made the announcers "look like prostitutes."[51]

On a lighter note, after Reggie Jackson grew a mustache, Finley offered a bonus to any player who did the same—the owner was as keen as ever to pounce on a new promotional gimmick. Most of the players eagerly obliged, with Rollie Fingers cultivating a waxed handlebar that one observer described as "Daliesque." Fingers became arguably the best relief pitcher of his era, and Catfish Hunter, Ken Holtzman, and John "Blue Moon" Odom (whose nickname predated his meeting Finley) formed a stellar starting rotation.[52]

While Oakland prospered on the field, Kansas City struggled. In an August game in Oakland, the A's' Sal Bando and the Royals' Ed Kirkpatrick started a benches-emptying brawl; afterward the A's swept the Royals in a series in which Kansas City failed to score a single run. Later that month, Kansas City manager Bob Lemon benched both Amos Otis and Fred Patek for a perceived lack of effort. "It's the first time anyone ever said I didn't hustle," said Patek, who quickly got back into the manager's good graces and reentered the lineup. Otis, who not long before had injured himself by hitting a wall while chasing a fly ball, sat out longer: "Sure I'm shy of the fences. Let [Lemon] run into one and see if he isn't."[53]

Just before the end of a disappointing season in which the Royals finished fourth with a 76-78 record, Ewing Kauffman fired Lemon, overruling the wishes of Cedric Tallis. The Royals owner cited a *Los Angeles Times* article that had quoted Lemon as saying that he was "just a couple of years from retirement and I'm going to get out as fast as I can run." Kauffman decided that the team needed a younger man to motivate the players. He named Jack McKeon, manager of Kansas City's top minor league team, as the Royals' new manager. "Starting in 1974, we expect to win [the American League pennant] five out of 10 years," Kauffman proclaimed.[54]

Oakland would reach the pinnacle first. The A's bested the Detroit Tigers in a dramatic best-of-five series to win the 1972 league championship. Oakland shortstop Bert Campaneris was suspended following the second game of the series for flinging his bat at a Detroit pitcher who had deliberately hit him in the leg. In the deciding fifth game, A's pitcher Blue Moon Odom came down with the dry heaves and was replaced by Vida Blue, who shut out Detroit the rest of the way to clinch the pennant. During the victory celebration, Blue asked Odom why he had left the game. Odom told him the truth: "The tension got to me." When Blue mockingly held his hands to his throat and made a gagging sound, Odom lunged at Blue until teammates pulled them apart. "We had what was surely the first championship clubhouse fight in history," manager Dick Williams recalled. "We had to get to the World Series before we killed ourselves."[55]

That World Series between the A's and the Cincinnati Reds was billed as "the battle of the mods and the squares, the longhairs against the conventionals, the shaggies against the clean chins." Like Hank Stram's Kansas City Chiefs, the Reds under manager Sparky Anderson prohibited facial hair and promoted an aura of clean-cut discipline. In contrast, the mustachioed A's were called "baseball's black sheep." Cincinnati was favored to win the series, especially with Oakland's Reggie Jackson out with a leg injury. But A's outfielder Joe Rudi helped seal one victory with a spectacular catch, previously unheralded Gene Tenace hit four home runs, and Oakland beat Cincinnati four games to three, with Rollie Fingers getting the series-clinching save. Five years after fleeing Kansas City as perennial losers, the A's were world champions. The team's celebration in the visitors' clubhouse in Cincinnati was loud and long, and it continued unabated during the flight back home. Even then there was a sour note as the A's' Dave Duncan confronted Charlie Finley: "You don't care about us. You only care about what we can do for you."[56]

The A's' Gene Tenace acknowledges the cheers during the victory parade through downtown Oakland after the A's won the World Series in October 1972. (Lonnie Wilson, untitled. Gelatin silver, 11 x 14 in. The Oakland Tribune Collection, the Oakland Museum of California, gift of ANG Newspapers.)

Writer John Krich lived in Oakland in 1972 and was skeptical of the city's investments in major league sports. The Coliseum, he said, had been "built with the funds that might have rehabilitated 100,000 homes." Charlie Finley was a "massa" whose promotional schemes were ill suited to "a city on welfare." But when Krich drove to Oakland's Jack London Square immediately following the A's' World Series victory, he encountered an unlikely congregation of celebrants from all classes. There were well-to-do denizens of the hills overlooking Oakland who "had arrived

to identify with the city they'd left behind." There were small-town dwell-
ers from beyond the hills who "bounced in the beds of their pickups."
And there were young people from the city itself in a motley collection
of vehicles. They "grinned broken-teethed from unmuffled Impalas,"
"boogaloed atop Eldorados," and "jigged to bagpipes that wailed from
VW busses."[57]

The same phenomenon repeated itself on a grander scale the next
day during what one city official said was the first parade in downtown
Oakland since the 1950s. Oaklanders who had treated the A's with apparent indifference in the past now turned out in huge numbers to
greet the victorious players, who temporarily set aside their internal
bickering to bask in the communal joy. "Seeing all those people, you'd
think we were in New York City," the A's' Sal Bando said. "There were
old people and young people, hippies and squares. It was beautiful. I
never thought I'd see that in Oakland." Even the Black Panthers turned
up in their leather berets and took advantage of the occasion to collect donations, accepting each one with a cheery "right on." The crowd
roared when Charlie Finley declared, "There are two baseball teams in
the Bay Area, and if one of them moves, it sure as hell isn't going to be
the A's." That evening Dave Duncan gave a victory dinner summation
of the "Hairs vs. Squares" World Series just concluded: "We showed it
doesn't matter what a person looks like on the outside. . . . We had what
it counts inside, heart and guts."[58]

The good feelings would not last. Baseball owners' relief over the best
news that most of them would receive during 1972—the U.S. Supreme
Court ruling against Curt Flood's lawsuit—would dissipate in the face of
new challenges to baseball's reserve clause. Oakland's attendance woes
would reemerge, along with new rumors of the A's potentially moving
elsewhere. Charlie Finley would trade away Dave Duncan. And the
"heart and guts" of baseball's defending champions would continually
be tested anew.

4 Chiefs vs. Raiders, Part II

PRO FOOTBALL PLAYERS' labor unity lagged behind that of their baseball counterparts. In July 1970, the National Football League Players Association ordered players not to report to training camp because of a dispute over pensions. The Kansas City Chiefs ignored the edict long enough to play in the annual College All-Star Game against top collegiate players. The Chiefs were unwilling to forego the extra pay that the game would give them, especially considering that the average NFL salary was then only $23,000. Michael Oriard was about to join Kansas City as a rookie. "Solidarity with the union would [have been] personally expensive," he would say of his soon-to-be teammates.[1]

The labor dispute was quickly settled, and although the union won a few concessions, the team owners maintained firm control over their players. Chiefs players had reason not to be overly concerned. They had earned the right to play in the College All-Star Game because they were the defending NFL champions. Kansas City was viewed as a state-of-the-art franchise that was about to move into a state-of-the-art stadium. Within two years, though, the Chiefs would be eclipsed by the team they had beaten to reach the Super Bowl, the Oakland Raiders. For all his innovations, Chiefs coach Hank Stram's conception of a team being "a group of people who think and look alike"[2] would increasingly seem outmoded, whereas the Raiders' acceptance of unique personalities would serve them well as professional football entered a more flamboyant era. In addition, Kansas City's vaunted new stadium seemed to distance the Chiefs from their fan base even as the Oakland Coliseum seemed to help bring fans and players together. Still, the Raiders experienced ongoing frustration as they repeatedly failed to win the championship that they believed was their due. And both the Oakland Coliseum and Kansas City's Arrowhead Stadium became enmeshed in a broader debate over the funding, location, and beneficiaries of big-league sports facilities.

* * *

Hank Stram was on top of the world in the first half of 1970. The Chiefs coach flew all over the country for awards and speaking engagements; he also appeared in TV commercials and on the shows of Ed Sullivan, Johnny Carson, and David Frost. Everywhere he was lionized for epitomizing the "Football of the Future" that employed multiple formations and camouflage. Stram noted that he had instituted that style of play years before: "But we weren't the world champions then. Now that we are, we're being copied. And to be copied is the greatest compliment."[3]

Of his players, Stram said that it was "ridiculous to think they can't absorb" what was asked of them on the field given that off the field they were "engineers, lawyers, bankers, stock brokers, salesmen, [and] artists." Many players on the Chiefs as well as the Oakland Raiders lived in their respective communities year-round, and they were active both in business and in charitable work. Chiefs players' business interests in Kansas City ranged from restaurants to an advertising firm. In Oakland, members of the Raiders similarly oversaw enterprises that included restaurants, nightclubs, and liquor stores, with guard Wayne Hawkins serving as a bank executive and linebacker Dan Conners running a sports mouthguard company.[4]

Yet there were limits to what certain players could accomplish. "It's almost impossible for a black to go into business in this town unless it's a bar," said Kansas City's Mike Garrett in 1970. His teammate Otis Taylor said that he did not receive endorsement offers the way that such white teammates as Len Dawson did, and Taylor communicated his anger in the bluntest way possible: "I'm supposed to be a superstar but I'm a super nigger." One former member of the Oakland Raiders expressed cynicism about pro football players' off-field endeavors. Chip Oliver said that the average player who had been in the NFL for several years mainly sought "to keep his name in front of the public and his business associations going. And since he doesn't care about the game anymore, the quality of football declines."[5]

Oliver had left football after the 1969 season to work in a Bay Area fruit juice bar. "Football is a silly, childish game," he said. "It would make as much sense for men to beat each other over the heads with bats." Oliver would write a memoir, provocatively titled *High for the Game,* that said he had taken mescaline before football practice; he also said that players routinely took amphetamines (which the Raiders called "rat turds"). Oliver's memoir appeared soon after another recently retired NFL player published his own tell-all book. Dave Meggyesy wrote in that book that he wanted to reveal "what's really behind the video glitter of the game—the racism and fraud, the unbelievable brutality that affects mind as much as body." He also excoriated football's "maudlin and dangerous pre-game 'patriotism'" directed toward the flag and national anthem. Meggyesy had written his book at Oakland's Institute for the Study of Sport and Society, which had been founded by former college athlete Jack Scott. Calling sports "conservative, narrow and encrusted," Scott declared that "you shouldn't feel badly just because you lose. The final score should be almost incidental."[6]

Such comments reflected the changes that had begun sweeping over sports in the 1960s and that would continue during the 1970s. There had been the so-called revolt of the black athlete[7] with African American pro football players challenging the racism they encountered; there also were the beginnings of a labor revolution in baseball. Dave Meggyesy's and Chip Oliver's books had much in common with the contemporaneous ones written by baseball players Jim Bouton and Curt Flood in that they all exposed the seamier side of big-league sports. Athletes were becoming more willing to express their individuality and question authority.

Still, when it came to the punishing physicality of professional football, most NFL players held views that differed sharply from those of Meggyesy and Oliver. "It's no flower-tossing thing," said one of the Oakland Raiders about football. "And it's become the world's most popular sport because it is so violent and exciting." In fact the NFL promoted violence as one of the essential elements that made the game so compelling. To mark its fiftieth anniversary in 1970, the league published a commemorative book featuring an essay titled "A Game for Our Time."

"Professional football is basically a physical assault by one team upon another in a desperate fight for land," the essay proclaimed. It also suggested that football spectatorship compensated for the loneliness and alienation of contemporary urban life, with television—"the electronic core of the nation"—being especially well equipped to show "the ferocity developed within the momentary sieges of the scrimmage." Television's *Monday Night Football* debuted in 1970 and became an immediate hit in no small part through its vivid, up-close depictions of that ferocity.[8]

The second-ever telecast of *Monday Night Football* showcased the Kansas City Chiefs, who raced to a 31–0 lead over the Baltimore Colts before winning 44–24. The Colts had long been a power in the National Football League, and Kansas City's rout of them seemed to auger well for the Chiefs now that they and other one-time American Football League teams had merged into the NFL. However, the Chiefs and the Oakland Raiders (who continued to play in the same division) soon discovered that they could not dominate their opposition to the degree that they had in the AFL. Both teams struggled to win consistently during the first weeks of the 1970 season, and after one Oakland loss, team executive Al Davis wondered out loud if he should replace coach John Madden.[9]

The Raiders' fortunes soon turned thanks to the unlikeliest of heroes. Forty-three-year-old George Blanda had been on shaky ground in Oakland after criticizing how he had been used in the AFL championship loss to the Chiefs the previous January. During summer training camp, Al Davis had referred to the kicker-quarterback as a "sour old guy" and had briefly placed him on waivers. Yet Blanda had remained with the Raiders, and in the middle of the 1970 season he suddenly began working miracles. He entered a game against Pittsburgh and threw three touchdown passes to beat the Steelers. The following week in Kansas City, his last-minute forty-eight-yard field goal gave the Raiders an improbable tie with the Chiefs. The week after that, he came off the bench again as the Raiders played the Cleveland Browns in Oakland. Blanda tied the score with a touchdown pass with less than two minutes to play, and then following a Raiders interception, he moved them into position for a fifty-two-yard field goal attempt to win the game. "The odds against this must be about 76 million to a half," Oakland radio announcer Bill King told his listeners. Then Blanda kicked the ball: "That's got a *chance*.

That is—*good!* It's good! Holy Toledo! . . . George Blanda has just been elected king of the world!"[10]

Over the next two weeks, Blanda clinched two more Raiders wins with a touchdown pass against Denver and a field goal against San Diego. Oakland radio station KNEW promoted its broadcasts of the games by mixing highlights of Bill King's play-by-play calls with "America the Beautiful" and the "Hallelujah Chorus" along with narration parodying an old-time radio serial: "George has done everything. What does he do for an encore? . . . Find out this weekend!" Despite his age and grizzled countenance, Blanda seemed oddly more in sync with the times than did his much younger teammate Daryle Lamonica, the quarterback whom Blanda frequently replaced during games (often to Lamonica's frustration). One sportswriter described Lamonica as "a throwback to the type of pro athlete the nation idolized in the 1950s—friendly, patient, smiling." In contrast, Blanda's irascibility resonated with the iconoclasm that big-league athletes would increasingly express during the 1970s. "It's certainly a pleasure to be here to answer these ridiculous questions," Blanda told a Raiders Boosters lunch that had just given him a standing ovation. "I talk to 11- and 12-year-olds who make more sense."[11]

While Blanda was performing his heroics, the Chiefs also had managed to right themselves and keep step with the Raiders, setting up a late-season showdown in Oakland to decide the division winner. Kansas City led early in the game, but then the Raiders took charge behind fullback Marv Hubbard. Like Blanda and other members of the Raiders, Hubbard displayed a decidedly idiosyncratic personality. He was renowned among his teammates for regularly punching out a plate glass window next door to an Oakland bar that the team frequented, as well as for regularly plunking down money in advance to pay for the damages. Hubbard also nurtured an ongoing grudge against the Chiefs: "I have an intense hatred for them. They're the biggest bunch of cheap shot artists around." During the December 1970 game against Kansas City, a collision with Chiefs linebacker Willie Lanier left Hubbard woozy but unbowed ("what's the matter, Willie, can't you hit me any harder?" he claimed he said to Lanier), and his rushing led Oakland to a 20–6 victory over the Chiefs. The Raiders went on to lose the AFC championship game to Baltimore, but George Blanda was still named NFL Player of the Year.[12]

The Raiders' Marv Hubbard celebrates after scoring a touchdown against the Chiefs in Oakland in December 1970. (AP Photo)

The Chiefs had finished out of the playoffs largely owing to a pallid offense, inviting mockery of Hank Stram's so-called "Football of the Future" and "Offense of the '70s." "We'll move the ball the coming season," Stram promised during 1971 training camp. The Chiefs already had traded away Mike Garrett after he announced that he would soon quit football to play baseball instead. "You are a chattel," Garrett had said of life as an NFL player. (He eventually chose to remain in the NFL with San Diego.) Ed Podolak was now anchoring the Kansas City running game, and rookie wide receiver Elmo Wright supplemented the passing attack. Wright brought a new and unusual flamboyance to Stram's straight-laced Chiefs with his exuberant high-step after scoring touchdowns, immortalizing himself as the "Father of the End Zone Dance." The routine offended some traditionalists. "The average fan knows Elmo Wright is showboating when he goes into his dance and the average fan probably gets slightly disgusted at it," one sportswriter opined, while adding that it seemed to reveal what the NFL had become: "Pro football, there's no denying, is a television production. It's a great game, but it's built around a show business theme."[13]

Not even Wright could compare to Otis Taylor, who would be the Chiefs' biggest star in 1971 as he led the NFL in receiving yards. "People [in Kansas City] talk about him constantly, like 11th century Spaniards adding to the epic of El Cid or Wagner savoring the triumphs of Siegfried," *Sports Illustrated* commented. "Everyone has a favorite Otis Taylor play to recall." Most memorable would be a game-winning touchdown against Washington in which Taylor caught the ball one-handed while a defensive back pinned his other arm to his side. Taylor said that he regularly practiced for such circumstances: "God did give me two hands to catch with, and if the ball comes when I can't use one of them, I'll use the other."[14]

Oakland's most explosive wide receiver, Warren Wells, missed the 1971 season. Already on probation for attempted rape, he had gotten into further trouble for gun possession and drunk driving before finally having his probation revoked after being stabbed by a woman who said that he had beaten her after she refused to become a prostitute and give him her earnings. Al Davis unsuccessfully lobbied for Wells's release from prison during the season, which suggested that Davis was willing to overlook almost anything that a player might do provided that he could produce on the field. (As it happened, Wells never again played in the NFL.) But the Raiders still had receiver Fred Biletnikoff, and they had replenished their defense by drafting safety Jack Tatum and linebacker Phil Villapiano, both of whom established their own unique personas: Tatum as "The Assassin," known for his crushing hits on opposing players; and Villapiano as "Foo," known for once brawling with the Hells Angels.[15]

When the Raiders and Chiefs met for the first time in 1971, the Chiefs were leading 20–10 in the fourth quarter when Oakland coach John Madden again replaced Daryle Lamonica with George Blanda. In short order, Blanda threw a touchdown pass, and after Oakland got the ball back, he drove the Raiders to just short of the Kansas City goal line. Madden elected to have Blanda kick a field goal on fourth down rather than go for a winning touchdown, and the game ended in a 20–20 tie. Oakland guard Gene Upshaw had faced off against his younger brother Marvin, a Chiefs defensive lineman. "The only people that can be happy are my parents," the elder Upshaw said of the tie.[16]

The December rematch in Kansas City would determine the division title, which Oakland had won each of the previous four seasons. Past experience had made many Kansas Citians apprehensive, if not cynical. One fan (whom the *Kansas City Times* described as "brave, if not wise") made his doubts plain to the Chiefs' Willie Lanier: "When the pressure is on you guys, you're like children. Oakland will win, and win easily." Indeed it looked late in the game as though the Chiefs would once more lose to the Raiders. George Blanda had come off the bench anew to give Oakland a 14–13 lead, and the Chiefs were facing a third-and-long at their own seven-yard line. "Get open," quarterback Len Dawson told Otis Taylor, and so Taylor did, pulling in a first-down pass and then three additional passes during the Kansas City drive. After Dawson threw to him once more and Oakland interfered with him, the Chiefs were in position for a short Jan Stenerud field goal that won the game 16–14. "His catches were splendid," said Hank Stram of Taylor. "I just can't describe them; I don't know enough adjectives."[17]

The Chiefs then met the Miami Dolphins in the playoffs on Christmas Day, with the scheduling designed to accommodate network TV. Some sportswriters and fans protested, and a sign at the game in Kansas City criticized NFL commissioner Pete Rozelle for putting profits ahead of holiday cheer: "Merry Chritma from Grinch Rozelle."[18] But fans cheered when the Chiefs jumped to an early lead. However, Kansas City never could pull away from Miami as the Dolphins shut down Otis Taylor. The Chiefs did benefit from an extraordinary game from Ed Podolak, who amassed 350 yards in total offense. His long kickoff return late in a 24–24 game set up Jan Stenerud for a thirty-one-yard field goal attempt that likely would give Kansas City the win.

Stenerud had left his native Norway nine years before to go to Montana State University on a ski jumping scholarship. The school's football coach had seen him kicking a football and invited him to join the team. "This is the land of opportunity," Stenerud had thought to himself. "If you are ready for it and some kind of occasion presents itself, who knows what can happen?" He would go on to help the Chiefs win the Super

Bowl. But Stenerud had been shaky at times in 1971, and he already had missed a field goal in the playoff game against Miami because of a botched fake kick. Now, with the season on the line, his thirty-one-yard attempt went just wide, and the game moved into overtime. Stenerud had one more chance to win it for the Chiefs, but the Dolphins blocked his kick. Finally, Miami made a field goal during the second overtime period to win 27–24. The longest game in NFL history ended in a hush, as described by the *Kansas City Star:* "Not since Billy Graham called for silent meditation at an outdoor religious rally have 50,000 persons been so quiet."[19]

Stenerud was inconsolable after the game. "I feel like hiding," he said. "It's totally unbearable." Hank Stram sat alone in the Chiefs locker room staring into nothingness: "It has to be the toughest loss we've ever had."[20] It would be the last-ever football game at Kansas City's Municipal Stadium; the next season, the Chiefs would play in brand-new Arrowhead Stadium. But coming on the heels of their loss to Miami, the Chiefs' move to their new home represented a decisive turning point in the franchise's fortunes even as the new stadium and other sports facilities came under critical scrutiny.

* * *

Controversy over Kansas City's Truman Sports Complex had started with the funding shortfall that had forced cancellation of the complex's rolling roof; then there were the frustrations over the strikes that had delayed construction. A November 1970 news conference seemed to offer happier news, at least at first. In addition to making the "Arrowhead" name official, the Chiefs announced that they were paying to install a stadium club and "Golden Circle" suites on the lines of similar amenities in the Houston Astrodome and other newer sports facilities. Owner Lamar Hunt said that the additions would ensure "that our fans have the most complete and luxurious stadium in the world."[21]

Only the most privileged fans would experience the complete luxuriousness that Arrowhead had to offer. Just 750 season ticket holders could become club members, and they had to pay an initiation fee and annual dues; the Golden Circle suites would go to corporate customers and their clients. As a result, according to Robert Lewis's history of the sports complex, there developed a "gnawing feeling that the Com-

plex had become the plaything of special interests," with suburbanites
from outside Jackson County enjoying the facilities without putting tax
money toward them. Some citizens sent angry letters to the *Kansas City
Star,* and the local *Wednesday Magazine* published an editorial: "The new
[complex] will cost $54 million without the rolling roof. It will return
tax-free revenue to a few people. It will provide pleasure to a majority
of people not paying for it. It will provide, for a few rich people, some
luxury to rival anything Ancient Rome could offer. But what about
the Jackson County taxpayer?" Three such taxpayers filed a lawsuit
against the stadium leases and the sale of revenue bonds intended to
help complete the complex. The lawsuit threatened to delay completion
indefinitely (prompting a Chiefs supporter to shout in the face of one of
the plaintiffs, "You're killing this deal!"). The plaintiffs agreed to drop
the suit in exchange for conditions that included allocating a portion of
stadium food and drink revenues to Jackson County and giving county
residents seating priority.[22]

The settlement also stipulated that a public meeting allow citizens
and media to question local officials and team executives. At times
the meeting was contentious. A reporter from the suburban *Raytown
News* asked whether there was "any significance that the Arrowhead
Club brochure shows no Negroes inside the premises." (Lamar Hunt
answered no, and the moderator quickly changed subjects.) Former
Jackson County official Charles Wheeler, who had criticized the sports
complex in the past, ripped local media for having been cheerleaders for
the complex and for "consistently wanting to overspend on all public-
budgeted projects." In response Chiefs radio announcer Bill Grigsby
accused Wheeler of exploiting the controversy "for private and personal
gain in your great desire for a broadened political future."[23] Wheeler in
fact would be elected Kansas City mayor the following March, defeat-
ing Dutton Brookfield, chair of the Jackson County Sports Complex
Authority. Even so, construction went ahead on the complex, including
on the stadium club and suites.

Soon a new controversy developed over a proposed sports arena in
Kansas City. It would provide a new home for the American Royal live-
stock show that was based in an increasingly decrepit building in the
West Bottoms stockyards district west of downtown; the new arena also
would offer a home for a potential National Hockey League franchise,

thus expanding the city's major league offerings into what was foreseen as "the boom sport of the '70s and '80s." In July 1971, Mayor Wheeler said that he would back building an arena in the downtown central business district. Former mayor H. Roe Bartle seconded the idea: "Downtown has been growing ill where cash registers were once ringing and singing." Other people promoted alternative sites in the stockyards, at the Truman Sports Complex, or in suburban Overland Park in Johnson County, Kansas. Overland Park seemed to gain the upper hand after the Kansas legislature approved creating a sports authority to build the arena. The city's mayor said that the arena would help bring Johnson County "into full partnership in the metropolitan area." Not incidentally, the arena also would help the county further its own big-league aspirations.[24]

In June 1972, the NHL awarded Kansas City an expansion team to begin play in 1974, apparently in Overland Park. The *Kansas City Star*'s Joe McGuff welcomed the news and suggested that it was inevitable for big-league sports facilities to locate in suburban areas: "As cities grow and road systems improve, the old pattern of concentrating businesses, hotels and entertainment facilities in one area becomes impossible to maintain." Yet the *Star*'s editorial page still lobbied for a downtown or stockyards site, saying that the postwar deterioration of Kansas City's urban core was a "trend that must be reversed." (Downtown Kansas City's decline paralleled that of other downtowns across the country during the postwar years as suburbanization accelerated, whereas the stockyards never had recovered from the flood of 1951.) Complicating matters for Overland Park was that some business owners and taxpayers there objected to a proposed motel and restaurant tax to help fund an arena, with Johnson County restauranteurs calling the proposal "totally unreasonable." After Johnson Countians rejected the tax in a November 1972 referendum and after Kansas City's R. Crosby Kemper Jr. announced a gift toward building an arena in the stockyards instead, it appeared as though the debate over the site finally had been resolved.[25]

Then new obstacles emerged. The city council in Kansas City could not agree on a bond issue to supplement Kemper's gift; the council also considered changing the arena location. "I have never seen such a lack of leadership or such a total failure at the city level," fumed Kemper. There were fears that the NHL might move the expansion franchise to a different city. The council and Mayor Wheeler settled on $5.6 million bond issue for the stockyards site, but a Jackson County citizens group sued to stop it. Although voters had approved general revenue bonds for an arena, that vote had occurred back in 1954, and the citizens group felt that a new referendum was needed given the problems that Kansas City now faced: "Urban blight is spreading; public hospitals are overcrowded and understaffed; streets are filled with chuckholes; police and firemen are underpaid. People are suffering. Can the council ignore these needs and spend [millions] on a sports palace?" In response Mayor Wheeler criticized the group for ignoring "positive growth ethics" and for purportedly wanting "to see Kansas City shrink and crack." In March 1973, the group abandoned its suit in exchange for a tax on arena admissions to pay off the bonds; and in November 1974, following delays by a construction strike (the city was still not totally free of such shutdowns), Kemper Arena finally opened in the stockyards.[26]

The new arena's contributions to Kansas City's major league image did not fully work out as planned. Kemper Arena did for a short time host both the Kansas City Kings of the National Basketball Association and the Kansas City Scouts of the NHL. The Kings had arrived in town without much fanfare in 1972 after the NBA's Cincinnati Royals sought a new home because of poor fan support. Team members had been expecting to move to San Diego and were unhappy about going to Kansas City instead; they were especially displeased to learn that they also would have to play multiple games in Omaha because Kemper Arena did not yet exist and there were not enough open dates in Kansas City's old Municipal Auditorium. (At first the newly transplanted team was called the Kansas City–Omaha Kings.) The Kings boasted a superstar in Nate Archibald and made the playoffs by their third season in Kansas City, but they never would draw consistently well there, especially not after the Kemper Arena roof collapsed during a 1979 storm and the team temporarily had to move back into Municipal Auditorium. The franchise left for Sacramento in 1985.[27]

As for the hockey franchise that had been a prime motivation for building the new arena, the Scouts would last all of two years. They were utterly overmatched on the ice; in their last twenty-seven games of existence, they did not win once. When their coach Bep Guidolin was asked if it seemed like a nightmare, he replied, "You gotta sleep before you can have nightmares." The Scouts also experienced constant chaos in the front office and received little support from the city. Thus the franchise moved to Denver in 1976 after having "disappeared down a sinkhole caused by mismanagement, deceit, incompetence and apathy everywhere from Kemper Arena to City Hall," according to one sportswriter's postmortem.[28]

Oakland lost its own NHL team that same year. Ten years earlier, the city had lured the Seals away from San Francisco into the new Oakland Coliseum Arena. *Oakland Tribune* sports editor George Ross had said that the team promised "a spectacular 'spinoff' of potential benefits" to the city. But the Seals achieved little success even—or especially—after Charlie Finley bought them in 1970. Finley, whose baseball team had a live mule as a mascot, presented a skating mule (two tandem skaters in one big mule costume) at his hockey team's games. Such promotions failed to attract hockey fans and also inadvertently prolonged games (while the mule skated, the Zamboni waited). Finley sold back the team to the NHL, and it was finally moved to Cleveland. Bay Area sportswriter Art Spander commented that the Seals' travails highlighted the folly surrounding cities' quest for major league franchises: there were simply "too many teams" and "too many people trying to squeeze every last dollar out of the customer."[29]

Professional basketball would bring some athletic glory to Oakland, although the city never received the full credit that it felt it deserved. The Oaks of the American Basketball Association won the ABA title in 1969 but soon left town. Then the NBA's San Francisco Warriors moved to Oakland in 1971. They were owned by Franklin Mieuli, a Bay Area radio-TV producer with an iconoclastic personality on par with those of Charlie Finley and Al Davis. Rather than rename his team the *Oakland* Warriors, he called them *Golden State* instead, presumably to give them broader marketing appeal. The new name annoyed Oakland sports boosters. After the Warriors and their star player Rick Barry won the 1975 NBA title despite being heavy underdogs, Oakland Mayor John Reading told a victory rally, "They call themselves Golden Staters, but you know and I know they're Oakland's own." The *Oakland Tribune* made a point of referring to the team as "Oakland," and years later, longtime Oakland sportswriter Dave Newhouse called "Golden State" a "repugnant" name with "no governor, mayor or zip code." As of 2018, the Warriors—once again NBA champions—would still be based in

Oakland, but they were preparing to move back to San Francisco into a new arena.[30]

Although development of the Oakland Coliseum Complex had aroused some controversy in the 1960s, that controversy never had grown quite so heated as the ones that at times would envelop Kansas City's Truman Sports Complex and Kemper Arena. In part that was because the complex had been built relatively inexpensively. "Costs were far below those of most other new stadiums. Cost overruns were almost nonexistent," wrote Bill and Nancy Boyarsky in a 1974 critique of municipal spending on sports facilities. They also noted that the Coliseum had been more commercially successful than competing facilities. Still, it had not yet generated enough revenue to allow Oakland and Alameda County to stop paying rent (the arrangement under which the Coliseum had been built stipulated that the rent would pay off bonds and help operate the facility until it became self-sustaining). The Coliseum also had done little to increase property values or reduce property taxes.[31]

At heart, said the Boyarskys, the sports complex pointed to rival political and economic systems that offered competing visions for Oakland. "In the early sixties, the white system was building the Oakland Coliseum Complex to beef up the city's economy," they wrote. "During those same years, the black system was building a new ghetto consciousness. Each represented one segment of society's attempt to cure the social ills besetting Oakland." Ultimately the Coliseum had "done nothing to end the decay and despair" of the African American community.[32]

Addressing that "decay and despair" would be a focal point of Bobby Seale's 1973 run for Oakland mayor against John Reading. The Black Panthers' cofounder campaigned alongside fellow Panther Elaine Brown, who was running for city council. According to Brown, they sought to empower Oakland's African American citizens: "Black folks were talking proud, declaring they would no longer allow a rich white minority to retain domination over the politics of a city that was half black." In the months prior to the election, the *Black Panther* newspaper produced what historian Robert Self would call "a remarkably coherent body of critical journalistic work" that targeted the city's power elite. As Brown later put it, "We had attacked every institution in the city of Oakland."[33]

Among those institutions was the Coliseum. The *Black Panther* allowed that the sports complex had "provided Oakland residents with many thrills and much excitement; it has been a definite plus for our city." However, "the businessmen who run the Coliseum, the teams operating there, the contractors and construction companies who built the Coliseum, and the Reading administration, who claims 'credit' for the construction, have run a 'con game'" by reaping "fantastic profits" at Oakland citizens' expense. The newspaper singled out *Tribune* publisher William Knowland as well as local industrialist Edgar Kaiser, who the newspaper said had provided much of the Coliseum's steel and concrete. The paper also charged that Oakland's big-league sports teams paid little in taxes compared with the teams in San Francisco. Bobby Seale and Elaine Brown proposed raising the A's' and Raiders' rents while ending the city's own payments: "City support for the Coliseum is unnecessary considering the Coliseum makes good money, as do the teams who use the facilities there."[34]

Although Seale made it into a runoff against John Reading, both Seale and Brown ultimately lost their campaigns. Black support had not been directed solely toward them; there had been other African American candidates for mayor, and an African American newspaper, the *Oakland Post,* had endorsed Reading (who was white) as well as the city council incumbent whom Brown was trying to unseat.[35] Operations continued as before at the Coliseum. But it did not offer the luxury boxes or other tony features that Kansas City's Arrowhead Stadium and other new stadiums did, and in due course the Coliseum's perceived shortcomings would be among the factors prompting the Raiders' Al Davis to start looking for a new home for his team.

* * *

It had been touch and go on whether Arrowhead would open in time for the 1972 football season, but Chiefs general manager Jack Steadman and Jackson County presiding judge George Lear had helped keep construction on track while mediating disputes among the architects, contractors, and unions. On August 12, Kansas City opened the stadium by hosting the St. Louis Cardinals in a preseason game. The festivities included four military jets flying so low over Arrowhead that a number of the 78,000 attendees "thought they'd had it," according to the stadium manager. "Some were so shaky we had to calm them down." Arrowhead was still not quite finished, and dignitaries were feted in a suite with

Kansas City's Arrowhead Stadium. The stadium accommodated far more spectators and much more parking than the Chiefs' previous home, Municipal Stadium. (Ichabod / Wikimedia Commons / CC-BY-SA-3.0)

a bare concrete floor and plasterboard walls. Among those dignitaries was Mayor Charles Wheeler, who had criticized the building of such suites. "This is just a one-shot thing," he smilingly said of his presence there as opposed to being out in the stands.[36]

The media, which enjoyed a luxurious facility in Arrowhead with ample food and liquor, touted the stadium's other features. Along with the "Presidential Suite" that could be rented for $18,000 annually, there also were the two scoreboards ("Big Chief" and "Little Wolf") and the two hundred "Arrowettes" (young women ushers who had been hired through an open audition in which they had been asked to dress in miniskirts and heels). Then there was the artificial surface cared for by a

"Turf-O-Matic" cleaning machine. Artificial turf manufacturers had run ads in the *Sporting News* claiming that it improved athlete safety and the quality of play: "And on TV, viewers should have better pictures because the light reflected from AstroTurf has a remarkably uniform character."[37]

Yet just as new sports stadiums stirred debates over their costs and benefits to citizens, they also stirred debates over their impact on athletes, particularly in connection with the artificial surfaces that the new facilities featured. By 1972 the media already had highlighted disaffection toward such surfaces among many football players and coaches, with one coach comparing them to "putting a throw rug over a driveway." After the Kansas City–St. Louis game, four Chiefs and five Cardinals reported foot, ankle, or knee injuries that seemed partly attributable to the Arrowhead surface. The Chiefs' equipment manager also reported the loss of seventeen pairs of football pants whose knees "looked like they were just burned right in two." Complaints among the Chiefs and other NFL players about artificial turf would mushroom during the coming years; quarterback Len Dawson would recall getting blood poisoning from chemicals used on the turf. The NFL players union called for a moratorium on the installation of artificial surfaces, but teams continued to play on them.[38]

Beyond health concerns, running back Ed Podolak said that the Chiefs lost a competitive advantage when they moved to Arrowhead from Municipal Stadium, where they had gone undefeated during the 1971 regular season. The old stadium had natural grass, and the Chiefs' large offensive and defensive lineman played more effectively on it than on artificial turf, where quickness was an advantage. The team lost something else as well: Municipal Stadium had been smaller and fans were closer to the field. "I felt that we players were the focal point of all our fans' attention," the Chiefs' Michael Oriard would say. "I sensed the fans' presence, felt bound to them by a common passion." Arrowhead was much larger and separated the Chiefs from their fans while also giving spectators plenty of distractions from the game itself. Oriard felt that Municipal Stadium offered "the heroic game I had discovered in my youth," whereas Arrowhead presented football as "big business and mass entertainment" geared toward television, much as artificial turf manufacturers asserted that their product improved the TV viewing experience.[39]

The Chiefs' biggest problem by 1972, according to Ed Podolak, was that they "were aging" and consequently "started going downhill." That impending decline was not readily apparent at the start of the season. On the contrary, the Chiefs were considered among the favorites to make the Super Bowl. ("Where is their weakness?" the Raiders' Al Davis asked rhetorically.) Coach Hank Stram had just signed a ten-year, $1 million contract that had given him total control over the team's football operations. "I feel I have the best coaching job, the best contract, the best complete situation in pro football," Stram said.[40]

Then the regular season began with a September rematch against Miami at Arrowhead. The temperature was ninety-one degrees, with high humidity; it was estimated to be 120 degrees on the artificial turf. Sixty fans were treated for heat exhaustion. The Dolphins—headed toward a perfect season and Super Bowl championship—dominated the game and won easily. The Chiefs went on the road to win their next three games, but then they returned home to lose to the Cincinnati Bengals. Next came a game at Arrowhead against the Philadelphia Eagles, who were so awful in 1972 that four of their season-ticket holders sued them for refunds. The Eagles quickly jumped to a big lead and held on to beat the Chiefs. Before the game, the U.S. flag at Arrowhead was accidentally displayed upside down as an apparent distress signal.[41]

Hank Stram dismissed charges that the Chiefs were past their prime: "We're not old. We're just more experienced than most teams." In contrast, the Oakland Raiders continually added young talent while moving past the likes of Ben Davidson and Warren Wells. "We never want to make the mistake of keeping a veteran with a year or two left instead of taking a rookie with 10 years ahead of him just because the vet knows more," coach John Madden would say.[42] In 1972 Oakland's stellar rookie crop included wide receivers Mike Siani and Cliff Branch, center Dave Dalby, cornerback Skip Thomas, and defensive lineman Otis Sistrunk. George Blanda was relegated mostly to placekicking, and Ken Stabler took over as the backup quarterback to Daryle Lamonica.

The Raiders led the Chiefs in the division race as the two teams prepared to play for the first time at Arrowhead. "Normally the home field might be worth an advantage, but the Chiefs have literally done nothing in their spacious grid palace," the *Kansas City Star* commented. Oakland's Marv Hubbard gave the Chiefs and their fans whatever additional spark they may have needed. "When we go to Kansas City, we're going to kick some rear," Hubbard promised in remarks that were picked up by the Kansas City media. More than 82,000 spectators turned out for the game, and the Chiefs thrilled the standing-room-only crowd by soundly beating Oakland 27–14, their first regular-season win in their new stadium. "We want Hubbard!" the crowd chanted toward the end of the game. Afterward the Raiders' running back, who had fumbled twice, said that fans also had saluted him in a different way: "I was coming off the field and two girls and a man in the stands spit in my face."[43]

The spitting incident embarrassed some Kansas City residents while also stirring a minor dust-up in the media. A letter to the *Star* said that "there were a few persons from Lower Slobbovia [at the game] and it must have been some of these who were involved as surely no Kansas Citian would do such a despicable thing." Nonetheless Glenn Dickey of the *San Francisco Chronicle* wrote that Chiefs fans "give pro football a bad name" and "go to church on Sunday morning and then spend three hours in the afternoon yelling variations of 'Kill 'em.'" In response, Kansas City area sportswriter Steve Cameron accused Dickey of perpetrating "one of the worst pieces of journalistic irresponsibility ever allowed by a major metropolitan newspaper." Cameron said that it could provoke violence among Oakland fans the next time the Raiders and Chiefs played at the Coliseum.[44]

Cameron need not have worried: by the time the teams did meet again in Oakland late in 1972, little remained at stake. The Raiders had virtually sewn up the division, while the Chiefs had resumed their losing ways. A low point had come the previous week on a frigid day at Arrowhead against San Diego. The Chiefs were out of the game by halftime, and a water main break knocked out the stadium plumbing, leaving fans who had loaded up on hot chocolate and coffee in dire straits. Things would be even worse against Oakland. Already riddled with injuries, the Chiefs lost Len Dawson after the Raiders' Otis Sistrunk hit him in the jaw. Oakland fans displayed a sign reading, "Nobody Spits on Hubbard," and then they took up their own "We want Hubbard!" chant as he ran for ninety-six yards in the Raiders' 26–3 win.[45]

The Chiefs did win their final games to salvage a winning season, but as far as the playoffs were concerned, they only could indulge in schadenfreude at the expense of the Raiders, who fell victim to perhaps the most famous play in NFL history. Oakland led the Pittsburgh Steelers 7–6 with only seconds left to play and the Steelers facing a fourth down. A desperation pass ricocheted backward when Pittsburgh's Frenchy Fuqua and Oakland's Jack Tatum collided, and Pittsburgh's Franco Harris plucked the ball out of the air to score a winning touchdown for the Steelers. The furious Raiders protested—then and always thereafter—that the fluke play had been illegal. "They were obsessed with the Immaculate Reception," said Bay Area sportswriter Betty Cuniberti, referring to the play by its popular label. "It was such a wonderful fuel for their strange engine": that is, the Raiders' abiding sense that it was them against the world.[46]

Al Davis set the prickly tone for the Raiders from the organization's top, which by now he occupied largely by himself. He had greatly expanded his powers in 1972 by playing the team's co-owners off each other and wrangling a new ten-year contract for himself. The details did not become public until April 1973 when the *Oakland Tribune*'s George Ross reported that co-owner Wayne Valley was suing to nullify Davis's new contract and expel him from the Raiders. (Valley, who had feuded with Davis for years, felt that Davis had snookered him in arranging the deal.) Ross and the *Tribune* had long maintained a cozy relationship with Davis, for which Ross did not apologize: "This guy was the number-one sports source in Oakland and he had a fantastic knowledge of the game and what was going on around the league, [so] as a journalist you accept it, you appreciate it, and you use it. Listen, if Al was using me, I was using him too."[47]

But Ross's story about the lawsuit permanently estranged him from Davis. "Al's sense of loyalty is absolute," Ross would say. "You're either on the team burning down the enemy fort, or *you* are the enemy." Davis's break with the *Tribune*—one of Oakland's staunchest boosters—also signaled a cooling of the relationship between the Raiders and Oakland. As early as 1968, Davis had expressed resentment toward the city's pursuit of the A's and other big-league teams. "The Raiders worked a long time to build up this city's image and pride in itself," he had said then. "Now, all of a sudden, we are supposed to have this great big happy family of Oakland teams. The Raiders don't want any part of that." Davis also had warned that should the opportunity arise for him to move elsewhere, "I won't feel that I am initiating the breaking of any trust with Oakland." Now Davis had his new contract (a judge would uphold its essence despite Wayne Valley's legal challenge), and it would give him greater power not just to leave town himself, but also to take the Raiders with him.[48]

But all seemed well with the Raiders heading into the 1973 season. The team continued to play in the Coliseum on natural grass (artificial turf was just being introduced when the facility opened in 1966). The grass frequently was soggy because of the stadium's proximity to the Oakland Estuary, and the sogginess appeared to work to the Raiders' advantage. So too did the fans who came to the Coliseum. Kansas City's Michael Oriard would scornfully say that the suites in Arrowhead Stadium were occupied by "social elites" who spent the game "sipping cocktails, nibbling on hors d'oeuvre, and following the game on closed-circuit television." The Oakland Coliseum was different. In the fond words of the Raiders' Ken Stabler, it was a "little ol' bullring filled with blue-collar crazies" consisting of "everyone from bikers to longshoremen." Rather than sip cocktails, Raiders fans "drank out of the same bottle," according to one fan: "And when they were done, they threw it at somebody."[49]

The Raiders continued to draft well in 1973, picking future Hall of Fame punter Ray Guy and linebacker Monte Johnson, and one sportswriter predicted a potential "runaway year" for them, whereas Kansas City seemed "headed for the twilight era." But the Chiefs' magic was not quite gone yet. They beat Oakland 16–3 early in the season at Arrowhead, holding the Raiders to their lowest offensive output in five years, with the game's only touchdown coming on a Willie Lanier interception return. The loss persuaded Oakland coach John Madden to make Ken Stabler the starting quarterback over Daryle Lamonica. Even though Kansas City fans reveled in beating the Raiders, a sign at Arrowhead indicated growing impatience with the Chiefs and especially with their coach: "Stram's defense is nimble / Stram's defense is quick / But the 'offense of the '70s' / Resembles a bunch of hicks."[50]

The defense kept the Chiefs in the division race until they met the Raiders again in Oakland in December. This time the Raiders and Marv Hubbard ran all over the Chiefs in a 37–7 win. "They just kicked the hell out of us," said Hank Stram in the funereal Kansas City locker room. About the only real blows that the Chiefs were able to land came in the fourth quarter after Oakland's George Atkinson hit Kansas City's Ed

Podolak in the face by the Chiefs sideline: "a total cheap shot," according to the Raiders' Phil Villapiano. A brawl followed—the biggest between the two teams since Ben Davidson speared Len Dawson three years earlier—and Villapiano received the worst of it while ending up under the Chiefs bench. "Everyone starts punching me," he would recall. "I'm getting *kicked*." Some Oakland fans tried to join the fight before police intervened.[51]

The Chiefs once more salvaged a winning year by winning their season finale, but ominously there were more than 35,000 no-shows at Arrowhead, and a Chiefs official ordered the removal of a "Stram Must Go" sign from behind the team's bench. In the playoffs, the Raiders exacted revenge for the Immaculate Reception by beating Pittsburgh, but then they lost to Miami in the AFC championship. Frustration over their postseason failures was beginning to grow. "The world knows that the Raiders always come up short in their final game," wrote the *Oakland Tribune*'s Ed Levitt. "It's as if every season is four quarters too long."[52]

Off-field events soon diverted attention from Oakland and Kansas City's worries. In the first months of 1974, the new World Football League signed several NFL stars to lucrative contracts. Among them were Raiders quarterbacks Daryle Lamonica and Ken Stabler. Lamonica—unhappy over having lost his starting role in Oakland—would join the Southern California Sun in 1975, with Stabler scheduled to go to the Birmingham Americans in 1976. Chiefs defensive lineman Curley Culp also signed with the WFL. However, neither he nor Stabler would ever play in the rival league, for it folded after just two seasons, beset with money troubles. (One WFL game erupted in a benches-clearing fight. A coach raced onto the field threatening to fine any of his players who did not return to the sideline. "Fined from what?" asked one player, sparking great laughter among the combatants on both sides and ending the fight.)[53]

Adding to the NFL's concerns was a players strike significantly more serious than the brief labor dispute of 1970. Union head Ed Garvey said that the players sought "to end the suffocating paternalism and the suppression of constitutional rights in the National Football League." At issue was what Michael Oriard would call "a thorough system of 'owners' and 'owned'" that included arbitrary fines, curfews, and restrictions on player movement similar to baseball's reserve clause. The strike lasted past the opening of summer training camps, but gradually player solidarity crumbled. Raiders stars including Ken Stabler, George Blanda, Fred Biletnikoff, and Jim Otto crossed picket lines to report to camp, along with top players on other teams. (The Chiefs demonstrated greater solidarity as Len Dawson, Otis Taylor, Willie Lanier, and Buck Buchanan, among others, stayed out of camp.) By August the strike had fizzled out entirely, and many strikers—including the Chiefs' Oriard— would be cut or traded in seeming retaliation.[54]

Oriard later pondered the reasons why NFL players had not displayed the same unity that major league baseball players had during their strike of 1972. Football rosters were larger than baseball rosters, and they were more prone to divisions between star players and role players as well as between starters and reserves. In addition, according to Oriard, "the 1974 strike shone a harsh light on the well-worn platitudes about the importance of the team." Strikebreakers who "bluntly looked out for 'Number 1'—the ones who put self above team or union—were actually the ones in the vanguard of a cultural revolution, as the 1960s gave way to the 'Me Decade' of the 1970s."[55]

Under John Madden and Al Davis, the Raiders were more tolerant of this new individualism than were Hank Stram's Chiefs. (Davis's catch-phrase "just win, baby" suggested that he cared only about whether a player could help his team win.) By 1974 the so-called Raider Nation was burgeoning as the team's unique talents and personalities were on constant display. They were regulars on *Monday Night Football*, building an 11-1-1 record on the program while Madden was coach. It was during a 1974 Monday night game that the camera showed the steaming bald head of Oakland's Otis Sistrunk as sportscaster and former player Alex Karras quipped that Sistrunk came from "the University of Mars." It was also during 1974 that Steve Sabol wrote words to accompany a rousing musical theme for NFL Films: "The autumn wind is a Raider / Pillaging just for fun / He'll knock you 'round and upside down / And laugh when he's conquered and won." And in 1974, Raiders fan and future actor Tom Hanks graduated from Oakland's Skyline High School. Years later he still could mimic John Facenda, the stentorian voice of NFL Films, narrating Raiders-Chiefs highlights: "'*The Raiders came out in the second half like men possessed. The Kansas City offense suddenly found itself floundering, unable to put together so much as a good combination for a first down. In the meantime, the Raider defense was swarming'*—you know, that kind of stuff just made us feel wonderful."[56]

The state of the two franchises had become such that the *Oakland Tribune* would comment wistfully that "football's hottest rivalry may never be the same." The Raiders, en route to a 12-2 season, easily dispatched the Chiefs in Oakland 27–7, and after clinching the division, they beat the Chiefs again 7–6 in Kansas City despite resting several starters. Not so long before, Oakland coach John Madden had engaged in gleeful gamesmanship with Hank Stram, telling him (truthfully) that there were rats in the Chiefs locker room at the Coliseum: "The next time you come here, there won't be any more rats—but today you have to live with them." Now Madden could not work up much excitement about beating the Chiefs, saying only that "we did enough to win and I guess that's what is important." Marv Hubbard, who used to boast about kicking the Chiefs' rears, now displayed more pity than swagger: "They [still] can hit. They may be old but I felt it just the same." As for Kansas City fans who once hung signs saying, "The Only Good Raider Is a Dead Raider," they now hung ones wistfully recalling the Chiefs' vanished glory days: "How Sweet It *Was.*"

Hank Stram's biggest move to try to reverse his team's slide would backfire disastrously. Mindful of Curley Culp's planned departure to the World Football League and unhappy with what he perceived to be Culp's intransigence, Stram traded him to the Houston Oilers, along with Kansas City's first-round draft pick the next year. Culp (who remained with Houston after the WFL collapsed) would be named the 1975 NFL defensive player of the year, and the Oilers used the draft pick they obtained from the Chiefs to select future Hall of Famer Robert Brazile. The main player the Chiefs received in return, John Matuszak, ended up achieving his greatest professional success not with Kansas City but with Oakland.

The Chiefs finished 5-9 in 1974, their worst-ever season, and *Kansas City Star* sports editor Joe McGuff had seen enough. Much as the *Oakland Tribune* had boosted the Raiders, the *Star* had been mocked for uncritical coverage of the Chiefs, with Bay Area sportswriter Glenn Dickey calling the paper "an important arm of the Chiefs' public relations staff." But now McGuff minced no words: "No one in the Chiefs organization seems willing to admit just how bad the team is or to level with the public and say that the time has come for a major rebuilding program. . . . The public is waiting for strong, decisive action but sees no sign of it."[57]

Just after Christmas, Chiefs owner Lamar Hunt announced Hank Stram's dismissal. Hunt and general manager Jack Steadman had met with area business leaders who told the Chiefs executives that interest in the team as reflected by season-ticket sales was dropping precipitously. Kansas City magazine publisher Tom Leathers offered an appraisal of Stram that would be consistent with many other observers' assessments of the Chiefs coach: he had been "loyal to a fault." Stram had tenaciously supported longtime players who he felt supported him and his authority, whereas "the rebel—even the rebel who played well—soon found his name on the waiver list" or else was traded, as had been the case with Curley Culp. For his part, Stram never apologized for sticking too long with his veteran players. Instead, he would blame the Chiefs' decline on an increasingly corporate-minded and profits-oriented culture that had been fostered by Jack Steadman and that had been exacerbated by the move to Arrowhead. "Could a football team really be operated like an MBA program?" said Stram. "I didn't believe so."[58]

Meanwhile, the Raiders tried to reverse their playoff woes. They beat the Miami Dolphins with a miraculous last-minute touchdown pass from Ken Stabler to Clarence Davis, a player with "legendarily bad hands" who somehow snagged the ball while being surrounded by three Dolphins. (The play would earn its own moniker: the "Sea of Hands" catch.) In the AFC championship game played at the Coliseum, Oakland led Pittsburgh 10–3 heading into the final quarter before everything fell apart once more for the Raiders—they lost 24–13. Marv Hubbard, who had rushed seven times for a total of six yards, was succinct in his remarks to the media: "Just use the same quotes from last year, and the year before that."[59]

The Raiders and Chiefs would both have to wait until next year. For the Raiders, the playoff agonies would not yet quite be over. For the Chiefs, the losing had just begun.

5

A's vs. Royals, Part II

IN MANY WAYS, baseball provided a happy antidote to the frustrations of Oakland and Kansas City sports fans in the mid-1970s. While the Raiders repeatedly fell short in the postseason, the A's extended their run of world championships; as the Chiefs went downhill in Arrowhead Stadium, the Royals blossomed as up-and-coming contenders in their new ballpark. Kansas City promoted its sports complex as part of a broader strategy of remaking itself and raising its national profile. Similarly, Oakland pursued ambitious new city projects to build upon the momentum it had established by constructing the Coliseum and upgrading its port. Both cities wanted to curb the white flight to the suburbs that had accompanied the deterioration of the cities' public schools and downtowns. However, Kansas City's and Oakland's efforts toward that end were not helped by their decisions to locate new sports facilities outside their central business districts. Their efforts at renewing themselves and becoming "big league" beyond just sports attracted criticism that reflected longstanding conflicts over class and race. And members of the Royals and especially the A's rebelled against what they saw as heavy-handed interference by management, even as baseball's labor revolution accelerated.

* * *

Some major league teams that had sought new stadiums during the 1950s and 1960s had done so partly because of changes in the areas where their old stadiums were located—in particular, people of color moving into previously white-majority neighborhoods.[1] That was not the case with Kansas City's Municipal Stadium, which had been situated in a predominantly African American district from the start. The stadium had been built in 1923 to host the minor league Kansas City Blues; its location at 22nd and Brooklyn east of downtown was near the site of the team's previous ballpark. The neighborhood had seen a significant influx of African Americans following the turn of the century, and by 1920 it was already 75 percent black. Yet the ballpark was conveniently located for both white and black baseball fans to watch not only the Blues but also the Monarchs of the Negro leagues. It was within walking distance of the African American business and entertainment center at 18th and Vine; it also was within walking distance of the white neighborhood that began a few blocks away at 27th Street, which for years would mark the unofficial southern boundary of the African American community.[2]

Kansas City's segregation was rigidly enforced through covenants and lending practices reflecting what sociologist Kevin Fox Gotham has called "the deliberate and organized efforts of the real estate industry to market racial exclusivity as requisite for neighborhood stability"—the same "racial exclusivity" that made it difficult for many African American athletes to find satisfactory places to live. The city's public housing and public schools were equally segregated. Prior to 1954, African Americans were restricted to Lincoln High School next to Municipal Stadium plus a vocational school. After the U.S. Supreme Court's *Brown* decision outlawed state-sanctioned school segregation, the Kansas City school district adopted new attendance zones, with Troost Avenue becoming a key demarcator. Troost—a north-south street running through the heart of the city—was already a racial dividing line; not many African Americans lived west of there. Now people residing west of the street were directed toward one set of schools while those east of the street were directed toward a different set of schools, including many that up until then had excluded African Americans. The east side's Central High School, whose student body had been 100 percent white in 1954, became 99 percent black by 1962. Residential patterns followed suit, driven by rampant fear-mongering and blockbusting. The African American population rapidly moved south and east past its old borders, but what became known as the "Troost Wall" held firm in the west.[3]

Oakland's history had been similar. When African Americans moved in growing numbers to such areas as East Oakland in the 1960s, unscrupulous realtors pressured white residents into leaving. "They hounded us to sell the house at that time so that they could give it to [African American buyers] at about twice the price," one white homeowner recalled. As whites left neighborhoods, public high schools such as Castlemont in East Oakland became increasingly identified as "black," while school zoning helped ensure that the new Skyline High School in the Oakland Hills was "white." Disparities among schools fueled resentment. "Many students are bitter," one high schooler told the city's board of education. "They feel Skyline has better books and more facilities because [its students] live in a richer area." In 1966 a citizens group tried to organize a three-day boycott of Oakland schools to protest inequitable conditions; the boycott degenerated into violence when youths assaulted five teachers at Castlemont High and then broke storefronts along several blocks of East 14th Street near the newly opened Oakland Coliseum.[4]

The fans who packed the Coliseum for Raiders games were in many ways a diverse lot (the "blue-collar crazies" who included "everyone from bikers to longshoremen," as quarterback Ken Stabler remembered them). But sportswriter Frank Deford observed in 1968 that the sports complex failed to attract some potential spectators, specifically many "Negroes who live quite near the complex but cannot afford to visit it" and "San Franciscans who would not go to Oakland under any circumstance." In addition, said Deford, the strategic decision to place the Coliseum far from downtown and closer to the suburbs near East Oakland inadvertently forced the city to rely on "the support of the rich and powerful suburbs around it to retain the only eminence it ever has had." By the late 1960s, the East Bay suburbs were booming in no small part because of white flight from Oakland, and they increasingly represented what one critic would call a "white noose" that hindered the city's development.[5]

Kansas City had pursued an aggressive annexation program from the 1940s to the early 1960s that helped ensure that it had room to expand and maintain an adequate tax base. But it too experienced white flight to its suburbs as the racial makeup of its neighborhoods and schools changed, consistent with the postwar experiences of other U.S. cities. White fans did turn out in impressive numbers at Municipal Stadium during the baseball A's' first years there as Kansas Citians celebrated their new big-league status. (One resident of a white, blue-collar neighborhood recalled that as a youth he and his friends would take a city bus and then walk "unafraid, and sometimes stridently, through several blocks of the black section surrounding the stadium" to go to A's games.) Kansas Citians also supported the Chiefs at Municipal Stadium after the team began winning regularly, supporting historian Neil Sullivan's contention that sports fans "will visit where they might not live" and "will set aside any misgivings they might have to get to the games, especially if the team is a contender."[6]

As the years went by, though, the old stadium and its environs were increasingly viewed as places where fans could end up with "missing teeth and missing pocketbooks," according to a Kansas City sportswriter. The A's' consistently awful performance and the constant controversy surrounding owner Charlie Finley also drove down attendance. After the A's were replaced by the Royals in 1969, local fan Bill James was struck by the stark difference between Finley's ramshackle operation and Municipal Stadium's new residents: "[The Royals] seemed antiseptic, colorless, mechanically efficient and with not much personality to like or dislike. This was a very welcome change. We had moved from the slums to the suburbs."[7]

James was speaking metaphorically, but when the Royals left their old stadium in 1973 for the new Truman Sports Complex, they literally moved from the inner city to a new suburban-like home, albeit one still within the city limits. The once-bustling African American neighborhood surrounding Municipal Stadium had already been suffering from a loss of population and housing stock, and that deterioration continued after the stadium was abandoned and demolished. A 2010 report would pronounce the area as having long been "neglected, forgotten and poorly served," although the addition of a Negro Leagues Baseball Museum and other improvements offered signs of hope.[8]

On the other hand, the new Royals Stadium, with its vast parking lots, was connected by freeways facilitating access from the suburbs north of the Missouri River and in Kansas; it was also situated next to Kansas City's eastern suburbs. The ballpark offered features and diversions similar to those in Arrowhead Stadium next door: artificial turf, a stadium club, a giant center-field scoreboard, and a colorful lights-and-fountains water spectacular. Unlike the multipurpose stadiums that other cities (including Oakland) had erected, Royals Stadium was designed solely for baseball, and many people would call it the best ballpark in the big leagues. Attendance during the Royals' first season there would increase by more than 90 percent over their final season in Municipal Stadium. But just as in Oakland, locating the new sports complex far from Kansas City's urban core did nothing to resuscitate a downtown that "already was dying," according to historian James Shortridge; the later decision to put Kemper Arena in the stockyards (which were not easily accessible from downtown) also did little to help, even if Kansas City had managed to keep the arena from locating across the Kansas state line in Johnson County. Furthermore, the new baseball stadium invited the same criticism that neighboring Arrowhead did: as Michael MacCambridge later wrote, it represented a trend of professional sports venues becoming "more corporate, more affluent, and more white."[9]

The two stadiums at the Truman Sports Complex did differ in one key aspect in 1973—Arrowhead's football tenant was aging and declining; Royals Stadium's baseball tenant was a young team on the rise. The Royals had installed artificial turf because it drained more easily than natural grass, making it less likely that people who had driven to the stadium from out of town would encounter a rainout (another example of a team catering to fans who lived outside the team's host city). The turf stirred some of the same complaints that the Arrowhead surface did, with Kansas City outfielder Lou Piniella recalling that "my ankles were sore, my knees were sore, and the field was really, really, really hot." But for the youthful Royals who were built on speed and defense, the turf presented a competitive advantage, especially when no other American League stadium had a full artificial surface and opposing teams were unused to playing on one. A sportswriter described what happened to fielders on one visiting team soon after the stadium opened: "Balls jumped up and slammed against their bodies, rolled swiftly between outfielders and caromed off the high outfield fences for extra bases."[10]

The turf also lent itself to the aggressive style brought to the Royals by their newest member, who would belie perceptions that the team was bland or antiseptic. Hal McRae was the last key Royal obtained by general manager Cedric Tallis, who once again had turned to the National League for a ballplayer frustrated by a lack of playing time.

While with the Cincinnati Reds, McRae had adopted the same brand of play epitomized by his teammate Pete Rose, never hesitating to crash into an opposing player to try to jar the ball loose or break up a double play. "I don't like to be intimidated on the field," McRae said. "If there's any intimidation, I'm going to do it." He struggled mightily at the plate after having been dealt to Kansas City until coach Charley Lau began working with him on his swing. Even with McRae slumping, the Royals got off to a scorching start in 1973 in trying to displace the Oakland A's at the top of their division.[11]

As was their wont, the A's had had an eventful off-season. Charles Finley lavished them with diamond World Series championship rings that he said had cost him $1,500 apiece. He also traded away first baseman Mike Epstein, who had fought with Reggie Jackson and manager Dick Williams the previous season. After catcher Dave Duncan held out for a higher salary, Finley traded him too. (Duncan—never a Finley fan—took a parting shot at the A's owner: "I am a human being with an identity of my own and I think this is something he tries to strip away from everyone around him.") Once the season began, the A's seemed listless; the wild enthusiasm with which Oaklanders had greeted them following their World Series win had faded back into apathy. "Look how drab this place is," said third baseman Sal Bando of the Coliseum. "It's so dead, so gray, no fans. The players call this place the Oakland Mausoleum."[12]

One bright spot for the A's was their new center fielder Bill North, obtained through another Finley trade. Manager Dick Williams would say that North was "the only player I've ever seen literally strut on to a world championship team." Like Hal McRae, North was an aggressive African American player who did not mind making enemies. In the first game of an A's-Royals series at the Coliseum in May, he charged the mound and began slugging Royals pitcher Doug Bird for no apparent reason. North later said that it was payback for Bird having beaned him in the head in the minor leagues three years previously: "I'd made my mind up that one day we'd see each other again." While the Royals threatened retaliation, the American League suspended North for the remainder of the series.[13]

As the season wore on, griping and grumbling emerged among both teams. At first new Royals manager Jack McKeon had charmed Kansas City fans and sportswriters, with one writer saying, "If fans love him, it is only because he loved them first." (Lou Piniella would tartly recall that "McKeon had the bullshit.") But the manager clashed with some of his players—Piniella among them—and he also began clashing with the Royals' front office, charging that it was not doing enough to strengthen the team. At the same time, the A's' Joe Rudi and Reggie Jackson were complaining about occasional benchings by Dick Williams. "I can't play here and be happy," Jackson said. Even so, the A's returned to their winning ways and had taken over first place by the July All-Star break, with the Royals in second.[14]

The 1973 All-Star Game was played in Royals Stadium. A capacity crowd heartily cheered Hank Aaron, who was nearing Babe Ruth's all-time home run record; it heartily booed a congratulatory message from President Nixon, who was under siege from Watergate. Kansas Citians saved their biggest jeers for Dick Williams and members of the A's, showing their contempt for all things Oakland.[15] When play resumed after the All-Star break, the Royals managed to stay close to the A's, and in September the two teams squared off in Kansas City in their first truly meaningful series: an A's sweep would all but eliminate the Royals from the pennant race, whereas a Royals sweep would pull them into a virtual tie for first heading into the season's final weeks.

The series was lionized by a Kansas City sportswriter: "They clomped on one another like rabid animals, neither wishing to release the death-grip on the throat, neither asking nor giving a quarter." In the opener, the A's overcame two four-run deficits to win 10–7. The game was marked by another altercation involving Bill North, who got into a shoving match with the Royals' Kurt Bevacqua. Afterward Dick Williams said that the "bush" Kansas City fans had gotten what they deserved for having booed the A's during the All-Star Game. In the second game of the series, the Royals came from behind with two outs in the bottom of the ninth to beat the A's 10–9. Carl Taylor—a backup player whose previous claim to fame had been a literal meltdown in which he had set his belongings ablaze in the Kansas City clubhouse—got the winning hit. In the series finale, light-hitting Cookie Rojas hit two home runs to lead the Royals to a 6–5 victory. *Kansas City Star* sports editor Joe McGuff predicted that the Oakland series would "stand as a starting point for all of the Royals' future successes."[16]

Those future successes would have to wait. The A's won the division after taking two of three games from Kansas City when the two teams met again in Oakland later in September. A's fans heaped invective upon the Royals, one of whom claimed that he had "never heard anyone booed that much anywhere, and that includes Marv Hubbard and Ben Davidson in Kansas City." Passions were even more heated among the A's themselves. While Oakland was beating Baltimore to repeat as American League champions, teammates Rollie Fingers and Blue Moon Odom nearly got into a brawl, and team owner Charlie Finley unleashed a profane tirade at American League president Joe Cronin. A's outfielder Angel Mangual pleaded to be traded: "This place is too crazy for me. Why kill your mind with so much trouble?"[17]

The World Series against the New York Mets only escalated the craziness. The A's lost a game when infielder Mike Andrews—never noted for his defense—made two errors. Afterward Andrews was pressured into signing a statement saying that he was too injured to remain on the roster; Charlie Finley blamed him for Oakland's defeat and in effect was firing him. The move infuriated the A's players, several of whom protested by wearing makeshift labels with Andrews's uniform number on them. Finley called a midnight news conference to defend his actions, but cut it short after the media pressed him on Andrews's true condition; Dick Williams told his players that he could take no more and would quit after the series; and baseball commissioner Bowie Kuhn ordered Andrews's reinstatement. Despite it all, the A's rallied to win the championship four games to three behind resilient pitching and the hitting of Reggie Jackson. Once again Oaklanders turned out in vast numbers for a victory parade through downtown. The *Oakland Tribune*'s Ed Levitt wondered how many of those fans actually had paid to see the team play during the regular season.[18]

Charlie Finley was excoriated for his conduct during the series, with sportswriters calling him an "egregious busher," a "jolly green gewgaw," and "a bigger jerk than I ever imagined he could be." Finley's own players were no kinder. "Please don't give that man the credit," Reggie Jackson said in response to the suggestion that Finley deserved praise for molding the A's into champions. Nor did the controversy cease during the offseason. Dick Williams attempted to join the New York Yankees as

The Oakland A's overcome off-field controversies to celebrate their second consecutive World Series title in October 1973. (Russ Reed, untitled. Gelatin silver, 8 x 10 in. The Oakland Tribune Collection, the Oakland Museum of California, gift of ANG Newspapers.)

manager, but Finley blocked him, saying that he was still under contract to the A's (Williams temporarily left baseball altogether). Bowie Kuhn fined Finley for his actions during the World Series and placed him on probation; Finley responded by suing the commissioner. When a sportswriter tried to interview Finley during the baseball winter meetings in December, an enraged Finley scratched his face. In his calmer moments, the A's owner maintained a confident demeanor: "I ain't the least bit concerned."[19]

During the mid-1970s, the cities of Kansas City and Oakland would both try to do the same: project confidence and positivity in the face of turmoil while proving their naysayers wrong. Even in the face of suburbanization and urban blight, they sought to show the world that they were still big-league cities that would survive and thrive.

* * *

Kansas City boosters saw the 1973 All-Star Game as a coming-out party not just for Royals Stadium but also for the city generally, and they took out a full-page ad in the *Sporting News* to spread the word. "Comparing the Kansas City of 1960 (when we hosted the first of two Major League All Star Games that year) with the Kansas City of 1973 is like comparing the cotton flannels of Honus Wagner's time with the flashy knits of Amos Otis," said the ad in contrasting a famous player of yesteryear with one of the Royals' current stars. Apart from promoting the Truman Sports Complex and the soon-to-be-built Kemper Arena, the ad touted the new Kansas City International Airport—"the world's most innovative and convenient supersonic jetport"—which had opened the previous fall. The airport was designed to allow travelers to park close to their gates and walk a minimal distance to board their planes. There was talk of building a monorail to connect it to downtown, several miles away.[20]

The ad also boasted of a new "mammoth convention center completely free of interior columns." Voters would narrowly approve funding for the downtown center in 1973 after the *Kansas City Times* editorialized that the city needed to reclaim the convention hub status that it had "forfeited in the years of stagnation when Kansas City was either unwilling or unable to keep up with more progressive places." Like sports facilities, new convention centers were becoming increasingly popular among cities determined to reinvigorate "benighted urban hubs," as historian Jon Teaford would write.[21]

Then there was what the *Sporting News* ad called the "city-within-the-city" that Hallmark Cards had just opened a mile south of downtown. Hallmark had been buying property near its Kansas City headquarters for years with an eye toward creating a mixed-use development to counter blight. The result—Crown Center—featured a hotel built on "Signboard Hill," once covered by unsightly billboards. It also featured underground parking, restaurants, office buildings, residential towers, a department store with three themed levels ("Earth," "Elegance," and "Excitement"), and a boutique center called "West Village" that according to the *Kansas City Star* offered "such offbeat items as backpacking gear, Mexican copperware, recipes for homemade wine, neon art, unicycles, stained glass items, mobiles, guitars and banjos, and military miniatures." Crown Center ran its own ad in the *Star* promoting the new shops: "Long live optimism! Down with pessimism! . . . There's plenty to be optimistic about, because you live right here in 'Optimicity.'"[22]

Such advertisements dovetailed with a broader campaign called "Prime Time" that was headed by Hallmark's president. Prime Time's stated goal was "to focus national attention on Kansas City as a model of urban self-improvement to erase the city's former image as an isolated 'cowtown'"; it also sought to "rekindle pride, confidence and involvement" among Kansas Citians. The campaign followed the example of such cities as Atlanta that had cultivated a big-league image in the 1960s through vigorous self-promotion. Prime Time produced a television commercial displaying beauteous images of Kansas City with a solo guitar accompanying the narration: "There's a city with more public greenspace than San Francisco, including the second-largest urban park in America; with more fountains than any place but Rome, more boulevard miles than Paris, and cleaner air than Honolulu." The commercial concluded with Prime Time's slogan: "Kansas City: one of the few livable cities left."[23]

Prime Time's creators considered the campaign a rousing success. Hallmark's public relations director recalled looking through the *Readers' Guide to Periodical Literature* to assess how the press had reported on U.S. cities. During the 1960s, "Atlanta received nine out of every ten favorable stories about how America was solving its urban crisis. Then, during the early years of the 1970s, Kansas City took over that role. We received more favorable publicity than any other city and the Prime Time program was responsible for virtually every placement." So-called competitive boosterism had moved beyond just trying to take other cities' sports teams—now it extended to garnering the most upbeat media coverage.[24]

Nevertheless, the Prime Time campaign and the Crown Center development raised a few eyebrows. Kansas City native Richard Rhodes wrote in *Harper's* that the city "ought to be a serene and unpretentious place. It isn't, because its leading citizens believe its virtues misunderstood," with such initiatives as Prime Time serving as overcompensation. In the *New Yorker,* fellow Kansas City native Calvin Trillin said that he felt as though "an old friend, someone who had always been an unassuming and quietly dressed businessman, suddenly turned up in a bushy mustache and bell-bottom hip-huggers and a buckskin jacket: there is a terrible temptation to say, 'Oh, come off it.'"[25]

It was in reaction to Crown Center that Trillin coined the term "domeism" to describe the compulsion of one-time minor league cities to erect major league–size airports and stadiums and cities-within-cities as proof that they had truly arrived. He allowed that Crown Center looked good, but it was "a beautifully designed island cut off from a black neighborhood and a Mexican-American neighborhood." And he questioned whether typical Kansas Citians were really interested in buying the exotic goods offered by West Village. (It turned out they were not, and in time West Village was remodeled into more orthodox retail and entertainment space.) Crown Center did attract out-of-town visitors, especially after it opened a second hotel, and it was praised for being an imaginative, privately financed endeavor toward urban rejuvenation. But it did not halt suburbanization, and even with the new convention center, Kansas City's downtown north of Crown Center continued to languish, "whether measured by the significantly smaller work force, by the increase in the number of closed shops and empty offices, or by continued demolitions," as historian George Ehrlich writes.[26]

In Oakland, city boosters had been planning their own "domes" while touting the city's own virtues and successes, especially those that had raised its status in relation to San Francisco. Of particular satisfaction were the Port of Oakland, whose explosive growth had corresponded with the decline of San Francisco's port; and the Coliseum complex, which had lured the hockey Seals and the basketball Warriors from across the bay. Such developments produced what *Oakland Tribune* publisher William Knowland called "shock value" for San Francisco: "Sometimes it's hard for older brother to realize that younger brother has grown up."[27]

Oakland wanted more than enhanced standing in the sports and industrial worlds, however. It wanted cultural cachet as well. Toward that end, the *Tribune* and civic leaders had urged passage back in 1961 of a bond issue that would build a new city museum to replace three older facilities. "Cultural facilities make the difference between a city that people want to invest in and one they don't," said one business executive. "They are the difference between a good city and a poor city." Voters approved the bonds and also approved putting the new museum by Lake Merritt, not far from the city center. (Just prior to the vote, the *Tribune* had quoted New York architect Philip Johnson as urging Oakland to avoid locating the museum far from downtown: "Suburban atmosphere [is] inimical to culture.") The new museum would focus on California history, science, and art. It would not be ready until 1969, but as it prepared to open, critics were hailing it as a triumph of architecture and design. "No structure in San Francisco, just across the Bay, can equal it," said the *New York Times*.[28]

Oakland's most ambitious new project was City Center. First proposed in 1965, City Center was conceived as "a major urban retailing, office, hotel and public open-space complex which will eliminate blight in the heart of Oakland and reestablish Oakland as the dynamic hub-city of the East Bay." The mixed-use project—similar in scope to Kansas City's Crown Center—was to be built largely through federal funds. It sought to take advantage of the new Bay Area Rapid Transit (BART) system and the new Grove Shafter Freeway along the west edge of downtown; the transit system and freeway were expected to bring thousands of additional people into downtown from across the Bay Area. The project also aimed at creating jobs, including for people of color. "Oakland has to go to work and do something that puts it on the map—outside of baseball and football—for reasons that deal with the long-term survival of its people," said John Williams, director of the Oakland Redevelopment Agency. "Like the port, City Center is part of that."[29]

Yet both City Center and the new Oakland Museum would spark intense controversy stemming from the same competing visions for Oakland that also stirred debate over the port and the Coliseum. The museum had hired a director and an education coordinator committed to creating a "museum for the people" during "a time of crises, of demand and change; a time when the tyranny of relevance will not allow this institution . . . to stand on the sidelines or serve only a few." Such commitments were at odds with Oakland's conservative establishment that held more traditional views of what a museum should be. Just before the museum opened in 1969, the director was fired and the education coordinator quit. In the subsequent uproar, a community group called the Black Caucus called for a boycott of the museum. Negotiations between the city and the Black Caucus resulted in the hiring of a new director and a new coordinator charged with serving all sectors of the community, but tensions remained. In reviewing the new museum, the radical Bay Area magazine *Ramparts* said that "one looks in vain for something that shows how the Gold Rush also involved genocide against the Indians," or for anything showing "how Hispanic peoples were here first and were dispossessed; or about the virtual slavery of Orientals who built the railroads; or about the black people who were also part of California history."[30]

Meanwhile City Center was caught up in debates over the human costs of urban renewal. BART—considered key to the project's success—already had been the target of protests in the 1960s when the new transit system was routed through the historically African American neighborhood of West Oakland. "Besides displacing residents, BART encouraged the movement of jobs to the suburbs," historian Joseph Rodriguez writes in summarizing the protesters' stance. "BART became a symbol of elite bias in favor of regional mobility and individualism, in contrast to the local self-sufficiency and communalism that the West Oakland leaders supported."[31]

Such criticisms were renewed in the early 1970s when the *Black Panther* newspaper launched its comprehensive critique of Oakland's institutions. The paper charged that City Center was intended to become an "immense suburban shopping center" that would serve whites from outside the city while ignoring "the Black and poor communities of Oakland." Criticism of City Center intensified when the project encountered numerous delays, leaving a large swath of downtown razed with no new construction underway to fill it.[32]

Over time a new hotel was built, along with a substantial amount of new office space; there also would be a new convention center in keeping with what Kansas City and many other cities would construct. But scholar Mitchell Schwarzer has observed that City Center's original ambitions were unrealistic. Much as the Panthers had charged, the project had chosen to ignore "the working-class and African American women who had become the principal shoppers downtown" in favor of trying to attract white suburban shoppers who had little reason to travel to Oakland given that they already had plenty of retail services closer to where they lived. In addition, the demolition of more than twenty city blocks for the project produced "incalculable losses in human and architectural terms." City Center had sought to help make Oakland a viable contender to San Francisco for preeminence in the Bay Area. Instead, for a great many years, "it created a void at the heart of the city."[33]

* * *

The void in downtown Oakland paralleled a void within the leadership of the Oakland A's as the 1974 season approached. Charlie Finley had suffered a heart attack and was going through an acrimonious divorce while continuing to fend off rumors that he would move or sell his team, which seemed adrift. "Despite two straight world championships, this is a franchise that is not functioning," commented sportswriter Ron Bergman, adding that the team "lacked, among other things, a manager, a radio-television contract and signed contracts from most of their players who were finding negotiations for 1974 salaries extremely bitter."[34]

The salary negotiations corresponded with the latest changes to baseball's labor structure. For the first time, major league players were allowed to make their cases for increased wages before an impartial arbitrator (it had been a concession extracted from the owners the previous year). Arbitration reduced the owners' power to determine player salaries, as Finley soon discovered to his consternation. Reggie Jackson was among the A's using the process to request a hefty raise, which Finley grandiloquently argued that Jackson did not deserve. "He was the God of baseball, sent down from Olympus to set confused mortals straight on all questions pertaining to baseball," said players union head Marvin Miller of Finley's performance at the arbitration hearing. In the end, the arbitrator granted Jackson and some other members of the A's the salary hikes they had asked for, but the relations between the owner and his players were as toxic as ever. Seeking a new manager whom he could control, Finley picked Al Dark—the same manager whom he had fired seven years earlier during the A's' final season in Kansas City. The deeply religious Dark pledged fealty to the A's owner: "If Mr. Finley says [something] will be done, it will be done. The Bible teaches this."[35]

Once the season began, the A's players mocked their new manager's obeisance to Finley's whims. "I knew Alvin Dark was a religious man, but he's worshipping the wrong god—C.O.F.," said Vida Blue, referring to the owner by his initials. The A's also complained about the way that Dark handled the pitching staff; the World Series rings they had received from Finley (cheap in comparison with the previous year's rings); the poor upkeep of the Oakland Coliseum plus the continued poor attendance there; and the "designated runner" whom Finley had insisted on adding to the roster (champion sprinter Herb Washington, who would be inserted into games despite never having played baseball before). In June Reggie Jackson and Bill North brawled in the clubhouse. The fight injured both Jackson and catcher Ray Fosse, who separated a cervical disc while trying to act as peacemaker. The next day, Finley delivered a lengthy tirade at the team. Pitcher Rollie Fingers was unconcerned: "So what's new? Being on this club is like having a ringside seat for the Muhammed Ali–Joe Frazier fights."[36]

The Kansas City Royals were enduring their own tumult. During the off-season, they had traded Lou Piniella following tensions between him and manager Jack McKeon. The Royals also announced that they were closing their much-touted Baseball Academy in Florida to save money. Then in June they surprised everyone by firing general manager Cedric Tallis. Although Tallis had built the Royals into contenders, he had clashed with Royals owner Ewing Kauffman over the team's direction. Kauffman was highly competitive, particularly with Charlie Finley; the two men even pitched pennies for high stakes during baseball's winter meetings. Now sportswriter Dick Young suggested that Kauffman had "caught a severe case of Charleyfinleyitis" and was seeking to emulate his rival's imperious leadership style: "If Charley

Finley can run the A's by himself, and win pennants, why not Ewing Kauffman [with the Royals]?"[37]

There were bright spots for the Royals. Pitcher Steve Busby threw his second no-hitter in as many seasons. Hal McRae became one of the team's leading batters after assuming the role of designated hitter (which the American League had adopted the previous season after Charlie Finley had long pushed for it). And much as the A's had grown their own talent through their farm system, Kansas City was now doing the same with two promising infielders joining the roster. Frank White—who had been raised in Kansas City a few blocks from Municipal Stadium—had come through the Royals' Baseball Academy and hence was nicknamed "Academy Frank." Ewing Kauffman was said to be especially interested in White succeeding in the big leagues to prove that the academy had not been a folly.[38]

Kansas City's other young infielder was George Brett, a southern California native who had not impressed Frank White's wife Gladys the first time she met him: "He had the cutoff shorts, no shirt, and all this hair. And I thought, 'That's a baseball player?'" Brett became the Royals' starting third baseman early in the 1974 season. When he did not hit well at first, coach Charley Lau worked with him on his swing, just as Lau had done with Hal McRae the previous season and with players on other teams before that (including the A's' Joe Rudi). Brett's batting average rose accordingly. Many years later, he would compare Lau to "a security blanket."[39]

In August Ewing Kauffman gave manager Jack McKeon a new two-year contract despite anonymous quotes in the press from Kansas City players that the team had "no leadership on the field or on the bench." Kauffman's response regarding the players was terse: "To hell with them." The controversy seemed at first not to affect the play of the Royals, who pulled within four games of the division-leading A's. Then they collapsed, losing nineteen out of their next twenty-two games and finishing fifth in their six-team division. Just before the end of the season, McKeon fired Charley Lau, charging him with disloyalty. The move triggered widespread anguish among the Royals and a near-revolt against the men who ran the team. George Brett and Fred Patek wept, Hal McRae announced that he wanted to leave Kansas City to follow Lau, and Steve Busby said that the firing "makes us look like a bunch of blithering

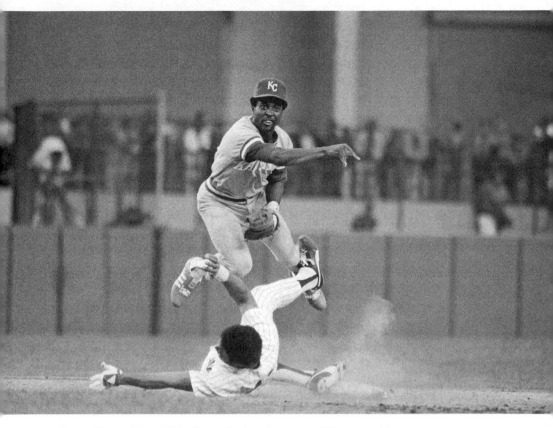

Royals second baseman Frank White displays his defensive prowess. White grew up in Kansas City near Municipal Stadium. (AP Photo)

idiots." *Kansas City Star* sportswriter Gib Twyman charged McKeon and the Royals with "having junked one of their most valuable assets for the most bankrupt set of so-called justifications."[40]

While the Royals crumbled, the A's managed to overcome their differences enough to win their division and then beat Baltimore for their third-straight American League pennant. Naturally the team still had problems. Attendance at the Oakland Coliseum lagged even behind the relatively lackluster performance of the previous season. (The A's had barely managed to attract a million fans during their world championship year of 1973, and then only because Charlie Finley had padded the announced attendance for the final home date.) Finley blamed the weak

turnout on negative media coverage in the Bay Area. In response, the
Oakland Tribune's Ron Bergman said that the poor attendance actually
stemmed from shoddy promotion by "the A's alleged organization,"
which he called "beneath disgrace."[41]

Any semblance of peace among the A's disintegrated before their
first World Series game against the Los Angeles Dodgers. In front of
the media, Blue Moon Odom needled Rollie Fingers about his marital
problems; Fingers responded by attacking Odom. Although Fingers
required stiches afterward, he was blasé about it. "Five stiches is not the
record," he said. "Our clubhouse brawl record is 15, held by many." There
were other commotions. Pitcher Catfish Hunter said that Charlie Finley
had violated terms of his contract, and therefore he should be released
from that contract. Rumors emerged—again—that the A's might move,
this time to a new domed stadium in either Seattle or New Orleans.
Reggie Jackson threatened a sportswriter over a magazine profile that
had talked about Jackson's household possessions (which included adult
magazines and a "color TV set with a Holy Bible and a pistol on it"), as
well as the player's relationship with one of Oakland's former "ballgirls"
(who was said to look "lovely in a lotus position and a green bikini").
Jackson's threats against the writer drew remonstration from the baseball
commissioner.[42]

Amid it all, the Dodgers expressed disbelief in their inability to beat
the A's, who would win the World Series four games to one. Fingers
won the series Most Valuable Player award for his relief pitching, second baseman Dick Green provided sterling defense, and Joe Rudi hit a
home run in the series-clinching game in Oakland after the game was
delayed by fans throwing debris on the field. For a third time, Oaklanders paraded joyously through downtown. "Nothing brings a town closer
together than winning a World Series—especially three in a row," wrote
Ed Levitt in the *Tribune*. "Who can worry about inflation when you're
thinking about Joe Rudi's game-winning home run?"[43]

Even as Charlie Finley claimed credit for the A's' continued success—
"I don't mind taking bows at all, as hard as I've worked"—he soon was
grappling with new challenges to his authority over his players. An arbitrator ruled that Finley had indeed violated Catfish Hunter's contract
by not regularly paying into an annuity as agreed, and therefore Hunter
was a free agent. Kansas City made a vigorous effort to sign him; Ewing

Kauffman had previously tried to buy Reggie Jackson and Vida Blue from the A's, and now he promised that the Royals would "go as far as fast as we can" after Hunter. In the end, Hunter signed with the New York Yankees instead, but the Royals still benefited in that Oakland had lost one of its best pitchers. "I think that it would be tough to win without him," lamented the A's' Ken Holtzman.[44]

Oakland's woes extended beyond Hunter's departure. Commissioner Bowie Kuhn was determined to solve baseball's Bay Area problem, with attendance for the San Francisco Giants having sunk even lower than that of the A's. Kuhn proposed moving the Giants to Toronto and having the A's split their home games between San Francisco and Oakland. Robert Nahas, who had played key roles in building the Coliseum and bringing the A's to Oakland, had grown disillusioned with Charlie Finley and his apparent disinterest in the city. But Nahas's resentment toward San Francisco was as strong as ever, and he resisted any move to share the A's: "San Francisco never gives us anything but problems. Why should we give up half our games?" Finley offered no cooperation; he held Kuhn in contempt and unsuccessfully tried to force the commissioner from office. Thus the status quo remained with the A's and Giants still residing—if not necessarily happily—on opposite sides of the bay.[45]

Conflict continued between the A's and their owner in 1975. A new round of contentious arbitration hearings provoked dismay from third baseman Sal Bando: "I wish that someday management would make it possible for newsmen to write about what we do on the field and not about all the crazy stuff that happens off the field." Yet even without Catfish Hunter, the A's still were formidable, and they opened a sizable division lead once the season began. In Kansas City, the turmoil that had engulfed the team the year before did not abate, and at one point pitcher Steve Busby threatened to quit the team. Complaints about manager Jack McKeon continued among other members of the Royals and in the Kansas City media. Finally, not long after the July All-Star Break, McKeon was fired. Ewing Kauffman had assumed responsibility for such actions in the past, but perhaps by now he had gotten over the worst of his "Charleyfinleyitis." He gave authority to general manager Joe Burke to dismiss McKeon.[46]

Kansas City's new manager, Whitey Herzog, immediately rehired Charley Lau as coach, and with stability and tranquility restored to the team, the Royals began to win. John Mayberry enjoyed his finest year, George Brett led the American League in hits, and rookie Dennis Leonard joined the pitching rotation alongside Steve Busby and Paul Splittorff. The Royals rode an eight-game winning streak heading into a key series in Oakland in September. It appeared that they had a legitimate chance to dethrone Oakland as division champions. "I'll go and hide if we don't win," the A's' Reggie Jackson said before the series opener.[47]

Hiding proved unnecessary. The A's swept the Royals in three straight games, crushing Kansas City's title hopes. "Actually, it was all over before it began," commented sportswriter Ron Bergman. "The A's have the Royals psyched out in the Oakland Coliseum, where the concrete is as grey as the skies overhead, the grass is real and slow, and the foul territories vast." Returning home from their disastrous trip to Oakland, the Royals' charter flight was forced to make an emergency landing arising from a bomb threat that apparently had come from the Bay Area. "Why would anybody in the Bay Area want to hurt us?" manager Whitey Herzog said. "Every time we play out there, we prove we're harmless." Kansas City had to content itself with a second-place finish and its best-ever season record at 91-71.[48]

With their fifth-straight division title in hand, the A's entered the American League Championship series against the Boston Red Sox with high hopes, but Boston swept Oakland in three games for the pennant. "Sure, I think it would have been different if we still had Catfish Hunter," said Reggie Jackson afterward. "But nobody on this earth, even in China, thought the A's would get beat in three." The *Oakland Tribune* eulogized the now-former champions, saying that they had stirred civic pride while also proving "that guys with long hair and short tempers, along with handlebar mustaches and outlandish behavior, can team together to be the best."[49]

Even as the A's promised that they would be back the following season, Reggie Jackson offered encouragement to Oakland's football team: "Maybe Al Davis and John Madden will take over where we left off. Come on Raiders—bring Oakland a championship!"[50] The A's would themselves make one more run at a championship in 1976, but Reggie Jackson would no longer be with them. As for the Raiders, they would realize their championship dreams, but not without controversy or travail.

6

"Triumph and Tragedy"

THE OAKLAND RAIDERS entered the 1975 season as favorites to win the Super Bowl, with coach John Madden doing nothing to discourage such expectations. "We used to say that we'd take one thing at a time," he said. "Now, from the start, the ultimate goal is the Super Bowl." The Raiders continued to infuse their lineup with new talent. Dave Dalby took over as center from Jim Otto, Mark van Eeghen supplanted Marv Hubbard at fullback, and Ted Hendricks—nicknamed "The Mad Stork" for his eccentricity and lankiness—joined the linebacker corps.[1]

In contrast, the Kansas City Chiefs were beginning a rebuild of uncertain duration. "The Chiefs are a football team in a state of decay," commented one sportswriter, "like some cities of the industrial northeast." To replace Hank Stram as head coach, Kansas City selected Paul Wiggin, previously the defensive coordinator of the San Francisco 49ers. Wiggin said that there would be no quick fixes: "We have to build from the draft and from within the organization."[2]

However, Wiggin was severely handicapped by having comparatively few draft picks; Hank Stram had traded many of them away. The players whom the Chiefs did draft in 1975 made no impact, and their top pick would be convicted of murder after he left the team. In addition, several players from Kansas City's glory years were gone or about to leave, including Bobby Bell, Otis Taylor, Buck Buchanan, and Len Dawson. There was little surprise when the Chiefs lost their first three games of the season while the Raiders were winning their first three, and Oakland was heavily favored to beat Kansas City when the two teams met in Arrowhead Stadium during the season's fourth week. As they had in the past, though, the Chiefs were able to conjure up some home-field magic against the Raiders, and they demolished Oakland 42–10. Warpaint—the team's equine mascot—galloped around the stadium after every Kansas City touchdown, reputedly prompting John Madden to quip after the game, "We couldn't beat the Chiefs, but we damn near killed their horse."[3]

Following Kansas City's upset of Oakland, the rest of the season unfolded according to expectations for both teams. The Chiefs finished at 5-9 for the second consecutive year while the Raiders won their fourth-straight division title. "We have the best team in football," said quarterback Ken Stabler before the playoffs. He repeated the prediction that this would finally be the year that the Raiders won it all: "We'll do it. I feel it. I believe it."[4]

Oakland narrowly beat Cincinnati in the first playoff round and then headed to Pittsburgh for the AFC championship. It was a bitterly cold day and the field was frozen, hindering the Raiders' offense. A last-minute rally fell short when a Stabler pass to wide receiver Cliff Branch was stopped shy of the goal line, and Pittsburgh won 16–10. Raiders head Al Davis denied media reports that he had second-guessed John Madden's play-calling. To make matters worse for Madden, a reporter after the game accidentally called him "Al," reinforcing the misconception that Davis was the real coach of the team and Madden a nonentity.[5]

NFL Films' retrospective on the Raiders' season—narrated as usual by John Facenda and including the Raiders' signature theme music "The Autumn Wind"—made much of the team's successes. "In 1975 the Raider organization maintained its total commitment to excellence," Facenda intoned. "In terms of consistent victory, the Raiders continued their complete domination of professional football." Yet once again, as Facenda acknowledged, "suddenly, disappointingly, another memorable year of glory ended in a single day of defeat." Only a Super Bowl win would "add the ultimate triumph of professional football's winningest team."[6]

The film's title—"Triumph and Tragedy"—seemed a considerable overstatement; the only "tragedy" associated with the 1975 Raiders was their continued inability to get over the hump in the postseason. But the title does provide an apt metaphor for Oakland's and Kansas City's big-league hopes and ambitions by the last half of the 1970s. Both cities would win titles they long had craved, and both would transform themselves in ways that would have seemed unthinkable only a few years previously. At the same time, the cities and the athletes who played there would experience crushing disappointments as well as genuine tragedies. Unqualified triumphs were difficult to come by, and success often came at a cost.

* * *

In December 1975, an arbitrator's decision changed baseball forever. The previous year, Peter Seitz had ruled that Oakland owner Charles Finley had violated Catfish Hunter's contract, allowing the pitcher to sign with the Yankees. Now Seitz ruled against baseball's reserve clause in a grievance filed by major league pitchers Andy Messersmith and Dave McNally. The decision would permit players to pursue free agency.[7]

Baseball owners—who had hired Seitz originally—reacted to the arbitrator's ruling by firing him; they also challenged the ruling in federal court. Needing to file that challenge in a city that hosted a major league club, the owners chose Kansas City. Royals owner Ewing Kauffman recalled that "they felt that a judge in New York would be too liberal and thought judges in Kansas City would be more conservative and more inclined towards their cause." In that they were mistaken. A judge said that the court had no responsibility "to act as some sort of guardian of what the Club Owners refer to in their brief as the national pastime," and Seitz's ruling was upheld.[8]

Still determined to fight, the owners locked players out of spring training, stirring fears that the 1976 season might be threatened. Commissioner Bowie Kuhn ordered the camps reopened, and the season began as scheduled. Among those most unhappy with the turn of events was Charlie Finley; with the end of the reserve clause, he stood to lose most of the A's' biggest stars. Finley suggested that the clubs make all players free agents, which would have saturated the market and driven down salaries. Fortunately for the players, the other owners did not listen. "All I can imagine is that they had such a fixation on power, such an abhorrence of the idea of the players winning any kind of freedom, that they refused even to consider an idea that clearly was in their economic interest," players union head Marvin Miller would say. In the end, the owners and the union agreed to a new deal ensuring that only a limited number of free agents would be available any given year: exactly what the union had wanted.[9]

Finley began unloading players whom he knew he could not sign. He traded Reggie Jackson and Ken Holtzman to Baltimore despite Jackson's stated desire to remain in the Bay Area: "I'm not quite as much Oakland as Lake Merritt is, but I feel like an Oakland-grown boy." Finley fired Al Dark as manager after Dark was quoted as saying that the A's owner would go to hell if he did not accept Jesus Christ as his personal savior. Chuck Tanner was named as Dark's replacement. Finally Finley declared—once more with feeling—that the A's absolutely would never leave Oakland.[10]

For the Kansas City Royals, the biggest news of the offseason had been the trade that they failed to complete. They had agreed to send Amos Otis and Cookie Rojas to Pittsburgh in exchange for outfielder Al Oliver, but Rojas vetoed the deal. (Certain longtime players had won the right to reject trades; it was another new change to baseball labor relations.) Hence Otis, who had been ill and played poorly the previous year, remained in Kansas City. His relationship with sportswriters remained touchy, and at times he would post a "No Interviews" sign by his locker, although he later admitted that he actually did it to get the writers' attention: "Any time I wasn't getting enough ink, I'd put up the sign. After a week, I'd take it down and reporters would be waiting at my locker." Regardless, he would go on to have one of his best seasons.[11]

Otis would not be Kansas City's only star in 1976. In May George Brett began a streak of six consecutive games with three or more hits. He enjoyed being what was described as a "young, single, ruggedly handsome" sports celebrity. ("I don't want to sound like Joe Bachelor," he said, "but I don't have any plans to get married for a while.") Brett and teammate Hal McRae would remain near the top of the American League batting race all season long. By mid-June, the Royals led their division with the best winning percentage in the league.[12]

Oakland, meanwhile, was in fifth place with a losing record, having been afflicted by injuries and indifferent play. "They don't look right without Reggie Jackson," said Kansas City's John Mayberry after the Royals swept a series with the A's. "They just look like they're waiting to get beat." Just before the June 15 trading deadline, Charlie Finley sold Rollie Fingers and Joe Rudi to the Boston Red Sox for $1 million each and Vida Blue to the New York Yankees for $1.5 million. "I will not be driven into bankruptcy by the astronomical, unjustified salaries ballplayers are demanding today," Finley declared. Three days later, commissioner Bowie Kuhn voided the sales, saying that they would make the A's uncompetitive in their division. The Royals, who would profit the most if the A's were weakened, vehemently opposed Kuhn's decision, and Finley branded Kuhn a "village idiot" and "24-carat kook." For nearly two weeks, the A's owner also refused to play Blue, Rudi, or Fingers. Only after the other A's threatened to strike did he relent and allow the team to return to full strength.[13]

In early August, Oakland trailed the first-place Royals by twelve games. Then suddenly the A's won nine in a row. They already had been swiping bases with abandon (their 341 steals would set an American League single-season record); now the A's were also hitting and pitching well while cutting into Kansas City's lead. "They can put it up in their clubhouse: 'Finley Says Kansas City Is Going to Choke,'" said Charlie Finley of the Royals. "It's supposed to make them mad. But the longer they read it, the more they're going to believe it."[14]

The Royals laughed off Finley's words, as well as similar remarks from A's manager Chuck Tanner. But two of their starting pitchers were injured and their hitters began to struggle, fueling charges that they were pressing too hard in their battle to hold off the A's. "I want to win it against them so bad," acknowledged Kansas City's George Brett. "We're a more civilized team. You don't see us popping off all the time." Indeed, much as they had often done in the past, the A's were sniping at Charlie Finley and he was responding in kind. "You can see he's not interested in winning," said Joe Rudi, to which Finley retorted, "They're not going to win in spite of me. They're going to win because of me."[15]

Despite their slump, the Royals still led Oakland in the division race late in September, but the teams had two series left to play against each other. The opening game of the first series in Kansas City was marked by high drama and intrigue. The A's—who had taunted Amos Otis by calling him a choker—beaned him in the head and knocked him out of the game. Later Kansas City manager Whitey Herzog led the umpires on a mid-game excursion to the Oakland bullpen, where they uncovered binoculars that the Royals claimed were being used to steal signs. Sign-stealing or not, Oakland lost the game to the Royals 3–1, and happy Kansas City fans burned an A's pennant in the stands.[16]

That celebration proved to be premature. Oakland pummeled the Royals in the remaining two games of the series, 11–1 and 8–1. "The Oakland A's are like a bad penny," commented the *Kansas City Times*. "They keep coming back."[17] Heading into the final week of the season, the two teams had one more three-game series to play in the Oakland Coliseum, which had been the site of no small heartbreak for Kansas City's big-league teams in the past. Although the Royals still led the A's by 4½ games, if the A's could sweep Kansas City, they would seize all the momentum in their quest to cap an unlikely late-season surge and repeat as division champions for the sixth straight year.

The Royals and A's had brawled before, but what happened in the first game topped anything that had happened between the two teams in the past. After Sal Bando homered for the A's, Royals pitcher Dennis Leonard beaned Oakland's Don Baylor, who charged the mound. "I didn't hear him say anything, but I saw fire in his eyes," Leonard said. The ensuing fight left players with bloody lips and a twisted knee. Order was briefly restored, and then a new battle erupted between the Royals bullpen and Coliseum fans seated nearby. "One guy had a bottle and somebody threw a jug at us," said Kansas City's John Wathan. "One guy wanted to fight, so we tried to oblige him. But we couldn't get him to come out of the stands." Spectators hurled beer on the Kansas City players, and a Royal grabbed a spectator's umbrella and began swinging it wildly at the fans until security guards broke up the melee. The A's went on to win the game 8–3 and then beat Kansas City again the next night 1–0. "This might be the biggest collapse in history," Royals manager Whitey Herzog said apprehensively. The A's' Bill North looked toward the series finale: "This is the one, baby. This is the one we've got to win."[18]

Herzog turned to Larry Gura to pitch the game for the Royals. Gura had been obtained earlier in the season and had been used sparingly until then. Herzog also reinserted Amos Otis into the lineup; he had slumped since his beaning and had sat out the first two games in Oakland. It all worked beautifully for Kansas City: Otis drove in two runs with a double and a home run, and Gura shut out Oakland 4–0. "The mighty A's," said the Royals' John Mayberry. "We'd chased 'em and chased 'em, and now it was our turn." The next night, the California Angels beat the A's to clinch the division for the Royals, and Fred Patek and Cookie Rojas celebrated by jumping into the fountains beyond the outfield wall at Royals Stadium. Inside the champagne-drenched Kansas City clubhouse, coach Charley Lau picked up a baseball. "This little thing can cause a lot of grief and a lot of happiness," he said. "And there's usually a lot more grief than happiness. But maybe once in a career, once in a lifetime, it's all worth it."[19]

The day after the regular season ended, the front page of the *Oakland Tribune* pictured the A's' Rollie Fingers, Joe Rudi, Don Baylor, Gene Tenace, and Sal Bando enjoying their own champagne celebration. They were commemorating their free agency (along with that of Bert Campaneris) and their freedom from Charlie Finley. "The destruction of one of the finest, and perhaps most unusual, baseball teams ever now is complete," commented *Tribune* sportswriter Ron Bergman. Vida Blue, who would be left behind with whatever remained of the A's, unleashed his frustrations to the media: "I hope the next breath Charles O. Finley takes is his last. I hope he falls flat on his face, or dies of polio."[20]

The Royals moved on to play the New York Yankees in the American League championship series, with the teams splitting the first four games between them. In the deciding fifth game in New York, the Yankees led 6–3 in the eighth inning when George Brett tied the score with a three-run home run. The game remained tied heading into the bottom of the ninth. New York's Chris Chambliss homered on the first pitch from Kansas City's Mark Littell to win the pennant for the Yankees, 7–6. New York fans surged onto the field and forced Chambliss to race to the dugout before he could touch home plate.

Kansas Citians followed the game on radio and television. Among them, as reported in the next morning's newspaper, was a hefty cab driver watching on a miniature TV. He announced his intention to celebrate all night at Crown Center if the Royals won. Then Chambliss hit his home run. "There ain't going to be no party tonight," the cabbie said glumly.[21]

Joe McGuff took a longer view. The *Kansas City Star* sports editor had covered Kansas City baseball since the days of the minor league Blues and remembered the city's excitement at becoming big league with the arrival of the A's. He also recalled the bleak years under Arnold Johnson and Charlie Finley when at times he "could scarcely stand to go to the park, let alone write about the team." Then the A's had left town to win multiple championships in Oakland while the expansion Royals experienced growing pains. But now the Royals had won the first-ever title for a major league baseball team in Kansas City, and McGuff saluted the achievement while acknowledging his city's cow-town roots: "Kansas City is identified with steaks and agriculture and for many years the city also had a national reputation for producing bumbling baseball teams. But no more."[22]

The Royals' title capped a banner year for Kansas City. The city had reaped national attention by hosting the 1976 Republican National Convention at Kemper Arena. Although the delegates found themselves scattered among far-flung hotels, one attendee commented that "the outstanding attitude of the people" compensated for the logistical problems. The convention had been preceded by a flurry of laudatory media coverage in everything from the *New York Times* to *National Geographic,* seemingly realizing the fondest ambitions of the city's Prime Time promotional campaign. Kansas City was praised for being "a bustling place" that was "about as agreeable a settlement as the nation has produced" in addition to being "light years ahead of larger, older cities in warding off urban malaise." The coverage included photos of the Truman Sports Complex, Crown Center, and the Kansas City International Airport—all of which had opened within the past four years—as well as of such longtime civic treasures as the Nelson-Atkins Museum of Art and the Country Club Plaza shopping center. "I'm certain of one thing," a journalist wrote. "In years ahead we'll see more, not less, of that special excitement—that special spirit—in this place called Kansas City."[23]

Instead, the next few years would sorely test the city's optimism. One high-profile effort at urban rejuvenation ran afoul of one of the city's least-savory group of residents. A historic collection of buildings just north of downtown Kansas City had been transformed by the early 1970s into an arts and entertainment district called River Quay, which promoted itself as a "community rich in leisure, arts, fashion, craftsmanship and 19th century flavor." Soon thereafter the city evicted several seedy bars downtown to make way for construction of the new convention center and an accompanying hotel (although the hotel would not be built until almost a decade later). Some of those bars moved into River Quay, along with organized crime.[24]

The Mafia had been active in Kansas City for years and had been linked to sports gambling. In 1969 major league pitcher Jim Bouton and his teammates were read a list of places to avoid in the city because they were gambler hangouts: "We expected to hear about three or four names. There must have been twenty-five." There also had been rumors of gamblers being connected to the Kansas City Chiefs, culminating in the news report just before the 1970 Super Bowl that quarterback Len Dawson would be called before a grand jury, although nothing ever came out of the rumors. Now the Mafia battled for control over River Quay and the strip clubs and porn theaters that had opened there. Rival mob factions took to killing one another and blowing up buildings in the district. By the end of 1977, River Quay was effectively dead.[25]

Other crises and calamities would strike the city. In the spring of 1977, teachers in the Kansas City public school district went on strike for the second time in four school years; the strike would last seven weeks. (Before long, "People moving into the metropolitan area tried to avoid the district entirely if at all possible," historian James Shortridge would write.) In September 1977, heavy rains produced flash flooding that killed twenty-five people and inflicted millions of dollars of damage on the Country Club Plaza. In January 1978, a fire in downtown's low-rent Coates House left twenty-eight people dead. In June 1979, a violent storm caused Kemper Arena's roof to collapse. Worst of all, in July 1981 two skywalks fell during a dance in the lobby of Crown Center's Hyatt Regency hotel. The disaster killed 114 people.[26]

Even a joyous moment for the city—the Royals' 1976 division championship—was marred by an incident suggesting that certain social ills continued to wound and divide people. In the final game of the regular season after the Royals had clinched the division, Hal McRae held a tiny lead over George Brett in the American League batting race. If Brett made an out in his last at-bat, McRae would win the batting title. When Brett lofted the ball to the outfield, Minnesota Twins outfielder Steve Brye pulled up short, and the ball bounced over Brye's head for an inside-the-park home run, making Brett the batting champion. It had seemed a routine fly ball ("the worst outfielder in the American

The Royals' Hal McRae (left) congratulates teammate George Brett for hitting an inside-the-park home run against the Minnesota Twins. The hit would win Brett the 1976 American League batting title. Soon after this photo was taken, McRae erupted in anger at the Twins, believing that they had conspired against him in the batting race. (AP Photo/John Filo)

League could have made the catch without unduly straining himself," wrote the *Star*'s Joe McGuff), and McRae was convinced that the Twins had allowed it to drop for a hit because Brett was white whereas McRae was African American.[27]

The Twins (including at least one of their black players) vehemently denied McRae's charges, and Brett was crestfallen over the way the batting race had ended, although it did not affect the two teammates' friendship. The American League conducted an investigation but turned up nothing to prove that Minnesota had colluded in favor of Brett. McRae's take-no-prisoners style of play had made him unpopular among some people in the league, but Brett was just as aggressive; years later in his Hall of Fame induction speech, he would say that McRae had "taught me how to play the game of baseball." The most noticeable difference between the teammates seemed to be their skin color.[28]

McRae had been enraged during the game and nearly had gotten into a fight with the Twins. Afterward, although he was no happier, he sounded resigned. "It's too bad things are like that in 1976," he said. "But they'll probably always be like that. This is America."[29]

* * *

As the 1976 baseball season concluded, the Oakland Raiders already were well on their way back to the NFL playoffs. Per usual they had worked in new players while discarding old ones. Dave Casper (nicknamed "The Ghost") took over at tight end and became one of Ken Stabler's favorite receivers, while John Matuszak joined the defensive line. Matuszak had previously been with the Chiefs—they had acquired him in the ill-fated Curley Culp trade—but his time with them ended after he ingested a near-fatal combination of pills and alcohol and finally exhausted coach Paul Wiggin's patience. Then Al Davis took a chance on him. "When most of the NFL thought I was nothing but a pain in the ass, Al didn't care," Matuszak would say. "He helped save my career." Just before resuscitating Matuszak, Davis and the Raiders had unceremoniously terminated the career of forty-eight-year-old George Blanda by waiving him during training camp. "Nobody ever accused the Oakland Raiders of being a sentimental organization," commented Bay Area sportswriter Wells Twombly. "This is a war they are engaged in and the Raiders are a paramilitary outfit, which is why they wear those stark and uninteresting [silver and black] uniforms. Those are convict colors, men-against-the-world colors."[30]

Without Matuszak, the Chiefs went 5-9 in 1976 for the third straight year. (They would be worse the following year—going 2-12—and Paul Wiggin would be fired as head coach.) The Raiders would lose only once during the 1976 season, a rout at the hands of the New England Patriots. The loss prompted a players-only meeting led by Raiders veterans Gene Upshaw and Willie Brown. "They said, 'If you want to win the Super Bowl, we are not losing any more games,'" recalled the Raiders' Otis Sistrunk. "After that, we were rocking and rolling." Near the end of the season, Oakland hosted the Cincinnati Bengals. A Cincinnati win would put the Bengals in the playoffs while Oakland's chief nemesis—the Pittsburgh Steelers—would miss them. The Raiders already had clinched home-field advantage throughout the postseason, so they had the option of resting their starters and in effect purposefully losing to Cincinnati. "I couldn't even think of an NFL team ever laying down," the Raiders' Phil Villapiano would say. "Especially against a team like the Bengals. Because we hated them too. We hated everybody." Oakland won easily.[31]

To ensure a rematch with the Steelers, the Raiders first needed a playoff win against the Patriots. The prospects seemed bleak when the Raiders trailed 21–10 in the fourth quarter, but quarterback Ken Stabler led them to two touchdowns in the closing minutes to win the game. Thus, for the third-straight season, Oakland met Pittsburgh for the AFC championship, with the game to be played in the Coliseum. The Raiders had experienced years of postseason frustration—especially at the hands of Pittsburgh—and they emphatically put an end to it by dominating the Steelers 24–7, earning Oakland its first Super Bowl trip since January 1968. The victory touched off wild celebrations in Oakland's Jack London Square and the Coliseum parking lot. Already there was a clamoring for Super Bowl tickets. "The political people will get first crack," grumbled one fan. "I became a season ticket holder in 1962 in response to [an Oakland] Tribune appeal to save the Raiders. Now I'll probably be treated like a second-class citizen." The prevailing mood, though, was one of ecstasy. "Tell [Al] Davis he no longer owns the Raiders," another fan yelled. "The people own the Raiders."[32]

All that remained between Oakland and the world championship were the Minnesota Vikings. Before the Super Bowl, sportswriter Jim Murray memorably compared the two teams: "The Vikings play football like a guy laying carpet. The Raiders play like a guy jumping through a skylight with a machine gun." The game itself was no contest. No longer would John Facenda of NFL Films have to lament an Oakland season ending in disappointment. "From the outset for the Oakland Raiders—professional sports' outstanding organization—there was never a question about the Super Bowl," Facenda said in a film marking the Raiders' 32–14 triumph. "This game, this season, this league, this decade belonged to the Silver and Black." The film preserved the game descriptions of Raiders radio announcer Bill King. "Jascha Heifetz never played a violin with more dexterity then Kenny Stabler is playing the Minnesota Viking defense this afternoon," King exclaimed. He also commemorated "Old Man Willie" Brown's long interception return for Oakland's final touchdown. When after the game the Raiders lifted John Madden to their shoulders (and just before they accidentally dropped him), King remarked upon the coach's "ear-to-ear" smile: "He looks like a slit watermelon!"[33]

No player—not even "Old Man Willie" Brown—had been with Oakland longer than wide receiver Fred Biletnikoff. He was one of only a handful of Raiders still on the team who had played in the Super Bowl against Green Bay nine years previously. Biletnikoff was high-strung under the best of circumstances. He took seemingly forever to dress before games, making certain that his uniform was just so, with exactly the right pair of cleats and precisely the right amount of Stickum to help him grab passes. (Teammates Ken Stabler and Pete Banaszak enjoyed tormenting him by telling him that his uniform looked awful, prompting him to take everything off and start all over again.) Biletnikoff also was notorious for smoking copiously and vomiting before every game. Prior to the 1976 season, he had expressed unhappiness over not having received a multiyear contract, and he had said that he might leave the Raiders. But Biletnikoff's performance in the January 1977 Super Bowl won him the game's Most Valuable Player Award. "I just kept fighting and fighting," he said, and he wept.[34]

Back in the Raiders' hometown, *Oakland Tribune* publisher Joseph Knowland wrote a front-page editorial celebrating the victory. "The 1977 Super Bowl reflects the spirit of this City of Oakland where things

Oakland's Fred Biletnikoff (left) and Ken Stabler celebrate the Raiders' Super Bowl victory in January 1977. (AP Photo)

happen that don't seem possible," the editorial said. "Something seems to spell out C-H-A-M-P-I-O-N-S once you pass the city limits sign."[35]

The past few years had been tumultuous for the *Tribune*. William Knowland had committed suicide in 1974, having racked up steep gambling debts while becoming increasingly paranoid that he might be kidnapped. Son Joseph had then taken over as publisher. The *Tribune* was less overtly right-wing than it had been in the past; while William Knowland was still alive, he had even hired a registered Democrat as political editor, and now his son was trying to modernize the paper. Other family members wanted to unload it, though, and they succeeded in forcing its sale later in 1977. Gannett acquired the newspaper two years later, and the company did something that would have appeared inconceivable back in the *Tribune*'s most reactionary days: it made an African American the paper's editor and later its publisher. Robert Maynard sought to improve what in his words had been "the horrible relationship between the Oakland community and the *Oakland Tribune*" through improved news coverage and a much more diverse staff. In 1983 Maynard bought the paper himself.[36]

The changes at the *Tribune* accompanied other momentous changes in the city of Oakland. Two major new edifices—the Wells Fargo Building and the Clorox Building—had been built downtown as the City Center project gained momentum after many delays. A new shopping center also had opened in Jack London Square as part of an effort to revitalize the city's waterfront. Most remarkable was the transformation of Oakland's leadership. In 1977 the city elected Lionel Wilson as its first African American mayor. Elaine Brown, the one-time chair of the Black Panther Party, had steered Wilson's campaign, and she assumed a leading role in getting the Grove Shafter Freeway completed to facilitate access to City Center. Not long before, Brown and the Panthers had asserted that the construction of freeways and City Center harmed the black community, but now Brown saw such projects as generating jobs and influence for African Americans. By the end of the 1970s, by which time blacks outnumbered whites in Oakland, not only was Oakland's mayor African American; so too were the city attorney, the symphony director, and the heads of many city agencies, including the Port of Oakland. According to writer Ishmael Reed, Oakland had become "a model for black power" representing a change "from a feudal backwater run by a few families to a modern city with worldwide recognition."[37]

Just as was the case in Kansas City, though, social progress and civic transformation in 1970s Oakland were clouded by controversy and calamity. The biggest tragedy symbolized the difficulty of finding common ground across intractable social rifts during angry and often violent times.

Following the protests over Oakland's public schools that had begun in the mid-1960s, the schools had become ensnared in even more heated disputes. Efforts to hire a new superintendent sparked clashes between the largely white school board and the city's Black Caucus, culminating in multiple arrests during a board meeting. Finally, Oakland hired Marcus Foster as superintendent in 1970, and tensions began to ease.

Foster could be blunt, telling a national meeting of school administrators that cities put African Americans such as himself into power only after matters had become especially dire: "Don't be deceived by these moves and think they come about by rightness and righteousness. They are motivated by institutional racism when they ask superblacks to come in and rescue the enterprise." But Foster also demanded shared accountability in improving schools, and in Oakland he won the respect of both African American activists and the conservative white establishment, with *Tribune* publisher William Knowland saying that he had "never met another communicator like" him.[38]

In 1973 a new controversy developed over strategies to reduce violence within Oakland schools. One side called for a security crackdown against troublemaking students; the other side, which included the Black Panthers, argued that the students were victims of racism and that better facilities and teaching methods would curb the violence. Foster supported a compromise that would encourage students to carry identification cards but would avoid regularly putting armed police in schools, as some people had demanded. The superintendent remained resolutely optimistic about the future: "We are going to make it in Oakland, and history may record that our schools have led the way."[39]

Unbeknownst to Foster, a small group of self-proclaimed revolutionaries who called themselves the Symbionese Liberation Army were plotting his assassination. The SLA represented a perversion of the radical ideals of justice and empowerment that had inspired many activists in Oakland and elsewhere in the Bay Area. According to the SLA, the Oakland school superintendent was an Uncle Tom and a puppet of the white establishment. In November 1973, Foster was leaving a routine school board meeting when he was gunned down with cyanide-laced bullets. The SLA announced that they had assassinated him because of his "fascist" school safety plan. Revulsion toward the killing was so widespread that the SLA kidnapped heiress Patty Hearst the following February partly to divert attention from Foster's murder.[40]

The void that his death left in Oakland would endure. According to biographer John Spencer, Foster's murder had "cut short one of America's most promising efforts to sever the links between race, socioeconomic status, and achievement": concerns that had long been the center of contention in Oakland. A close colleague of Foster asserted that he had "come to epitomize the yearnings of parents, of teachers, of administrators, of community and political leaders, [and] of the students themselves" to unite behind a shared vision for turning around Oakland's public schools. When Foster was murdered, it meant more than just the loss of a respected educator—it also meant "the loss of an imagined future, one that everyone had the right to want, to need, and in fairness, to expect."[41]

Concerns over race, of course, were not limited just to Oakland or its schools. They also extended to professional sports, as the McRae-Brett incident in Kansas City had demonstrated. Nor was professional sports immune from violence; on the contrary, pro football had long embraced it. Even as the Oakland Raiders were on their way to their greatest triumph—their first Super Bowl win—they were enveloped in a controversy that not only tarnished them and the rest of the NFL, but also foreshadowed a grim future for many football players in Oakland, Kansas City, and elsewhere.

By the mid-1970s, the Raiders' reputation as renegades had been firmly established and had been embraced by the players themselves. "We wear black," said quarterback Ken Stabler, who added that in the movies, "the white hat is usually the good guy and the black hat is the bad guy." The bad-guy aura had a devil-may-care side that reflected John Madden's coaching philosophy. "If you give [players] individuality and if you give them some freedom, then they can be and play the way they are," Madden said. The Raiders exercised that freedom through such stunts as Ted Hendricks riding a horse onto the practice field while wearing a German army helmet. In addition, according to Ken Stabler's tell-all memoir, they indulged in as much sex and inebriation as they could handle, especially during training camp: "Without the diversions of whiskey and women, those of us who were wired for activity and no more than six hours sleep a night might have gone berserk."[42]

The Raiders' image also had a menacing side, as Stabler acknowledged: "We've got some physical players on our team. If that's the way you have to play to win, then that's the way we'll play." Oakland's reputation for bending the rules and intimidating the opposition dated back at least to Ben Davidson and the "Eleven Angry Men," but it would be burnished by their "Soul Patrol" defensive backfield: Willie Brown, Skip Thomas (nicknamed "Dr. Death"), George Atkinson, and Jack Tatum (nicknamed "The Assassin"). A 1975 book on the Raiders—ironically subtitled *The Good Guys*—declared that "Tatum's best hits border on felonious assault." In his own memoirs, Tatum said that he and Atkinson competed to see how many wide receivers they could knock out of games. He added that rival teams "all treat the Raider malice with a special intensity, and football fans love it."[43]

The image of "Raider malice" would backfire on Oakland starting in January 1976 when the Raiders lost to the Pittsburgh Steelers in the AFC championship game. George Atkinson had given Steelers wide receiver Lynn Swann a concussion, and Pittsburgh head coach Chuck Noll had charged Oakland with taking "cheap shots." The following September, the two teams met again in Oakland to open the 1976 regular season. The Raiders twice rallied from a two-touchdown deficit in the fourth quarter to beat the Steelers, but the dramatic victory was marred by another Atkinson hit on Swann, this time when Swann was nowhere near the ball. Television cameras showed that Atkinson had blindsided the Pittsburgh receiver and dropped him as though he were "felled by an axe," according to the *Oakland Tribune*. The newspaper also quoted Swann after the game: "If someone dies on the field, I hope it's not me. But that depends on how many times I play against Oakland." Chuck Noll suggested that Atkinson's hit had been "with intent to maim," and the Pittsburgh coach added, "You have a criminal element in all aspects of society. Apparently we have it in the NFL, too."[44]

Atkinson rebutted Noll's charges: "With some of the things that their team does, I don't see why he's so upset. It's just football." (Atkinson would later say that he had been retaliating for Pittsburgh's Mel Blount having dumped Oakland's Cliff Branch on his head.) The Oakland defensive back then filed a libel and slander suit against Noll and the Steelers that went to trial in July 1977. Noll was forced to acknowledge under oath that the NFL's purported "criminal element" included several of his own players, while the Steelers' lead attorney theatrically decried what he called the "secret love of violence, the spectacle of liking to see others hurt, happiness at pain, enthralled by the love of blood. That's the America of George Atkinson." The jury decided that Atkinson had not been slandered, but *Sports Illustrated* opined that "the ugliness of [the trial] had stained everything and everyone involved."[45]

The Atkinson-Swann case did not have explicitly racial overtones in that both players were African American. However, Swann had attended the University of Southern California, where he had developed a persona that sportswriter Frank Deford would call "California Golden Universal—and race is no function of this persona, only style and outlook and eternal youth." Swann was known for his smile and grace and for having studied dance. In contrast, Atkinson had come from a small, historically black college in the South. He had faced allegations of embezzling money, concealing a weapon, and threatening to castrate a man. In a contest of public images between Swann and Atkinson, Swann was certain to win. Nor would the reputation of the Raiders or the "Soul Patrol" be helped when in 1978 Jack Tatum paralyzed New England wide receiver Darryl Stingley during a pass attempt.[46]

Yet in many ways, the Raiders were no worse in their conduct than any other NFL team, as Atkinson had implied when he said that it was "just football." Similarly, Tatum suggested that although such accidents as the Stingley injury (which had resulted from a legal hit) were regrettable, they were an unavoidable part of the game: "Believe it or not, receivers and defensive backs have been slamming into each other ever since the forward pass was invented." In highlighting that football's violence extended beyond a few villainous players or teams, the Atkinson-Swann case undercut the NFL's carefully tended myth that hitting and pain merely served the noble pursuit of athletic excellence. The case also suggested that football might damage young men beyond repair. "It is a wonder more players don't become lifelong cripples," the Oakland Tribune's Ed Levitt had written just after Atkinson's blindside hit on Swann.[47]

Over time, the prophecy of crippling injury came true for many NFL players. Oakland center Jim Otto, who had started 210 consecutive games, would undergo multiple knee replacements before finally having his leg amputated. ("It's all about priorities," said Otto. "I'd rather be a disabled Hall of Famer than a healthy, retired scrub.") When the Raiders held a team reunion in 2017, longtime offensive lineman Henry Lawrence was struck by the condition of several of his former teammates: "There were just so many things happening with them. Guys with hip replacements, knee replacements, and the list goes on and on."[48]

By the twenty-first century, as one historical account notes, medical researchers would increasingly assert that not only could football "break your neck"; it also could "unleash a cascading series of neurological

events that in the end strangles your brain, leaving you unrecogniz-
able."[49] Although chronic traumatic encephalopathy—CTE—can be
definitively diagnosed only by examining the brain after death, evidence
suggests that CTE affected several men who played with the Raiders or
Chiefs during the 1960s and 1970s.

Jim Tyrer's longevity as an offensive lineman rivaled that of Jim Otto.
Tyrer had started nearly every game for the Chiefs from 1961 (when
they were still the Dallas Texans) through 1973. "Among all the Chiefs
I played with, he seemed the most responsible, the most controlled,
the most conscientious and stable," his teammate Michael Oriard said.
Tyrer was noted for preparing himself for life after football by pursuing
multiple business ventures off the field. By 1980, however, he had been
out of football for six years and his business endeavors had soured.
Consistent with CTE symptoms, Tyrer was increasingly morose and
paranoid, while seeming to have difficulty focusing his attention. On a
September Sunday, he attended a Chiefs home game. "Instead of watching the game, Jim seemed to be staring at it," a friend later said. Early
the next morning in the Tyrers' Kansas City house while their three
youngest children slept, Tyrer shot his wife to death and then killed
himself. No one could make sense of his actions, but soon afterward,
his former Chiefs teammate Dave Hill said that "Jim would have been
better off if he'd never played football."[50]

In the years that followed, other former players began displaying neurological symptoms. Ceasar Belser had excelled for Kansas City on special teams, which were notorious for their high injury rate. "Ceasar has
knocked out three runners and maimed one," his teammate Mike Garrett wrote in 1969, adding that Belser was "one of the leading jokesters
on the team." Prior to his 2016 death, Belser was diagnosed with brain
trauma and dementia; his family (including son Jason, also a former
NFL player) donated his brain for CTE research. Star wide receiver Otis
Taylor—who had said that he always "wanted the defensive back to pay
a price when he tried to bring me down"—would be bedridden with a
feeding tube by 2016. His family sued the NFL, saying that Taylor had
sustained "multiple repetitive traumatic head impacts" during his career
and had suffered convulsions as early as the season that the Chiefs won
the Super Bowl.[51]

Among the Raiders, Ken Stabler's brain was diagnosed with CTE following the ex-quarterback's death in 2015. In his memoir, Stabler had said that NFL players "wear the best helmets that technology can produce, but when your head inside that helmet bangs off the [artificial] turf your brain gets scrambled. It happened to me while playing for the Raiders." Henry Lawrence was afflicted with headaches, blackouts, and violent thoughts; during a business meeting, he suddenly had begun screaming, "Where's my gun?" And George Atkinson, who twenty years earlier had sued over suggestions that his aggressive play verged on criminality, suffered from depression and mood swings: "I don't wish what is happening to me on anyone else at all."[52]

In 2017 a neuropathologist announced that of 111 deceased NFL players whose brains had been examined, 110 were found to have signs of CTE. (They included Tom Keating, a defensive lineman who had played for both the Raiders and the Chiefs.) Yet for years the NFL had fought to discredit research indicating that football's routine physical contact injured brains. Even some former players who appeared to be affected by head trauma still suggested that such outcomes were inevitable. "Football is a collision sport," said George Atkinson. "If you don't have a certain mentality you will get run out of the game." And football's boosters remained resolute in the game's defense. For them, whatever tragedies may have befallen individual players from playing the sport, the bigger tragedy would be if the sport were eliminated altogether. "If we lose football, we lose a lot in America," said the president of the Pro Football Hall of Fame. "I don't know if America can survive."[53]

By 2017 the city of Oakland was pondering its own future without professional football. It already had lost the Raiders once. Now it was about to lose them again.

Conclusion

THE ANNOUNCEMENT IN 2017 that the Oakland Raiders were leaving for Las Vegas culminated years of controversy surrounding Oakland's football and baseball franchises. Although Kansas City had not faced as direct a threat of losing the Chiefs or Royals, it too had experienced controversy over what it should do to maintain its big-league status.

The sports rivalry that had flourished between the two cities in the 1960s and 1970s cooled by 1977, the year that both the Kansas City Chiefs and the Oakland A's (who had been depleted by free agency) sank into last place. That same year, baseball commissioner Bowie Kuhn revived the idea of relocating one Bay Area franchise and having the remaining franchise split its games between Oakland and San Francisco. A's owner Charlie Finley was in poor health and he was willing to sell the A's to oil magnate Marvin Davis, who would move the franchise to Denver. But Finley still needed to get out of his lease with the Oakland Coliseum, and Robert Nahas and others in Oakland continued to resist losing the A's or dealing with San Francisco. It appeared that a compromise finally was achieved in the spring of 1978, but it collapsed after Finley—who had sued the baseball commissioner in the past—threatened to sue again, this time over Kuhn's veto of a sale of Vida Blue to Cincinnati.[1]

Next came efforts to find local owners for the A's. In the fall of 1978, furniture store owner Ed Bercovich announced that he represented a group of fellow Oaklanders (reportedly including Al Davis) who wanted to buy the franchise. After that deal failed, another group declared its hopes of acquiring the A's and keeping the team from moving. The group included executives of Clorox and of Kaiser Industries, two corporate mainstays in Oakland; and it was headed by the president of Combined Communications, the company that had bought the *Oakland Tribune* from the Knowland family. Combined Communications president Karl Eller already had other business investments in downtown Oakland. "This is actually a continuation of our effort to rebuild the community," he said of the bid to buy the A's. "I'm not so much interested in the baseball business as the Oakland business."[2] Even as Eller spoke of his ambitions for the city, Combined Communications and the *Tribune* were being acquired by Gannett, and this latest attempt to secure the A's' future also came to naught.

By then Finley's team had hit bottom. In 1979 the A's lost 108 games, a record of futility unmatched even by the Kansas City A's in their worst seasons. A game at the Coliseum in April drew a paid attendance of 653, although the actual attendance seemed significantly lower. The city of Oakland, Alameda County, and the Coliseum sued Finley for breach of contract, charging that he had failed "to endeavor in good faith to obtain maximum occupancy of the Stadium by the public by failing to reasonably promote attendance at Oakland A's baseball games." The A's' operation had been pared back to the point that it could scarcely function. (One person still in the team's employ was Oakland teenager Stanley Burrell, whom Finley had named as an honorary club vice president. He later gained fame as hip hop artist MC Hammer.) Media coverage of the team had shrunk as well. The *Oakland Tribune* stopped sending a reporter to cover the A's on the road, and for a time the team broadcast its games only on a low-power student radio station in Berkeley.[3]

Bowie Kuhn tried one last time to broker a sale of the A's to Marvin Davis and move the team to Denver. The parties reached a new compromise in November 1979 to pay the Coliseum $4 million to release the A's from their lease. But then Al Davis announced his intention to move the Raiders to Los Angeles, potentially leaving Oakland without either football or baseball. The city refused to let the A's go, and in 1980 Finley finally sold his team to the Walter Haas Jr. family, owners of the Levi Strauss company; they kept the franchise in Oakland as a civic gesture. Finley declared that he no longer could financially compete in baseball. "During the time we were winning championships, survival was a game of wits," he said. "It is no longer a battle of wits, but how much you have on the hip."[4] Before selling the team, though, he had acquired new young talent, most notably future Hall of Famer Rickey Henderson, who had grown up in Oakland. In 1981 following a strike-interrupted major league season, the A's swept Kansas City in an intra-divisional playoff series.

Looking back at his efforts to fix the problems with Charlie Finley and the A's in the late 1970s, Bowie Kuhn observed that "East Bay baseball was merely a pawn in a larger game to accommodate Al Davis and the enormously more popular Raiders," a team that generated more than twice the annual revenue than the A's did for the Oakland Coliseum.[5] While the baseball team struggled, the Raiders continued to win. In January 1978, they returned to the AFC championship game for the fifth consecutive season but lost to Denver. At the end of the following season, John Madden resigned as coach to pursue a broadcasting career, and Tom Flores replaced him.

The relationship between Al Davis and the city of Oakland became increasingly strained. George Ross, the *Oakland Tribune* sports editor who had helped bring Davis to the city, came to believe that "a deficiency on the part of the town [was that] it took him for granted." Yet Davis also had "resisted going out in front, didn't like to go speak to crowds. He and the town really were two separate trucks going past each other."[6]

In 1979 after the NFL's Los Angeles Rams announced that they would move to nearby Anaheim, Davis seized the opportunity to move into the stadium the Rams were vacating, the Los Angeles Memorial Coliseum. His stated rationale was to remain financially competitive—to ensure that he had enough "on the hip" to keep up with rising player salaries, as Charlie Finley would put it. "Pay TV is where it's going to be all at," Davis said. "It won't matter the size of the stadiums. But can you imagine two million viewers paying 10 bucks a head? That means the smart pro clubs have to be in the big TV markets"—bigger, apparently, than even the sizable Bay Area market. In early 1980, the Raiders formally announced an agreement to play in Los Angeles.[7]

The announcement triggered a lengthy, complex, and contentious succession of negotiations and lawsuits involving the Raiders, the NFL, and Oakland. Talks between the team and city over a new stadium lease had broken down over the lease's length and the construction of luxury boxes. When Davis indicated that the Raiders intended to leave Oakland, Mayor Lionel Wilson joined the fray. The city continued to cope with challenges that included crime, drugs, and unemployment, and according to one of Davis's biographers, the mayor "understood the political and socio-economic implications of a town with much blight losing not only a revenue-maker but a unifier of all classes." Wilson and the head of Kaiser Industries proposed substantially sweetening the terms of a new Raiders lease, but the Oakland Coliseum board rejected those terms. At the same time, with other NFL teams opposing the Raiders' move (league rules required that three-quarters of the teams approve it), the Raiders joined the Los Angeles Coliseum Commission in suing the NFL for violating federal antitrust laws.[8]

In February 1980, Oakland filed its own suit that sought to seize control of the Raiders from Al Davis via eminent domain. The attorney representing Oakland in the suit said that the franchise was so "important to the social, economic, sociological and psychological life of the city" that Oakland was justified in taking over the team to protect the public interest. Three years earlier, when Oakland had gone to the Super Bowl, a fan had exclaimed, "Tell Davis he no longer owns the Raiders. The people own the Raiders." In effect the city was now trying to use eminent domain to make that sentiment a reality (even though Oakland officials vowed to sell the team to new private investors should the suit succeed). The Raiders countered that the team was not nearly so essential to Oakland as the city claimed, and eventually the courts agreed—the eminent domain suit failed.[9]

Amid all the litigation, Al Davis and the Raiders moved their offices to Los Angeles, but for the time being the team itself continued to play in Oakland. Fans there expressed their unhappiness during the 1980 season by showing up in substantially smaller numbers at the Coliseum. The low point occurred in October in a game against winless Kansas City. Barely 40,000 fans saw the Chiefs do something they had almost never done before: they routed the Raiders in Oakland, taking a 31–0 lead in the first half before winning 31–17. Quarterback Dan Pastorini—whom the Raiders had obtained in a controversial trade in exchange for Ken Stabler—broke his leg during the game, and some Oakland fans cheered as he was carried off the field. The injury made veteran Jim Plunkett the new starting quarterback, and he led Oakland into the playoffs (but not before fans protesting the team's move boycotted the first minutes of a Monday night game at the Coliseum). In January 1981, the Raiders overcame all the drama surrounding them to win their second Super Bowl by beating Philadelphia 27–10.[10]

The following season would be the Raiders' last in Oakland for many years to come. The team sank to its first losing record since 1964, finishing at 7-9 and again playing before diminished Coliseum crowds. The Raiders' suit against the NFL finally was resolved in May 1982 as a jury decided that the NFL had indeed violated antitrust laws, freeing the team to play in Los Angeles. Al Davis had long fought with football commissioner Pete Rozelle; among other grievances, Davis believed that Rozelle had conspired against the Raiders in the George Atkinson–Lynn Swann case a few years previously. Now Davis blamed the commissioner for the Raiders having abandoned Oakland while absolving himself from responsibility: "When people get into the guts of this case, I think Oakland can sue Rozelle's ass. When they discover all the things he did behind my back, they're going to be awfully upset."[11]

The newly christened Los Angeles Raiders would win another Super Bowl in January 1984, but Davis soon grew unhappy in his new locale. Again there were disputes concerning lease terms and luxury box construction, this time at the Los Angeles Memorial Coliseum. Davis's dreams of a windfall from big-market pay TV also did not come to pass; revenue sharing among NFL teams—including the sharing of network TV revenue—meant that the Raiders likely would have remained financially competitive had they never left Oakland. In 1990 Davis announced that the Raiders would move back to their original home. "We've had fights and feuds, but that's just part of the egos of men," he said. The deal fell through: many in Oakland felt that mayor Lionel Wilson and the city had conceded far too much in trying to lure back the team, and Wilson was voted out of office the next year.[12]

Not until 1995 did the Raiders actually return to Oakland, as the Coliseum finally added luxury boxes and a new seating deck that was nicknamed (not necessarily affectionately) "Mount Davis." Even then Davis continued to bicker with the city and threaten to leave town again, and there were renewed concerns that Oakland had paid too exorbitant a price for the team's return. The controversy would come to a head after Davis's death in 2011.[13]

* * *

After dethroning the Oakland A's as American League West champions in 1976, the Kansas City Royals continued to reign over their division for the next few seasons. Their chief nemesis became the New York Yankees, who had beaten them for the American League pennant in 1976 and who would come to bedevil them as much as Charlie Finley's A's had (especially after Reggie Jackson joined the Yankees). Kansas City and New York met again in the league championship series in 1977 and 1978; both times New York won. Not until 1980 would the Royals finally defeat the Yankees to reach the World Series.[14] In 1985, with the last of the players from the franchise's earliest years (including George Brett, Frank White, and Hal McRae), the Royals won their first world championship.

The Kansas City Chiefs spent the rest of the 1970s and most of the 1980s in the doldrums. In 1989 their fortunes revived under new head coach Marty Schottenheimer and general manager Carl Peterson. The Chiefs-Raiders rivalry reignited while the Raiders were still in Los Angeles. "I don't like people that think they're above the law," Schottenheimer reportedly said of the Raiders, and he put a premium on beating them, which the Chiefs did regularly even after the Raiders returned to Oakland.[15] In Schottenheimer's ten seasons as coach, Kansas City went 18-3 against the Raiders, including a playoff victory in 1991. Arrowhead Stadium evolved into a raucous home for the Chiefs and gave them the home-field advantage they had seemed to lack when they first moved into the facility. But Kansas City never reached the Super Bowl under Schottenheimer, and he resigned after the 1998 season. Oakland did return to the Super Bowl in January 2003 behind quarterback Rich Gannon, who previously had played for Kansas City, but the Raiders lost to the Tampa Bay Buccaneers 48–21. As of 2019, that game represented the last time that either the Raiders or the Chiefs had appeared in the NFL championship. The two franchises continued to play in the same division, just as they had since the inaugural season of the American Football League in 1960, and the rivalry between them endured.

The rivalry between the Oakland A's and the Kansas City Royals did not reignite to the same degree, although on one notable occasion it was briefly renewed. The A's—led by "Bash Brothers" Jose Canseco and

Mark McGwire—regained their swagger in the late 1980s and won three consecutive American League pennants. They beat the San Francisco Giants in the 1989 World Series, but that triumph over the city across the bay was marred by an earthquake that killed sixty-three people, the majority of them in Oakland when the Cypress Freeway collapsed. In 1997 Billy Beane became general manager and systematically used statistics and research (what became known as sabermetrics or "moneyball") to help the A's return to the playoffs multiple times.[16] In Kansas City, the Royals fell on hard times after owner Ewing Kauffman's death in 1993. The nadir came when they lost more than one hundred games four out of five seasons between 2002 and 2006. The team began a slow rebuild under new general manager Dayton Moore, and in 2014 the Royals made the postseason for the first time in decades. Their first opponent was the Oakland A's, and in an epic winner-take-all wild-card game, Kansas City came from behind in extra innings to win. The Royals went on to the World Series but lost to the San Francisco Giants. The next season, the Royals beat the New York Mets to win their second world championship.

The sports facilities that Oakland and Kansas City had fought so hard to build in the 1960s and 1970s became the focus of new debate by the first years of the new century. The cities had erected the Truman Sports Complex and the Oakland Coliseum Complex far away from their central business districts with an eye toward placating countywide interests, accommodating automobiles, and saving money in land acquisition and construction. Kansas City's Kemper Arena was closer to downtown but still isolated from it.

Starting in the early 1990s, other cities had undertaken a new wave of sports-related construction in their downtowns. According to sports scholar Daniel Rosensweig, "retro ballparks" such as Baltimore's Camden Yards rejected the legacy of circular, multipurpose stadiums that "like cookie-cutter strip shopping centers failed to promote a sense of regional uniqueness, a specialness of place." Instead, retro baseball stadiums appealed to "a new urbanist ethos" through architecture that recalled the ballparks of the past while also providing a "themed environment for tourists, conventioneers, baseball fans, and others interested in experiencing a taste of the urban." The hope was that such themed environments would rejuvenate downtowns.[17]

Kansas City investigated building its own downtown retro ballpark. The Truman Sports Complex was now three decades old and needed repairs that Jackson County could not afford. There were concerns that the Chiefs or the Royals or both teams might leave if facilities were not upgraded. However, by 2005 the Royals chose to support renovating their current stadium and spending money on rebuilding their team as opposed to investing in a new ballpark. The Chiefs likewise advocated for renovations. In April 2006, Jackson County voters approved a sales tax hike to generate $425 million for the sports complex overhaul, with each team chipping in additional money and the state of Missouri providing tax credits. The *Star* backed the tax increase, and supporters of the measure vastly outspent opponents, although the opposition created a website sardonically named "saveourowners.com" that suggested the tax hike actually represented a windfall for the Chiefs and Royals' owners. Voters did reject paying for a rolling roof: the same rolling roof that had been dropped from the original construction of the sports complex because of cost overruns. Nonetheless, the renovations were intended to ensure that the Royals and Chiefs would remain in Kansas City at least until 2031.[18]

Although the city decided against a new baseball stadium, it did back constructing a new downtown sports arena with an accompanying real estate development. Kemper Arena had reopened following its 1979 roof collapse and had served as a hub for college basketball and other activities. By the end of the 1990s, though, leaders deemed its stockyards location too remote and the facility itself outmoded, with major sports tournaments relocating to newer venues in other cities. "These arenas are like computers," one college sports executive said. "An arena is going to go out of date every four or five years."[19]

In May 2004, Kansas City mayor Kay Barnes unveiled a proposal to build what would be called the Sprint Center, named after the telecommunications company. The arena, which would accommodate more than 19,000 people, would receive funding from both public and private sources, with the public funds to be raised by a hike in rental car and hotel fees. The facility was intended to become the linchpin of a new restaurant and entertainment center known as the Power & Light District, named after a nearby landmark building. The campaign over raising the fees was bitter, with Enterprise Rent-A-Car hiring sports

The Power & Light District in downtown Kansas City, with the Sprint Center at upper right.
(User:DanaWelsch / Wikimedia Commons / CC-BY-SA-4.0)

economists to argue that the new arena would be a poor investment. But voters approved the fee increase, and Mayor Barnes called the vote "a huge positive turning point for our city." By 2018 the Sprint Center and the Power & Light District received credit for having helped boost city tax revenue and downtown's resident population. As for Kemper Arena, the city sold it to developers who planned to convert it into a youth sports complex. The sales price was one dollar.[20]

In Oakland, the Coliseum Arena where the NBA's Golden State Warriors played was renovated in the mid-1990s. It took years for Oakland and Alameda County to find a company willing to buy naming rights to the overhauled arena, partly stemming from the Warriors' continual mediocrity; meanwhile, the city and county grappled with paying off the debt they had incurred by undertaking the renovations. In 2006 the computer company Oracle purchased the naming rights, and a few years later the Warriors drafted superstar guard Stephen Curry, who would

The Oakland Coliseum prior to an A's game with "Mount Davis" at center. (redlegsfan21 / Wikimedia Commons / CC–BY–SA–2.0

help them win three more NBA titles by 2018. By then, though, the team had announced that it would move to a new home in San Francisco, leaving Oracle Arena with a murky future.[21]

The Coliseum Complex's largest venue—the football-baseball stadium—had been full of excitement in 1995 when the Raiders announced their return, with one city booster declaring that "Oakland is now on the threshold of greatness." But the erection of "Mount Davis" to accommodate the Raiders did not help the A's, as the new seats blocked fans' views of the Oakland Hills while underscoring that the renovated stadium seemed much better suited for football than for baseball. After the Haas family sold the team to new owners, the A's began what would become a long and tortuous quest for a new facility. They attempted to obtain sites in suburban Fremont and in San Jose. (The San Jose location fell through after Major League Baseball ruled that the San Francisco Giants held territorial rights to the city. San Jose sued but lost in the U.S. Supreme Court.) The A's also examined multiple locales within Oakland.[22]

In 2017 the team finally settled on a site near Oakland's Laney College at the south end of Lake Merritt. The A's vowed to work with the college and the surrounding neighborhood to minimize disruptions and also to generate jobs and revenue for the area. But the community college district's board rejected the plan, saying that the A's' promises were too vague. "We're all really excited," one faculty member said. "Here's an instance where good old-fashioned organizing and grassroots organization worked." The A's resumed their search and looked at a waterfront site west of Jack London Square as well as at the existing Coliseum location as potential places for a new ballpark. For the time being, though, they would remain in what the *New York Times* pronounced as "a bland, charmless concrete monstrosity, the last of the unfortunate wave of multipurpose stadiums built in the 1960s."[23]

The Raiders continued to play in the Coliseum as well, but they already had their exit strategy in place. Al Davis's son, Mark, had assumed ownership of the team after his father's death in 2011, and he was unhappy that the franchise's income fell well short of competing teams with newer stadiums. Like the A's, the Raiders began searching for a potential new home. In 2015 they attempted to move back to the Los Angeles area to play in a new stadium to be built there, but the NFL rejected the plan in favor of instead allowing the San Diego Chargers and St. Louis Rams to move to Los Angeles. Oakland tried to entice the Raiders to stay, with a new stadium to be constructed at the Coliseum site. The Raiders turned down that proposal in favor of a competing bid from Las Vegas: a new stadium costing nearly $2 billion—$750 million of it in public money—that was scheduled to open in 2020.[24]

"We know that some fans will be disappointed and even angry," Mark Davis said. "But we hope they do not direct that frustration to the players, coaches and staff." But when Davis approached the leader of a fan group called "Forever Oakland" to discuss the Raiders' future in their new home, the fan cut him short: "There is no future."[25]

* * *

The Raiders' impending departure from Oakland invites a review of the Kansas City–Oakland rivalry and its significance for understanding past and present relationships between cities and sports teams. From a sports perspective, the rivalry stood out for its intensity and its inclusion of both football and baseball. The Chiefs-Raiders rivalry in particular featured what one sports historian has called "genuine animosity" and "genuine ill will" among players and fans. Oakland and Kansas City did not share geographic proximity the way that such cities as Chicago and Green Bay did in football or that New York and Boston did in baseball, but they did share the same division in both sports, and they frequently faced off to play for first place. "If you don't play big games that matter to each team, it's not going to be a [true] rivalry," a sportswriter has argued.[26] In the last years of the American Football League and the first years of the newly expanded National Football League, the Raiders and Chiefs did play big games for big TV audiences; more than once they also fought big brawls. Similarly, the A's and Royals played multiple late-season series with playoff implications, and when the A's finally were toppled from their longtime perch atop their division, it was the Royals who did the deed. Even when the stakes between the two cities' teams were not so high, the games still featured dramatic happenings as well as players with extraordinary talents and personalities. Many of those athletes would later be inducted into their respective sports' Halls of Fame.[27]

Beyond the pursuit of sports preeminence, the rivalry also featured the pursuit of civic preeminence, with Oakland and Kansas City representative of what was happening among many cities during the postwar years. "The metropolis appeared to be coming apart," historian Jon Teaford has observed of the typical U.S. city during that era. The decline of downtown and the loss of population to the suburbs resulted in "an increasingly dispersed metropolis with fewer bonds uniting its citizens." Cities turned to professional sports as a means of curbing those trends, especially cities west of the Mississippi River and in the Sun Belt that had never before hosted a major league franchise.[28] To land such a team implied that a city was not in decline—on the contrary, it had conspicuously established itself as being "big league" and as no longer being "minor league." The quest for big-league status was especially acute for Kansas City (which had long been burdened with a cow town image) and for Oakland (which had long been in the shadow of a more glamorous neighbor).

With a limited supply of big-league franchises, cities have felt compelled to compete to attract and retain those franchises by constructing new sports facilities and providing other incentives. "Rivalries among places are rooted in the pervasive competition for economic development and political favor; they are fueled by boosterism, the civic religion of being bigger and thus better than rival places," Michael Danielson has written. "Professional sports capitalized on those rivalries."[29] Kansas City and Oakland both poached teams from other cities and in turn were poached themselves as franchise owners profited from playing cities off one another. When Oakland lured the A's from Kansas City, the sports rivalry between the two cities assumed a new and more bitter dimension.

Neither Kansas City nor Oakland was big or wealthy enough to attract the equivalent of the baseball Dodgers or Giants. Instead they had to go after a team such as the A's, who were wretched both when Kansas City took them from Philadelphia and when Oakland in turn took them from Kansas City (although by then the A's had a bevy of young talent about to emerge). To get big-league football, the two cities had to turn to the American Football League—a league that for years many people refused to take seriously—and when Kansas City rejoined the major leagues in baseball, the city was forced to content itself with an expansion team that had to be built from scratch. The cities' teams featured motley sets of players. They included athletes who historically had not been highly sought after (as with AFL players from small African American colleges), or else who were seeming castoffs (as with onetime NFL players who found refuge in the AFL or ballplayers who had to go to an expansion franchise such as the Royals to play regularly). The teams included highly touted athletes as well: college football stars who took the money offered by such owners as Lamar Hunt to play in the AFL, or talented young baseball players who accepted bonuses to sign with the farm system of Charlie Finley's A's. Regardless of where they came from, professional athletes of the day confronted challenges that included racism and the often paternalistic and penurious control of the franchises that owned them. If Oakland and Kansas City hungered for respect, so too did the athletes who played in the two cities; they had multiple reasons to have chips on their shoulders.

The heyday of the Kansas City–Oakland rivalry corresponded with profound changes to professional athletes' working conditions. Not all of those changes were necessarily to the athletes' benefit. The widespread adoption of artificial turf appeared to contribute to player injuries and may well have exacerbated the neurological symptoms that many NFL players would develop later in life. (As the Raiders' Ken Stabler had said, "When your head inside that helmet bangs off the turf your brain gets scrambled.")[30] For years the NFL downplayed concerns about the game's physical impact on players. Many athletes paid a price to be "big league" just as cities did.

On the other hand, in keeping with the increasing challenges to authority that developed in U.S. society during the 1960s and 1970s, athletes became more willing to assert themselves and stand up for their rights. Baseball players won new freedoms, capped by the introduction of free agency. Unhappy members of the A's who in the not-too-distant past would have remained bound to Oakland against their will now had the opportunity to take their talents elsewhere for higher wages. In both baseball and football, the idea of "team" increasingly was contested. As former NFL player Michael Oriard put it, the "very notion of 'team'—as in everyone contributes, from the greatest star to the lowliest scrub—was a sacred idea in football, as old as the game itself." By the 1970s, though, professional athletes were more apt to look out for their individual interests, and Oriard contended that their relationships with fans were irrevocably altered: "The love affair of fans with 'their' [sports] heroes had always been built on illusions, of course, on a willed innocence that would never again be quite as easy to maintain."[31]

Illusions were not limited to fans. Kansas City's and Oakland's pursuit of big-league sports did not always produce the results that city boosters imagined would come about. When the A's came to Kansas City in 1955, they were greeted by cheering throngs. Six years later, the *Kansas City Star*'s Ernie Mehl—who had done as much as anyone to bring the team to town—wrote of "hopes never realized" and "promises broken" (and the city still had six more years of Charlie Finley to endure). Oakland built the Coliseum largely to attract major league baseball; after the A's arrived from Kansas City, fans greeted them with apathy. Later, when Kansas City built Kemper Arena in hopes of landing a National Hockey League franchise, that franchise lasted only two seasons before leaving town, and eventually the city's National Basketball Association team left as well. Oakland's investment in NHL hockey was little more successful than Kansas City's, and its NBA team refused to take the city's name. Neither city appeared to gain widespread economic benefits from big-league sports. One study said that the monetary impact on Kansas City of getting the Royals was "insignificant" and that construction of the Truman Sports Complex was in fact "significantly correlated with a reduction of that metropolitan area's share of regional income." In Oakland, as sports scholar Maria Veri notes, the presence of the Raiders did nothing to halt the loss of jobs or improve the lot of the city's poor: "The Raiders were not solely responsible for these deplorable conditions in Oakland, but given the city's acquiescence to the franchise's financial demands for public subsidization, one is left to question the cost of team affiliation."[32]

Some citizens challenged Oakland's and Kansas City's pursuit of professional sports and the cities' urban renewal initiatives, indicating that "the idea of a city" was being contested just as "the idea of a team" was.[33] Citizens filed lawsuits against construction of Kansas City's Truman Sports Complex and Kemper Arena. ("Urban blight is spreading; public hospitals are overcrowded and understaffed; streets are filled with chuckholes; police and firemen are underpaid," one group said in questioning civic priorities.) Such groups as the Black Panthers similarly challenged the operation of the Oakland Coliseum as well as the construction of major projects, including City Center. Some civic endeavors, such as the Oakland Museum, did win national praise, and the Kansas City Prime Time campaign capitalized on new urban developments to generate favorable publicity for the city. Nevertheless, the efforts to elevate Kansas City's and Oakland's status—whether through sports or other means—did not erase the two cities' class and race divides or stop white flight, consistent with the experiences of other postwar metropolises. And as years went by, some big-league franchises still left town despite cities' best efforts to hold on to them. "The Raider nation is the last of the blue-collar, salt-of-the-earth fan bases, and it absolutely breaks my heart to lose this team," said Oakland Mayor Libby Schaaf in 2017 after the Raiders announced that they would move to Las Vegas.[34]

Questions concerning the costs and benefits of big-league sports remain as pertinent today as they were in the 1960s and 1970s. Competitive boosterism ("the active participation of local elites in luring trade, industry, and investment to their own cities from elsewhere") is still very much alive, as indicated by Las Vegas's successful campaign to land the Raiders. A sportswriter for the *Las Vegas Sun* hailed the news in words strikingly reminiscent of those expressed in Oakland and Kansas City five and six decades previously. "The Raiders are all ours, and in the understatement of the century, that's a reason to celebrate," he wrote. No longer would Las Vegas be known only as a place to gamble, for it had at last joined the "elite fraternity" of big-league NFL cities: "We've grown up, Las Vegas. We've grown up together. Now, it's time to grow with the Raiders."[35]

Just as Kansas City's and Oakland's postwar pursuit of major league franchises foreshadowed franchise moves in the 2010s, the activism among African American athletes in the late 1960s foreshadowed a new wave of activism several decades later. "With the onset of the Black Lives Matter movement . . . any semblance of legitimacy regarding athletes' attitudes of individual economic primacy and political insularity dissipated," wrote Harry Edwards, who had helped lead athlete protests during the 1960s. Of particular note was the decision of some NFL players to take a knee during the national anthem to protest police brutality and the country's treatment of African Americans. However, the backlash against this practice suggested that resistance against political protest remained strong in sports, just as growing criticism of football on safety grounds sparked resistance among the game's defenders.[36]

New questions were raised about how cities might profit from professional sports. Mark Rosentraub has argued that a new sports facility can help revitalize a city if it is "an anchor for a broad-based real estate development plan" that adheres to the highest principles of "the art, practice, and science of urban planning and design," including density, a mix of uses, ease of movement, and distinctive architecture. Kansas City's downtown Power & Light District adjacent to the new Sprint Center could be seen as epitomizing some of those principles, although there were concerns that the city had assumed too much of a financial burden in building the arena and district—particularly while dealing with what the *Kansas City Star* described as "a mountain of debt and pension obligations."[37]

Oakland by the 2010s was seeing a downtown building boom that would have thrilled city leaders back in the 1970s, but the city also faced a shortage of affordable housing and angry disputes over gentrification, not to mention millions of dollars in public debt stemming from the Coliseum's renovation in the 1990s. Consequently, there was skepticism regarding any new concessions that might be made to get or keep major league sports franchises. The chancellor of the Peralta Community College District, which had rejected a plan to build a new baseball stadium near Laney College, said that "we need to do everything we can to keep the Oakland Athletics in Oakland." But, he added, "it's not just Peralta's job to do that. It's the whole community that needs to come together around that particular issue." Despite her unhappiness over losing the Raiders, Oakland mayor Schaaf declared that she did "not regret that we stood firm on no public funding for stadium constructions." And Bay Area sports columnist Marcus Thompson asserted that the Raiders' departure might prove beneficial. "Maybe the emotive, community element that fans cling to—which the NFL has mastered taking advantage of—will give way to logic and business savvy," he wrote. "Hopefully more [communities] will stand up to the influence of the NFL and demand that the billions the league will earn translate into real benefits to the cities and counties they inhabit. Maybe they can enter real, mutually beneficial partnerships one day. If that's what comes out of the Raiders leaving again, it will have been worth it."[38]

There remains the "emotive, community element" to which Thompson referred. Even if they did not receive substantial monetary returns, did Kansas City and Oakland still gain something important by investing in big-league sports? Did a sense of civic pride and unity emerge from the Raiders, Chiefs, Royals, and A's?

Sports historian Michael MacCambridge has aptly summarized the contradiction at the heart of the relationship between cities and professional athletics. "One of the central illusions of sport is that a group of athletes wearing a certain uniform can represent an entire city," he writes. "And one of the wonders of sport is that the repeated exercise of that illusion, through many years and many athletes, can serve to make it a reality." MacCambridge says that cities that were worried about not being perceived as big league developed an especially powerful connection to their sports teams: "Too often those feelings of loyalty are dismissed, but they were at the very heart of spectator sports in the late twentieth century."[39]

When Oakland's and Kansas City's sports teams overcame considerable obstacles to bring championships to their host cities, they did generate widespread feelings of pride and unity, even if those feelings were only temporary for some citizens. That was the phenomenon that writer John Krich witnessed after the A's won their first World Series in 1972 and he visited Oakland's Jack London Square to see people of different classes and races come together in celebration. Pride prompted the Chiefs' radio announcer to call the day after the team's 1970 Super Bowl victory "the greatest day in the history of Kansas City," and it prompted the *Oakland Tribune* to editorialize after the Raiders' 1977 Super Bowl win that "something seems to spell out C-H-A-M-P-I-O-N-S once you pass the city limits sign" into Oakland. And so it has continued in the years since. Following the Royals' 2015 World Series victory, the entire front page of the *Kansas City Star* consisted of an aerial photo of the massive victory celebration. The accompanying headline read, "A City United."[40]

In that regard, the concerted efforts of civic and business leaders in postwar Kansas City and Oakland to bring big-league sports to their cities paid dividends. Certain leaders and institutions were flawed or blinkered, but they still did promote and invest in their cities. The *Oakland Tribune*—which boasted on its editorial page that it was "Home Owned, Controlled, Edited"—joined other representatives of the city's establishment in pushing for construction of the Coliseum as well as other new urban developments in Oakland. They were motivated by financial interest, but as one analysis notes, they also were motivated by "civic pride, and the feeling that rank imposes obligations."[41] In Kansas City, the local business magnate who bought the expansion baseball team occasionally complained about how much money the team was costing him, but Ewing Kauffman also saw his purchase of the Royals as a philanthropic act (much as the Haas family did when they bought the Oakland A's in 1980). In fact Kauffman's estate bequeathed the Royals to a charitable foundation with the mandate that the foundation sell the team to new owners who would keep the team in Kansas City.[42]

The result would be that people came to identify the two cities by their sports teams, thus symbolically conferring upon those cities the big-league status they had craved. "You go around the world, and you say the word 'Oakland,'" said actor and former Oaklander Tom Hanks. "The next word is, 'Oh! You mean where the *Raiders* play?' And you say, 'Yes, exactly. That's exactly where Oakland is: it's where the Raiders play.'" The HBO television documentary *Rebels of Oakland* ended with a paean to the teams and fans of the 1960s and 1970s: "The success of the rebels of Oakland was proof positive to those in the city that they did not always have to live in someone else's shadow. The spotlight could and did shine on them." In 1976, the year that the Royals won their first division title, *Kansas City Star* sports editor Joe McGuff acknowledged that "life would have gone on in Kansas City without baseball." Then he put big-league baseball on par with the city's most celebrated jewels: "[Life] would also go on without the Nelson Gallery, the Philharmonic, the fountains, the boulevards, the Country Club Plaza, our colleges and universities. But who would want to live in a city without a soul?"[43]

McGuff—who back in 1967 had joined Ernie Mehl in helping talk American League owners into bringing baseball back to Kansas City—would go on to become editor of the entire *Star* before retiring in 1992. By 2005 he was incapacitated by Lou Gehrig's disease. Kansas City's baseball team was then at a low ebb, and when *Star* sportswriter Joe Posnanski visited him, McGuff labored mightily to articulate an urgent message: *We . . . half . . . keeep . . . Roh . . . alls.* Posnanski understood: We have to keep the Royals in town. "Joe wasn't a journalist. He did not even like the word," Posnanski recalled of McGuff after his death. "He was an old-time, ink-stained newspaperman, fighting to make Kansas City a better place, not for money or votes, but because he lived here."[44]

Cities and sports fans alike should maintain their skepticism regarding just how much professional sports can grant them in terms of prestige and prosperity. They should recognize that unrestrained boosterism never benefits all parties equally, and they should recognize when sports franchises finally are not worth keeping in town. And they should avoid letting nostalgia cloud their understanding of the ugliness that stained earlier eras or the grave mistakes that individuals and institutions made.

Nevertheless, fans of Kansas City, Oakland, and other cities can remember with pleasure the athletes and teams who fought to bring their
cities championships. And they can remember with pride the citizens—
sports fans and non-fans alike—who fought on multiple fronts to make
their hometowns better places: that is, genuinely big league.

Notes

Introduction

1. Wells Twombly, *Blanda* (Los Angeles: Nash, 1972), 25.

2. "Time of the Chipmunks," *Newsweek,* July 1, 1968, 62.

3. "Most of Raiders Like K.C. Chances," *Oakland Tribune,* January 5, 1970, 43.

4. The earliest published reference to the "Hiroshima" wisecrack appears to come from *Oakland Tribune* sportswriter Ron Bergman. Just after the A's' move to Oakland, Bergman attributed the remark to an unnamed "Midwest sportswriter." In later years, fellow sportswriters Wells Twombly and Shirley Povich explicitly attributed it to Joe McGuff, the sports editor of the *Kansas City Star*. However, in a 1973 book on the Oakland A's, Ron Bergman said that Stuart Symington had made the quip, and most subsequent sources also attribute it to Symington, with some erroneously claiming that he had said it on the floor of the U.S. Senate. See Ron Bergman, "Finley Charm Sweeps Oakland Off Its Feet," *Sporting News,* November 11, 1967, 29; Wells Twombly, "Charlie O., the Missouri Mule: Kicking the Sanctity of Baseball," *New York Times,* July 15, 1973, 36; Shirley Povich, "Charlie O. Finley Always Has the Last Word," *Washington Post,* May 28, 1984, C7; Ron Bergman, *Mustache Gang: The Swaggering Saga of Oakland's A's* (New York: Associated Features, 1973), 37.

5. Jim Scott, "Grid Team of '70s? Raiders Claim Tag Fits 'Em," *Sporting News,* June 13, 1970, 53.

6. Bob Valli, "Nahas Can Be Smug for 24 Hours," *Oakland Tribune,* October 19, 1967, 39.

7. John Beyer, "A New Museum for the West," *American West,* November 1969, 34.

8. W. A. Sparling, "The Coliseum Story," *Oakland-Alameda County Outlook,* September–October 1966, 14, Oakland History Room, Oakland Public Library.

9. "Why *You* Should Vote Tuesday," *Kansas City Star,* December 11, 1966, 16G.

10. "An Urban Center Scaled to a Grand Design," *Kansas City Times,* January 5, 1967, 14D.

11. See Bill Richardson, "Season Ticket Crush Sweeps Chiefs Off Feet," *Sporting News,* May 2, 1970, 53.

12. Bob Oates, "Other Chiefs Had a Hand—But Taylor Killed Vikings," *Sporting News,* January 24, 1970, 16.

13. Ted O'Leary, "A Percentage Player Makes His Pitch for K.C.," *Sports Illustrated,* January 8, 1968, 43; "Kauffman Heads Kansas City Club," *New York Times,* January 12, 1968, 77. See also Joe McGuff, "Kaycee Fans Stand and Cheer Royals' Boss," *Sporting News,* April 26, 1969, 5.

14. Twombly, *Blanda,* 45.

15. "Next Month in *Holiday,*" *Holiday,* February 1970, 104; Sol Stern, "Oakland: That Troubled Town Across the Bay," *Holiday,* March 1970, 74, 83.

16. "Is Oakland There?" *Newsweek,* May 18, 1970, 100.

17. B. Drummond Ayres Jr., "Kansas City Says Its Time Is Here," *New York Times,* March 23, 1973, 78.

18. See Robert O. Self, *American Babylon: Race and the Struggle for Postwar Oakland* (Princeton, N.J.: Princeton University Press, 2003), 153–55, 170–74.

19. "In Kansas City They Couldn't Go As Far As They Wanted," *Fortune,* October 1970, 98–101.

20. Monroe W. Karmin, "Racial Tinderbox: A Federal Study Finds Unrest Among Negroes Rising in Many Cities," *Wall Street Journal,* January 5, 1966, 1; "What We Want/What We Believe," *Black Panther,* July 26, 1969, 22; "We Want An Immediate End to Police Brutality and Murder of Black People," *Black Panther,* October 24, 1970, 8. See also "Youth Slain in Attack on Officer," *Oakland Tribune,* October 8, 1970, 22F.

21. Eddie Edmondson, "'No Response' Charged in Carter Death," *Kansas City Call,* November 4–November 12, 1970, 1–2; "FBI Into Bombing" and "Police React," *Kansas City Star,* October 16, 1970, 1–2. See also *Final Report: Mayor's Commission on Civil Disorder,* Kansas City, Missouri, August 15, 1968, Missouri Valley Special Collections, Kansas City Public Library; "Policemen 'Justified' in Fatal Shooting," *Kansas City Star,* October 6, 1970, 6.

22. "Black Boycott at Elmhurst," *San Francisco Chronicle,* October 29, 1970, 53; Mike Fancher, "Strife Splits Illinois Town," *Kansas City Star,* October 25, 1970, 12A; "Arsonist Wrecks U.C. Irvine Bank," *Oakland Tribune,* October 26, 1970, 1; "Nixon Blasts Egg-Tossers at San Jose: Many Deplore Vicious Attack," *Oakland Tribune,* October 30, 1970, 1, 20; "ANARCHY" (George Murphy campaign ad), *Los Angeles Times,* November 2, 1970, 25. Murphy ultimately lost his reelection bid to Democrat John Tunney.

23. Glenn Dickey, "Big Move Due for Raiders?" *San Francisco Chronicle,* Oc-

tober 30, 1970, 55; Joe McGuff, "Chiefs, Raiders Are Heated Foes," *Kansas City Star,* October 28, 1970, 5C; Joe McGuff, "Lamonica on Target," *Kansas City Star,* October 30, 1970, 17.

24. Glenn Dickey, ":03 Left, Blanda 48-Yard FG Ties KC," *San Francisco Chronicle,* November 2, 1970, 57.

25. See Blaine Newnham, "Davidson's Sweet Foul," *Oakland Tribune,* November 2, 1970, 41; Bucky Walter, "A Marx Brothers Finish in K.C.," *San Francisco Examiner,* November 2, 1970, 55; Dickey, ":03 Left," 53.

26. See Newnham, "Davidson's Sweet Foul," 43; Bill Richardson, "Chiefs Win Way to Super Bowl," *Kansas City Times,* January 5, 1970, 1A; "Interference Call Baffles Wilson," *Oakland Tribune,* January 5, 1970, 39. A video replay of Taylor's controversial sideline catch in the AFL championship game is in "1969 Kansas City Chiefs," *America's Game: The Super Bowl Champions,* NFL Films, 2006.

27. Gary D. Warner, "Tie May Spring Drive by Chiefs," *Kansas City Star,* November 2, 1970, 16A.

28. Ed Levitt, "It's Makeup, Not Mayhem, for Big Ben," *Oakland Tribune,* April 14, 1977, 51; Alan Hoskins, *Warpaths: The Illustrated History of the Kansas City Chiefs* (Dallas: Taylor, 1999), 167. See also Mark Ribowsky, *Slick: The Silver and Black Life of Al Davis* (New York: Macmillan, 1991), 194.

29. Jack Smith, "Ben Accused of Dirty Play," *San Francisco Chronicle,* November 5, 1970, 53; Bob Oates, "Chiefs May Appeal 17–17 Tie With Raiders," *Los Angeles Times,* November 4, 1970, G4; "Davidson of Raiders No Gentle Ben," *New York Times,* January 3, 1971, S2.

30. King's radio call is included in "Challenge of the '70s," NFL Films, 1970, available at https://www.youtube.com/watch?v=Fu1o9heRpZQ.

31. See Newnham, "Davidson's Sweet Foul"; Bill Richardson, "Otis: I Was Kicked Out," *Kansas City Times,* November 4, 1970, 1B; Dick Mackey, "Stram Crashes Referee's Gate," *Kansas City Times,* November 2, 1970, 2C; Joe McGuff, "Officials Raise Question As to Their Competency," *Kansas City Star,* November 2, 1970, 16A.

32. McGuff, "Officials Raise Question," 17A.

33. Ibid.; Mackey, "Stram Crashes Referee's Gate," 2C. See also Stephen B. Haynes, "'Ringside' Seats for 51,334 As Chiefs, Raiders Fight," *Kansas City Times,* November 2, 1970, 1A; Art Holst, *Sunday Zebras* (Lake Forest, Ill.: Forest Publishing, 1980), 186–91.

34. Ed Levitt, "The Big Rematch," *Oakland Tribune,* November 2, 1970, 41; John Hall, "Get Rid of Films," *Los Angeles Times,* November 4, 1970, G3. See also Gary D. Warner, "Chiefs Find Time to Jest," *Kansas City Times,* November 6, 1970, 11.

35. See Bill Richardson, "Storm Rages on in Chiefs' Dispute," *Kansas City Times,* November 2, 1970, 1B; Rich Sambol, "Fans Keep Phones Busy," *Kansas*

City Star, November 2, 1970, 16A; Joe McGuff, "Sporting Comment," *Kansas City Star,* November 4, 1970, 1E; "The Chiefs Fans Take It Hard," *Kansas City Star,* November 4, 1970, 4D.

36. McGuff, "Officials Raise Question," 16A–17A. See also William N. Wallace, "Rule in Spotlight in Raider-Chief Tie," *New York Times,* November 3, 1970, 43. The NFL later changed the rules to discourage a recurrence of what had happened in the Raiders-Chiefs game.

37. Joe McGuff, "Official Explains Call," *Kansas City Times,* November 2, 1970, 2C; Levitt, "The Big Rematch," 41.

38. See, for example, David Halberstam, *Summer of '49* (New York: Avon, 1990); Robert F. Garratt, *Home Team: The Turbulent History of the San Francisco Giants* (Lincoln: University of Nebraska Press, 2017).

39. See Filip Bondy, *The Pine Tar Game: The Kansas City Royals, the New York Yankees, and Baseball's Most Absurd and Entertaining Controversy* (New York: Scribner, 2015); Peter Richmond, *Badasses: The Legend of Snake, Foo, Dr. Death, and John Madden's Oakland Raiders* (New York: Harper, 2010).

40. See, for example, Richmond, *Badasses;* Jason Turbow, *Dynastic, Bombastic, Fantastic: Reggie, Rollie, Catfish, and Charlie Finley's Swingin' A's* (Boston: Houghton Mifflin Harcourt, 2017); Bob Gretz, *Tales from the Kansas City Chiefs Sideline* (New York: Sports Publishing, 2015); Steve Cameron, *Moments, Memories, Miracles: A Quarter Century with the Kansas City Royals* (Dallas: Taylor, 1992).

41. "The Origin of the Chiefs-Raiders Rivalry," *Chiefs.com,* 2016, available at https://www.youtube.com/watch?v=jcKy7nLzURc.

42. Bondy, *Pine Tar Game,* 51.

43. Jon C. Teaford, review of *City of Dreams: Dodger Stadium and the Birth of Modern Los Angeles,* by Jerald Podair, *American Historical Review* 122.5 (December 2017): 1648. For studies of other cities trying to change their image through big-league sports, see Jerald Podair, *City of Dreams: Dodger Stadium and the Birth of Modern Los Angeles* (Princeton, N.J.: Princeton University Press, 2017); William H. Mullins, *Becoming Big League: Seattle, the Pilots, and Stadium Politics* (Seattle: University of Washington Press, 2013).

44. Calvin Trillin, "A Reporter at Large: American Royal," *New Yorker,* September 26, 1983, 74.

45. Glen Gendzel, "Competitive Boosterism: How Milwaukee Lost the Braves," *Business History Review* 69 (Winter 1995): 531. See also John R. Logan and Harvey L. Molotch, *Urban Fortunes: The Political Economy of Place,* 20th anniversary ed. (Berkeley: University of California Press, 2007), 79–81.

46. Jon C. Teaford, *The 20th-Century American City: Problem, Promise, and Reality,* 3rd ed. (Baltimore: Johns Hopkins University Press, 2016), Kindle edition, chap. 8.

47. Michael N. Danielson, *Home Team: Professional Sports and the American Metropolis* (Princeton, N.J.: Princeton University Press, 1997), 110, 113.

48. James R. Shortridge, *Kansas City and How It Grew, 1822–2011* (Lawrence: University Press of Kansas, 2012), 204; Jim Miller and Kelly Mayhew, *Better to Reign in Hell: Inside the Raiders Fan Empire* (New York: New Press, 2005), Kindle edition. See also Marci D. Cottingham, "Interaction Ritual Theory and Sports Fans: Emotion, Symbols, and Solidarity," *Sociology of Sport Journal* 29 (2012): 168–85.

49. See, for example, James T. Bennett, *They Play, You Pay: Why Taxpayers Build Ballparks, Stadiums, and Arenas for Billionaire Owners and Millionaire Players* (New York: Copernicus, 2012).

50. Charles C. Euchner, *Playing the Field: Why Sports Teams Move and Cities Fight to Keep Them* (Baltimore: Johns Hopkins University Press, 1993), x.

51. George Lipsitz, *How Racism Takes Place* (Philadelphia: Temple University Press, 2011), Kindle edition, chap. 3.

52. See Robert A. Baade and Richard F. Dye, "The Impact of Stadiums and Professional Sports on Metropolitan Area Development," *Growth and Change* 21.2 (1990): 1–14.

53. Maria J. Veri, "Sons of Oakland: The Raiders and the Raz/Rais(ing) of a City," in *San Francisco Bay Area Sports: Golden Gate Athletics, Recreation, and Community,* ed. Rita Liberti and Maureen M. Smith (Fayetteville: University of Arkansas Press, 2017), 219. See also Ken Belson and Victor Mather, "Raiders Leaving Oakland Again, This Time for Las Vegas," *New York Times,* March 27, 2017, available at https://nyti.ms/2nFrhLL.

54. John Krich, *Bump City: Winners and Losers in Oakland* (Berkeley, Calif.: City Miner Books, 1979), 103.

55. Danielson, *Home Team,* 102.

Chapter 1. Striving for the Big Leagues

1. Lloyd Johnson, "Baseball in Kansas City," in *Unions to Royals: The Story of Professional Baseball in Kansas City,* ed. Lloyd Johnson, Steve Garlick, and Jeff Magalif (Manhattan, Kan.: AG Press, 1996), 2. Kansas City also hosted teams in the Union Association and the American Association, both of which were considered "major league" during the 1880s. In addition, the city had a team in the upstart Federal League in 1914–1915.

2. Darrell Garwood, *Crossroads of America: The Story of Kansas City* (New York: W.W. Norton, 1948), 321.

3. "Ten Lessons Kansas City Can Teach the Nation," *Coronet,* November 1955, 79.

4. Harry Haskell, *Boss-Busters and Sin Hounds: Kansas City and Its Star* (Columbia: University of Missouri Press, 2007), 331.

5. Ibid., 354–81.

6. George Ehrlich, *Kansas City, Missouri: An Architectural History, 1926–1990,* rev. and enl. ed. (Columbia: University of Missouri Press, 1992), 131. See also A. Theodore Brown and Lyle W. Dorsett, *K.C.: A History of Kansas City, Missouri* (Boulder, Colo.: Pruett, 1978), 253–62.

7. See Glen Gendzel, "Competitive Boosterism: How Milwaukee Lost the Braves," *Business History Review* 69 (Winter 1995): 530–66; Ernest Mehl, *The Kansas City Athletics* (New York: Henry Holt, 1956).

8. "Push for Majors," *Kansas City Star,* August 15, 1953, 2.

9. Bruce Clayton, *Praying for Base Hits: An American Boyhood* (Columbia: University of Missouri Press, 1998), 178. See also Johnson, "Baseball in Kansas City"; William A. Young, *J.L. Wilkinson and the Kansas City Monarchs: Trailblazers in Black Baseball* (Jefferson, N.C.: McFarland, 2016). Jackie Robinson also played for the Monarchs before breaking the major league color barrier with the Brooklyn Dodgers in 1947.

10. "Stadium and the Big Chance," *Kansas City Times,* August 14, 1953, 36; "Big League Uprising," *Kansas City Star,* August 25, 1953, 26. See also Jeff Katz, *The Kansas City A's and the Wrong Half of the Yankees* (Hingham, Mass.: Maple Street Press, 2007), Kindle edition, chap. 2.

11. "Push for Majors," *Kansas City Star,* August 15, 1953, 2.

12. Ernest Mehl, "Sporting Comment," *Kansas City Star,* September 30, 1953, 42; Ernest Mehl, "Sporting Comment," *Kansas City Star,* October 25, 1953, 2B.

13. C. E. McBride, "A Sports Cocktail," *Kansas City Times,* October 27, 1953, 17.

14. "Bond Vote Today," *Kansas City Times,* August 3, 1954, 1; Ernest Mehl, "Sporting Comment," *Kansas City Star,* August 3, 1954, 16. See also John E. Peterson, *The Kansas City Athletics: A Baseball History, 1954–1967* (Jefferson, N.C.: McFarland, 2003), Kindle edition, chap. 2; Katz, *Kansas City A's and the Wrong Half,* chap. 4; Mehl, *Kansas City Athletics,* 29–50.

15. Norman L. Macht, *The Grand Old Man of Baseball: Connie Mack in His Final Years, 1932–1956* (Lincoln: University of Nebraska Press, 2015), 533.

16. "It's a Home Run for Kansas City," *Kansas City Star,* October 13, 1954, 1. See also Macht, *Grand Old Man,* 521–70; Bruce Kuklick, *To Every Thing A Season: Shibe Park and Urban Philadelphia, 1909–1976* (Princeton, N.J.: Princeton University Press, 1991).

17. *The Kansas City A's in Action,* 1956, available at https://www.youtube.com/watch?v=dzEz0QexNEc. See also Bill Moore, "At Last, Opening Day," *Kansas City Times,* April 12, 1955, 1–2.

18. "A's-Yanks Deal Arouses Veeck," *Kansas City Star,* December 12, 1959, 8; Bill

Veeck with Ed Linn, *Veeck—As in Wreck* (Urbana: University of Illinois Press, 2001), 268.

19. See Jerald Podair, *City of Dreams: Dodger Stadium and the Birth of Modern Los Angeles* (Princeton, N.J.: Princeton University Press, 2017); Robert F. Garratt, *Home Team: The Turbulent History of the San Francisco Giants* (Lincoln: University of Nebraska Press, 2017); Neil J. Sullivan, *The Dodgers Move West* (New York: Oxford University Press, 1987); Lee Elihu Lowenfish, "A Tale of Many Cities: The Westward Expansion of Major League Baseball in the 1950s," *Journal of the West*, July 1978, 71–82.

20. Ernest Mehl, "A's Owner Rips Critics of His Trades," *Kansas City Times*, May 28, 1959, 8C.

21. Ernest Mehl, "Sporting Comment," *Kansas City Star*, March 10, 1960, 20. See also "Maris Would Rather Stay with the A's," *Kansas City Times*, December 12, 1959, 1, 34; Joe McGuff, "Arnold Johnson Dead," *Kansas City Times*, March 10, 1960, 1–2.

22. See Peterson, *Kansas City Athletics*, chap. 29.

23. Katz, *Kansas City A's and the Wrong Half*, chap. 2, chap. 13.

24. Ernest Mehl, "Sporting Comment," *Kansas City Star*, March 11, 1960, 29.

25. "Key to the A's at Turnstiles," *Kansas City Times*, July 22, 1960, 2.

26. See Peterson, *Kansas City Athletics*, chap. 15.

27. Joe McGuff, *Why Me? Why Not Joe McGuff?* (Independence, Mo.: Herald House, 1992), 158.

28. Peterson, *Kansas City Athletics*, chap. 17, chap. 30; Rex Lardner, "Charlie Finley and Bugs Bunny in K.C.," *Sports Illustrated*, June 5, 1961, available at https://www.si.com/vault.

29. See Joe McGuff, "Stadium Lease is Key to A's Future," *Kansas City Star*, August 18, 1961, 29; Harry Grayson, "Finley New Give-Away Plan Is Upsetting Other Owners," Chillicothe (Ohio) *Constitution-Tribune*, July 7, 1961, 2.

30. Ernest Mehl, "A's Ills Linked to Front Office Interference," *Kansas City Star*, August 17, 1961, 1–2.

31. "Finley 'Sick Enough' to Move out of K.C.?" *Detroit Free Press*, August 27, 1961, 4D. See also "Critics May Make A's Move—Finley," *Chicago Tribune*, August 19, 1961, C3.

32. See "Finley 'Salutes' Mehl," *Chicago Tribune*, August 21, 1961, C2.

33. See "Finley Seeks Frick Reversal," *Kansas City Times*, September 26, 1961, 16; "Finley Fires Frank Lane," *Kansas City Times*, August 23, 1961, 6.

34. See "Mehl Hurls First Pitch for Athletics," *Chicago Tribune*, April 11, 1962, C1; "Finley 'Sick Enough' to Move out of K.C.?"

35. Gene Fox, *Sports Guys* (Lenexa, Kan.: Addax, 1999), 74.

36. Jack Olsen, "Biggest Cheapskate in Big D," *Sports Illustrated*, June 19, 1972, available at https://www.si.com/vault.

37. Michael MacCambridge, *Lamar Hunt: A Life in Sports* (Kansas City, Mo.: Andrews McMeel, 2012), 107.

38. See Ibid., 109–30; Joe McGuff, *Winning It All: The Chiefs of the AFL* (Garden City, N.Y.: Doubleday, 1970), 33–72.

39. "A Pro Football Shift Possible," *Kansas City Times,* November 30, 1962, 14. See also Randy Covitz, "The Big Uneasy," *Kansas City Star,* August 29, 2004, 8; "Paper Reports Shift Proposals to Save A.F.L.," *Kansas City Times,* October 25, 1962, 10C.

40. James J. Fisher, "Bartle in Cloak-and-Dagger Role," *Kansas City Times,* May 23, 1963, 6A; "The Texans and Lamar Hunt: Big Assets to Area," *Kansas City Times,* May 23, 1963, 14D.

41. McGuff, *Winning It All,* 73. See also "Council Moves to Lure Texans," *Kansas City Times,* April 6, 1963, 1, 6.

42. Brown and Dorsett, *K.C.,* 261. See also "A's Owner for $1-A-Year Rent," *Kansas City Times,* March 9, 1963, 1, 8.

43. See James J. Fisher, "Aware of Pact Doubt," *Kansas City Times,* April 11, 1963, 1A–2A; "$1 A's Rental Plan Halted," *Kansas City Times,* April 12, 1963, 1.

44. G. Michael Green and Roger D. Launius, *Charlie Finley: The Outrageous Story of Baseball's Super Showman* (New York: Walker, 2010), Kindle edition, chap. 3; Peterson, *Kansas City Athletics,* chap. 22; Robert K. Sanford, "Grilling Heats Up Griddle Fete," *Kansas City Times,* May 23, 1963, 1A, 11A; McGuff, *Winning It All,* 78. See also Gendzel, "Competitive Boosterism," 551–58.

45. Bret Harte, *Stories and Poems* (London: Humphrey Milford, 1915), 502. See also Paul Brekke-Miesner, *Home Field Advantage* (Oakland, Calif.: Paul Brekke-Miesner, 2013), 11.

46. Beth Bagwell, *Oakland: The Story of a City* (Novato, Calif.: Presidio, 1982), 61.

47. Ibid., 254. See also Brekke-Miesner, *Home Field Advantage,* 11–18; Chris Rhomberg, *No There There: Race, Class, and Political Community in Oakland* (Berkeley: University of California Press, 2004), Kindle edition; Robert O. Self, *American Babylon: Race and the Struggle for Postwar Oakland* (Princeton, N.J.: Princeton University Press, 2003).

48. See Gayle B. Montgomery and James W. Johnson, *One Step from the White House: The Rise and Fall of Senator William F. Knowland* (Berkeley: University of California Press, 1998).

49. Edward C. Hayes, *Power Structure and Urban Policy: Who Rules in Oakland?* (New York: McGraw-Hill, 1972), 14, 190; Sol Stern, "Trouble in an 'All America City,'" *New York Times Magazine,* July 10, 1966, 22.

50. Bill and Nancy Boyarsky, *Backroom Politics* (Los Angeles: J.P. Tarcher, 1974), 195.

51. Rodney W. Stark, "Policy and the Pros: An Organizational Analysis of a

Metropolitan Newspaper," *Berkeley Journal of Sociology* 7.1 (Spring 1962): 15. Stark did not identify the newspaper in his article, but years later he confirmed that it was the *Tribune* (Rodney Stark, personal communication, June 7, 2017). See also *Discover the Friendly City—Oakland* (Oakland, Calif.: Oakland Economic Development Council, 1970), Oakland History Room, Oakland Public Library.

52. Montgomery and Johnson, *One Step from the White House,* 291. See also Frank Deford, "A City of Complexes," *Sports Illustrated,* April 1, 1968, available at https://www.si.com/vault.

53. Stern, "Trouble in an 'All America City'," 21; William F. Knowland, "Oakland Defended" (letter to the editor), *New York Times Magazine,* September 4, 1966, 12. See also "Key to the A's at Turnstiles," *Kansas City Times,* July 22, 1960, 2.

54. Brekke-Miesner, *Home Field Advantage,* 46. See also Paul J. Zingg and Mark D. Medeiros, *Runs, Hits, and an Era: The Pacific Coast League, 1903–58* (Urbana: University of Illinois Press, 1994), 110–12.

55. "SF-Oakland Rivalry Is Stirred Anew," *Daily Review* (Hayward, Calif.), January 29, 1960, 10; "Knowland Hails Grid Team Here," *Oakland Tribune,* January 31, 1960, 57. The Los Angeles Chargers moved to San Diego in 1961; they moved back to Los Angeles in 2017.

56. See "Grid Team Named 'Oakland Señors'," *Oakland Tribune,* April 5, 1960, 1; Alan Ward, "'Raiders' Rated as Solid Name," *Oakland Tribune,* April 15, 1960, 42.

57. Jeff Faraudo, "A Modest Beginning: Oakland Raiders Made Their AFL Debut 50 Years Ago Today," *Oakland Tribune,* September 10, 2010, Sports sec.; "Stadium Proposal Renews Hope for Major Loop Club," *Oakland Tribune,* November 4, 1960, 41.

58. See "Voters May Get Bid for Playing Site," *Oakland Tribune,* January 31, 1960, 57, 63; Dave Hope, "Site Dispute Slows Action on Stadium," *Oakland Tribune,* February 7, 1960, 1, 4; "Stadium Plans Get Big Boost," *Oakland Tribune,* December 6, 1960, 1, 10; "Stadium Backers Plan Financing," *Oakland Tribune,* December 7, 1960, 6; Ed Schoenfeld, "Sports Arena Takes Major Step Ahead," *Oakland Tribune,* March 17, 1961, 1, 53. See also Harriet Sternsher, *The Oakland-Alameda County Coliseum Complex,* March 4, 1967, Institute of Governmental Studies Library, University of California, Berkeley; Boyarsky, *Backroom Politics,* 189–203.

59. Ed Schoenfeld, "Nahas Honored at Coliseum Luncheon," *Oakland Tribune,* January 11, 1967, 2; John F. Lawrence, "Oakland Uses Sports to Give It an Image as a Big League City," *Wall Street Journal,* December 29, 1967, 3. See also Boyarsky, *Backroom Politics,* 196–97.

60. See "Oakland May Lose AFL Franchise," *News-Press* (Fort Myers, Fla.), November 3, 1961, 3B; "Easy Access and Lots of Parking Make Frank Youell Field a Gem," *Oakland Tribune,* August 22, 1962, 40; "A Pro Football Shift Possible";

"Civic Drive Ends Talk of Sale," *The Times* (San Mateo, Calif.), November 29, 1962, 21.

61. Ed Schoenfeld, "Council Flashes 'Go' on Stadium," *Oakland Tribune*, February 28, 1962, 1, 40; "Coliseum Near Realization," *Oakland Tribune*, March 1, 1962, 21.

62. Deford, "A City of Complexes"; George Ross, "Oakland on the Move," February 28, 1962, 35. See also Ed Schoenfeld, "Coliseum OK'd by Supervisors," *Oakland Tribune*, March 6, 1962, 1, 28.

63. "Alameda County Moves Forward," *Oakland Tribune*, March 11, 1962, FL9. See also Joan McKinney, "Bob Nahas—He Had a Dream," *Oakland Tribune*, June 13, 1976, People sec., 15, 17.

64. The *Tribune* touted the Coliseum's benefits in multiple articles in January–February 1963. See "Oakland—Stadium: 1962–1963" folder, Oakland History Room, Oakland Public Library.

65. See "Vote Ruled Out on Coliseum Approval," *Oakland Tribune*, March 29, 1963, 1–2; "Coliseum Project Opposition Wanes," *Oakland Tribune*, April 1, 1963, 1–2; George Ross, "We Get a Coliseum! Approval Opens Way for Majors," *Oakland Tribune*, April 9, 1963, 33–34.

66. Gerald Sturges, "Coliseum Sparks a New Boom," *Oakland Tribune*, May 3, 1964, 1. See also "Coliseum Demurrer Suit Filed," *Oakland Tribune*, December 11, 1963, 1, 7; George Ross, "Officials Hail Coliseum Decision," *Oakland Tribune*, December 27, 1963, 33, 35; Ed Schoenfeld, "Coliseum Hurdles Last Legal Bar," *Oakland Tribune*, February 25, 1964, 1–2; Ed Schoenfeld, "Ground Broken for Coliseum Complex," *Oakland Tribune*, May 15, 1964, 1–2.

67. See Fred Garretson, "Coliseum Magnet for A.L. Ball Team," *Oakland Tribune*, January 31, 1963, 14.

68. See Peterson, *Kansas City Athletics*, chap. 22; Leonard Koppett, "Athletics Deny Report on Shift," *New York Times*, July 9, 1963, 34; Bill Becker, "Oakland Appears Set to Build 2 Stadiums to Get One Ball Club," *New York Times*, August 4, 1963, 141.

69. William F. Woo, "Winter Rhubarb in Kansas City," *St. Louis Post-Dispatch*, Everyday Magazine, January 12, 1964, 1, 7. See also Peterson, *Kansas City Athletics*, chap. 22.

70. Ernest Mehl, "Sporting Comment," *Kansas City Star*, January 6, 1964, 8; George Ross, "Nod from A.L. Would Unroll Oakland Red Carpet for Finley," *Sporting News*, February 8, 1964, 6.

71. Frank Graham Jr., "Happiness Is Being Somewhere Else," *Saturday Evening Post*, April 4, 1964, 77. See also "Oakland's $6.5 Million Bid to Buy Indians Rejected," *New York Times*, September 24, 1964, 53.

72. See Peterson, *Kansas City Athletics*, chap. 32.

73. "Beatles Press Conference: Kansas City 9/17/1964," *Beatles Ultimate Experi-*

ence, available at http://www.beatlesinterviews.org. The Beatles had just played a one-nighter in New Orleans but had had no chance to tour the city. See also Peterson, *Kansas City Athletics,* chap. 17, 21, 23; Green and Launius, *Charlie Finley,* chap. 3; Lardner, "Charlie Finley and Bugs Bunny."

74. Bill James, *The Bill James Baseball Abstract 1986* (New York: Ballantine, 1986), 45; Bud Simpson, "Tall, Green and Handsome," *Northeast News* (Kansas City, Mo.), February 8, 2006, 4. See also Joe Posnanski, "Charlie, Oh! A's Became the Joke of the Baseball World After Their Move to KC Half A Century Ago," *Kansas City Star,* July 10, 2005, C8.

75. See McGuff, *Winning It All,* 78–79.

76. Although Native American sports imagery was not widely controversial among white sports fans in the early 1960s, the National Congress of American Indians had begun campaigning against demeaning depictions as early as the 1940s. By the 1970s, Native American activist Russell Means was suing to try to eliminate such sports caricatures as the Cleveland Indians' "Chief Wahoo." See, for example, J. Gordon Hylton, "Before the Redskins Were the Redskins: The Use of Native American Team Names in the Formative Era of American Sports, 1857–1933," *North Dakota Law Review* 86 (2010): 879–903; Russell Schneider, "Indians' Wahoo Symbol Facing a Legal Skirmish," *Sporting News,* February 5, 1972, 43.

77. MacCambridge, *Lamar Hunt,* 144. See also McGuff, *Winning It All,* 78–103.

78. "The Chiefs' First Training Camp," *Kansas City Star Video,* August 15, 2014, available at https://www.youtube.com/watch?v=-6tEuokJDZE.

79. McGuff, *Winning It All,* 80, 103–7; John Hall, "The Chief Appraiser," *Los Angeles Times,* June 16, 1965, pt. 3, 3. See also Bill Richardson, "Klosterman Had No Choice," *Kansas City Times,* January 6, 1966, 2D.

80. "Stadium Plan a Popular Idea," *Kansas City Times,* July 2, 1965, 5; Sid Bordman, "New Stadium Here Looms As Necessity to Preserve Pro Franchises," *Kansas City Times,* October 5, 1965, 13; Michael J. Kelley, "Cities to View Baseball Aims," *Kansas City Times,* November 26, 1965, 3.

81. Gendzel, "Competitive Boosterism," 553.

82. Wells Twombly, "Even the Mule Wore a Grin," *Sporting News,* November 11, 1972, 8; George Ross, "Oakland, You're Beautiful," *Oakland Tribune,* September 18, 1966, 47. See also Ed Schoenfeld, "$2 Million Cut Ordered in Coliseum Plans," *Oakland Tribune,* April 3, 1964, 49; George Ross, "Eastbay Goes Major League," *Oakland Tribune,* September 13, 1966, 3A–5A.

83. George Ross, "Man Who Shook AFL Charms Oakland," *Oakland Tribune,* January 21, 1964, 33; "'Hopeful Optimism' for Stadium Start," *Oakland Tribune,* January 21, 1964, 33.

84. See Michael McKenzie, *Arrowhead: Home of the Chiefs* (Lenexa, Kan.: Addax, 1997); Robert W. Lewis, *The Harry S. Truman Sports Complex: Rocky Road*

to the Big Leagues, June 1977, Missouri Valley Special Collections, Kansas City Public Library. See also Robert C. Trumpbour and Kenneth Womack, *The Eighth Wonder of the World: The Life of Houston's Iconic Astrodome* (Lincoln: University of Nebraska Press, 2016).

85. See McKenzie, *Arrowhead;* Lewis, *Harry S. Truman Sports Complex.* See also "Multi-purpose Stadium," *Wikipedia,* available at https://en.wikipedia.org.

86. Lewis, *Harry S. Truman Sports Complex,* 34.

87. Joe McGuff, "Sporting Comment," *Kansas City Star,* June 26, 1967, 12. See also "Bonds Would Keep Area Momentum Going," *Kansas City Star,* June 25, 1967, 1A; Michael J. Kelley, "Voters Say 'Yes' to All Bonds," *Kansas City Times,* June 28, 1967, 1A–2A.

88. Joe McGuff, "Sporting Comment," *Kansas City Star,* June 28, 1967, 1D; Fritz Kreisler, "Slumping A's Called 'Snake-Bitten' by Dark," *Kansas City Star,* June 27, 1967, 11. See also William Leggett, "Dark's Outlook Is Young and Bright," *Sports Illustrated,* March 13, 1967, available at https://www.si.com/vault.

89. "A's Fans Wait at Air Terminal," *Kansas City Star,* August 24, 1967, 1. See also Brent Musburger, "The Charlie O. Finley Follies," *Sports Illustrated,* September 4, 1967, 50–52.

90. Ed Schoenfeld, "Finley Picks Oakland For A's," *Oakland Tribune,* October 11, 1967, 1.

91. Fox, *Sports Guys,* 73.

92. Bart Everett, "A Scowl Is Worth 1,000 Words," *Kansas City Star,* October 22, 1967, 1A, 6A.

93. Ibid.; Fox, *Sports Guys,* 73–74. See also Gendzel, "Competitive Boosterism." After just one season in Seattle, the new expansion team the Pilots would move to Milwaukee in 1970 and become the Brewers.

94. Bob Valli, "Nahas Can Be Smug for 24 Hours," *Oakland Tribune,* October 19, 1967, 39; Joe McGuff, "City's One-Year 'Exile' Not Ideal, But May Be the Only Solution," *Kansas City Star,* October 19, 1967, 1A–2A.

95. See endnote 4 in the introduction.

96. 90 Cong. Rec. 29460 (1967) (statement of Sen. Symington); 90 Cong. Rec. 29473 (1967) (statement of Sen. Murphy).

97. Ron Bergman, "Finley Charm Sweeps Oakland Off Its Feet," *Sporting News,* November 11, 1967, 29.

98. Ibid.; "Joe DiMaggio 'Hitting Well' As Oakland Athletics' Veep," *News Journal* (Mansfield, Oh.), December 3, 1967, 4C.

Chapter 2. Chiefs vs. Raiders, Part I

1. Samuel J. Skinner Jr., "Kansas City Athletics Should Mean Jobs for Blacks," *Sun-Reporter* (San Francisco), October 21, 1967, 49; "Black Representation Missing in Oakland," *Sun-Reporter,* October 21, 1967, 51.

2. See Harvey Frommer, *When It Was Just a Game: Remembering the First Super Bowl* (Lanham, Md.: Taylor Trade, 2015), 147–48.

3. Jack Etkin, *Innings Ago: Recollections by Kansas City Ballplayers of their Days in the Game* (Kansas City, Mo.: Normandy Square, 1987), 10. See also Charles E. Coulter, *Take Up the Burden: Kansas City's African American Communities, 1865–1939* (Columbia: University of Missouri Press, 2006).

4. *Crossroads: A Story of West Oakland*, KQED-TV, 1996, available at https://www.youtube.com/watch?v=-M6ZO0W8Tbo. See also Donna Jean Murch, *Living for the City: Migration, Education, and the Rise of the Black Panther Party in Oakland, California* (Chapel Hill: University of North Carolina Press, 2010), Kindle edition, chap. 1.

5. Chris Rhomberg, *No There There: Race, Class, and Political Community in Oakland* (Berkeley: University of California Press, 2004), Kindle edition, chap. 3. See also Robert O. Self, *American Babylon: Race and the Struggle for Postwar Oakland* (Princeton, N.J.: Princeton University Press, 2003), 135–76.

6. Roy Wilkins with Tom Mathews, *Standing Fast: The Autobiography of Roy Wilkins* (New York: Viking, 1982), 60–61. See also Sherry Lamb Schirmer, *A City Divided: The Racial Landscape of Kansas City, 1900–1960* (Columbia: University of Missouri Press, 2002); G. S. Griffin, *Racism in Kansas City: A Short History* (Traverse City, Mich.: Chandler Lake Books, 2015); Kevin Fox Gotham, *Race, Real Estate, and Uneven Development: The Kansas City Experience, 1900–2010*, 2nd ed. (Albany, N.Y.: SUNY Press, 2014).

7. *Full Color Football: The History of the American Football League*, part 2, NFL Films, 2009, available at https://www.youtube.com/watch?v=16OJrm7CRrA; Randy Covitz, "Chiefs' Former Defensive Tackle to Be Inducted in August," *Kansas City Star*, January 28, 1990, 27A. See also Charles K. Ross, *Mavericks, Money, and Men: The AFL, Black Players, and the Evolution of Modern Football* (Philadelphia: Temple University Press, 2016); Gerald B. Jordan, "Bell Rings an End to Chiefs' Career," *Kansas City Times*, September 10, 1975, 1C, 3C; Joe McGuff, *Winning It All: The Chiefs of the AFL* (Garden City, N.Y.: Doubleday, 1970), 108–32.

8. Michael MacCambridge, *America's Game: The Epic Story of How Pro Football Captured a Nation* (New York: Random House, 2004), 198; McGuff, *Winning It All*, 74.

9. Bobby Bell, "Not-So-Welcome Wagon," *Kansas City Star*, August 29, 2004, 2. See also William S. Worley, *J. C. Nichols and the Shaping of Kansas City* (Columbia: University of Missouri Press, 1990); Judy L. Thomas, "'Curse of Covenant' Persists," *Kansas City Star*, February 13, 2005, A1.

10. Self, *American Babylon*, 161.

11. Monte Poole, "Former Raider Clem Daniels' Impact Goes Well Beyond Football," *Oakland Tribune*, March 1, 2012. See also Self, *American Babylon*, 100–111, 162–63.

12. Mark Ribowsky, *Slick: The Silver and Black Life of Al Davis* (New York: Macmillan, 1991), 127; Ross, *Mavericks, Money, and Men,* 60. See also Peter Richmond, *Badasses: The Legend of Snake, Foo, Dr. Death, and John Madden's Oakland Raiders* (New York: HarperCollins, 2010), 36–37.

13. *Full Color Football,* part 5, available at https://www.youtube.com/watch?v=1Uce_n4tXxc.

14. Richmond, *Badasses,* 48–49. See also Jack Olsen, *The Black Athlete, A Shameful Story* (New York: Time-Life Books, 1968), 179–80; Ribowsky, *Slick,* 143–44; McGuff, *Winning It All,* 95–97.

15. See "For Ordinance on Fair Rental," *Kansas City Times,* October 30, 1965, 1, 6; Kent Pulliam, "McClinton's Strength Is Game of Life," *Kansas City Star,* February 26, 1995, C1; Calvin Trillin, "U.S. Journal: Kansas City," *New Yorker,* May 11, 1968, 107–14; John T. Dauner, "Fair Housing Now Law," *Kansas City Times,* April 20, 1968, 1A, 8A.

16. See Poole, "Former Raider Clem Daniels' Impact"; Angela Woodall, "Owner of Oakland's Serenader Bar Dies at Age 77," *Oakland Tribune,* February 12, 2009; Ribowsky, *Slick,* 144; Jerry McDonald, "Art Powell and His Raiders Legacy," *Oakland Tribune,* April 8, 2015.

17. "A.F.L. Blasted for Site Move," *Kansas City Times,* January 12, 1965, 13; Bill Nunn Jr., "Change of Pace," *Pittsburgh Courier,* January 23, 1965, 23. See also Ross, *Mavericks, Money, and Men,* 73–76.

18. Ron Mix, "Was This Their Freedom Ride?" *Sports Illustrated,* January 18, 1965, 24–25.

19. *Full Color Football,* part 2.

20. Otis Taylor with Mark Stallard, *Otis Taylor: The Need to Win* (Champaign, Ill.: Sports Publishing, 2003), 53; Gerald Astor, "Big Little Chief," *Look,* November 14, 1967, 115.

21. See MacCambridge, *America's Game,* 130–34, 197–227; McGuff, *Winning It All,* 108–14, 130–32; Joe McGuff, "Sporting Comment," *Kansas City Star,* October 19, 1970, 11.

22. MacCambridge, *America's Game,* 228–30.

23. Edwin Shrake, "Thunder out of Oakland," *Sports Illustrated,* November 15, 1965, available at https://www.si.com/vault; Wells Twombly, "Davis Is Spoiling for a Fight," *Sporting News,* May 9, 1970, 52. See also Ribowsky, *Slick,* 161–76.

24. Ribowsky, *Slick,* 112. See also Glenn Dickey, *Just Win, Baby: Al Davis and His Raiders* (Orlando, Fla.: Harcourt Brace Jovanovich, 1991).

25. *Full Color Football,* part 2; "Chris Burford: 'I'd Never Hit a Little Guy!'" *Kansas City Town Squire,* November 8, 1968, 9. See also Gene Fox, *Sports Guys* (Lenexa, Kan.: Addax, 1999), 120–21; McGuff, *Winning It All,* 191–93.

26. Lamar Hunt, "Introduction," in Fox, *Sports Guys,* 8. See also McGuff, *Winning It All,* 59–107, 154–60.

27. Joe McGuff, "Sporting Comment," *Kansas City Star,* January 2, 1967, 18. See also Eugene Kozicharow, "Wolves Wail As Chiefs Prevail," *Kansas City Times,* November 29, 1965, 1–2; Edwin Shrake, "Four-Legged Halfbacks and Friendly Wolves," *Sports Illustrated,* November 28, 1966, available at https://www.si.com /vault; McGuff, *Winning It All,* 170.

28. "Ex-Raider Slams Davis," *Oakland Tribune,* April 12, 1965, 31; "Can They Pack Up the Packers?" *Life,* January 13, 1967, 72. See also Bill Richardson, "Stram Lauds Chiefs' Hurston," *Kansas City Star,* October 9, 1965, 6; Bill Richardson, "Frank Jackson Gets In Parting Words," *Kansas City Star,* July 16, 1966, 6; McGuff, *Winning It All,* 94–95, 98.

29. Tex Maule, "Stop Those Chiefs!" *Sports Illustrated,* January 16, 1967, available at https://www.si.com/vault; Frommer, *When It Was Just a Game,* 147– 48, 223–24; *Full Color Football,* part 3, available at https://www.youtube.com /watch?v=f5hTkCmK42M; McGuff, *Winning It All,* 185–86.

30. Joe McGuff, "Sporting Comment," *Kansas City Star,* August 24, 1967, 19. See also Michael J. Satchell, "Fans Overflow—Chiefs Overpower," *Kansas City Times,* August 24, 1967, 1A, 20A.

31. Dave Anderson, "Raiders 'Outcasts' Have Biggest Day, Routing Oilers, 40–7, for A.F.L. Crown," *New York Times,* January 1, 1968, 19; Edwin Shrake, "A Big Raid That Really Paid Off," *Sports Illustrated,* November 13, 1967, available at https://www.si.com/vault.

32. Ed Levitt, "Valley of Gold for 49ers?" *Oakland Tribune,* April 8, 1976, 39; Sol Stern, "Trouble in an 'All America City'," *New York Times Magazine,* July 10, 1966, 21; Anderson, "Raiders 'Outcasts' Have Biggest Day," 19. See also Ribowsky, *Slick,* 201.

33. Tex Maule, "A Romp for the Pack," *Sports Illustrated,* January 15, 1968, available at https://www.si.com/vault; Ribowsky, *Slick,* 207; Tex Maule, "Green Bay, Handily," *Sports Illustrated,* January 22, 1968, available at https://www.si.com /vault.

34. Self, *American Babylon,* 183–84. See also Rhomberg, *No There There,* chap. 7; Bill and Nancy Boyarsky, *Backroom Politics* (Los Angeles: J.P. Tarcher, 1974), 189–203.

35. "What We Want/What We Believe," *Black Panther,* July 26, 1969, 22. See also Jane Rhodes, *Framing the Black Panthers: The Spectacular Rise of a Black Power Icon* (Urbana: University of Illinois Press, 2017), Kindle edition, chap. 3–6.

36. "Off-Duty Pig's Last Act-of-Terror," *Black Panther,* August 2, 1969, 15. See also Griffin, *Racism in Kansas City,* 87–99; Steve Penn, *Case for a Pardon: The Pete O'Neal Story* (Shawnee, Kan.: PennBooks, 2013).

37. Amory Bradford, *Oakland's Not for Burning* (New York: David McKay, 1968), 200–201; "Our Community Challenged," *Oakland Tribune,* May 8, 1968, 1; "Citizens Pledged Against Coercion," *Oakland Tribune,* May 20, 1968, 3.

38. See Griffin, *Racism in Kansas City*, 128–29. See also Joel P. Rhodes, "It Finally Happened Here: The 1968 Riot in Kansas City, Missouri," *Missouri Historical Review* 91.3 (April 1997): 295–315; Eric Juhnke, "A City Awakened: The Kansas City Race Riot of 1968," *Gateway Heritage*, Winter 1999–2000, 32–43.

39. Lucile H. Bluford, "Many Questions on Police Action in Riots," *Kansas City Call*, April 19–April 25, 1968, 1.

40. See Taylor with Stallard, *Otis Taylor*, 99–103; Bill Richardson, "Chiefs' Stars Get Jump on March," *Kansas City Times*, April 11, 1968, 20; Olsen, *The Black Athlete*, 23–24.

41. "Citizens Join in Plea for End to Violence," *Kansas City Times*, April 12, 1968, 10. See also "Suffering a Back Injury," *Kansas City Star*, February 8, 1968, 2; Bill Richardson, "Chiefs Put Hammer on Williamson," *Kansas City Times*, February 16, 1968, 1B.

42. Alex Haley, *The Playboy Interviews*, edited with an introduction by Murray Fisher (New York: Ballantine, 1993). Haley's interview with Brown was originally published in *Playboy* in February 1968. See also "Curtis McClinton Scoring in New Job," *Sedalia Democrat*, August 8, 1971, 9A.

43. Harry Edwards, *The Revolt of the Black Athlete*, 50th anniversary ed. (Urbana: University of Illinois Press, 2017), 97.

44. Ibid., 30.

45. Michael MacCambridge, *The Franchise: A History of* Sports Illustrated *Magazine* (New York: Hyperion, 1997), 158–64.

46. Olsen, *The Black Athlete*, 27–28, 143–49, 173, 179.

47. Ibid., 177. See also Taylor with Stallard, *Otis Taylor*, 158; Paige Ricks, "Spotlight: Chris Burford, '60," *Stanford Magazine*, January/February 2011, available at https://stanfordmag.org/contents/the-rookies.

48. See Michael MacCambridge, *Lamar Hunt: A Life in Sports* (Kansas City, Mo.: Andrews McMeel, 2012), 194.

49. Ribowsky, *Slick*, 212, McGuff, *Winning It All*, 198.

50. Bill Richardson, "Chiefs T Party Spills Oakland," *Kansas City Star*, October 21, 1968, 19; Dick Mackey, "Stram's Full House Finds Raiders Asleep," *Kansas City Times*, October 21, 1968, 3C.

51. George Ross, "'Raiders' Best Ever Game,' Says Rauch," *Oakland Tribune*, November 4, 1968, 48; Tom Marshall, "This Was Bound to Come—Stram," *Kansas City Times*, November 4, 1968, 1C.

52. See Thomas Rogers, "Jets Cut for 'Heidi'; TV Fans Complain," *New York Times*, November 18, 1968, 1, 61; Jeff Miller, *Going Long: The Wild 10-Year Saga of the American Football League in the Words of Those Who Lived It* (Chicago: Contemporary Books, 2003), 289.

53. McGuff, *Winning It All*, 202–5; Bob Valli, "Raiders in Title Battle," *Oakland Tribune*, December 23, 1968, 29.

54. *Rebels with a Cause: The Story of the American Football League,* HBO Sports, 1995, available at https://www.youtube.com/watch?v=h8cW9ig8kCk.

55. John Madden with Dave Anderson, *Hey, Wait a Minute, I Wrote a Book!* (New York: Villard, 1984), 65–66. See also Bryan Burwell, *Madden: A Biography* (Chicago: Triumph Books, 2011), 69–70.

56. "Hank Stram," *Kansas City Town Squire,* July 1970, 20; Tom Leathers, "'Hair' May Be Hot on the Broadway Stage, But It's Not on the Football Field," *Kansas City Town Squire,* October 1969, 5. See also Bob Gretz, *Tales from the Kansas City Chiefs Sideline* (New York: Sports Publishing, 2015), Kindle edition, chap. 7.

57. Larry Felser, "AFL," *Sporting News,* August 16, 1969, 50. See also McGuff, *Winning It All,* 208.

58. George Ross, "From Omnipotence to Futility," *Oakland Tribune,* November 24, 1969, 52; Blaine Newnham, "Round 1 to Raiders," *Oakland Tribune,* November 24, 1969, 53.

59. McGuff, *Winning It All,* 226. See also Ed Levitt, "Cave-Man Football," *Oakland Tribune,* December 14, 1969, 53, 56.

60. See Dickey, *Just Win, Baby,* 78–79; Miller, *Going Long,* 337–39.

61. McGuff, *Winning It All,* 232–33. See also "50 Million Fans to Watch Raiders," *Oakland Tribune,* January 4, 1970, 45.

62. See the introduction for a discussion of these plays.

63. See Miller, *Going Long,* 341–43.

64. "Most of Raiders Like K.C. Chances," *Oakland Tribune,* January 5, 1970, 43; "Misquoted, Says Blanda," *Oakland Tribune,* January 6, 1970, 33–34. See also "QB Forgot Me—Biletnikoff," *Pittsburgh Post-Gazette,* January 7, 1970, 19.

65. Dave Anderson, "The Heat Is on Lenny the Cool," *New York Times,* January 11, 1970, sec. 5, 1.

66. Dick Gordon, "Grant 'Can't Stand the Luxury of Emotions,'" *Sporting News,* December 6, 1969, 29; Frommer, *When It Was Just a Game,* 71. See also "Hank Stram—Steve Sabol," *Chiefs Insider,* 2012, at https://www.youtube.com /watch?v=YVEQnRy5Ttw; Travis Vogan, *Keepers of the Flame: NFL Films and the Rise of Sports Media* (Urbana: University of Illinois Press, 2014).

67. "The Super Bowl" (Super Bowl IV), NFL Films, 1970, available at https:// www.youtube.com/watch?v=ujXDNwqeXo4.

68. "1969 Kansas City Chiefs," *America's Game: The Super Bowl Champions,* NFL Films, 2006; Michael J. Satchell, "Jubilant on Top of Football World," *Kansas City Times,* January 13, 1970, 1A; Charles Hammer, "Victory Makes a Cow Town Walk Tall," *Kansas City Star,* January 18, 1970, 27H; Gary D. Warner, "Chiefs Happy for Selves—and Len Dawson," *Kansas City Times,* January 12, 1970, 1C. See also "Empty Roads, Few Police Calls Are Signs of a Town Enraptured," *Kansas City Times,* January 12, 1970, 1A, 9A.

69. Joe McGuff, "Stram Finds Vindication for His Football System," *Kansas City Times,* January 12, 1970, 1C–2C; Dick Wade, "Stram Accepts Super Moment in Super Style," *Kansas City Star,* January 12, 1970, 3C.

Chapter 3. A's vs. Royals, Part I

1. Jim Bouton, *Ball Four* (New York: Dell, 1971), 1–9, 82, 357.

2. David Condon, "In the Wake of the News," *Chicago Tribune,* December 21, 1967, D1. See also Paul O'Neil, "You're A Good Man, Charlie O.," *Life,* September 6, 1968, 68–74.

3. See Paul Brekke-Miesner, *Home Field Advantage* (Oakland, Calif.: Paul Brekke-Miesner, 2013), 32–56.

4. George Ross, "The Day the A's Come West," *Oakland Tribune,* April 14, 1968, 3A. See also Ron Bergman, "Oakland Park Excellent—But Crowds Aren't," *Sporting News,* May 4, 1968, 7; "Hunter of A's Pitches Perfect Game!" *Chicago Tribune,* May 9, 1968, C1, C4; Jim "Catfish" Hunter and Armen Keteyian, *Catfish: My Life in Baseball* (New York: McGraw-Hill, 1988), 3.

5. George Langford, "New Oakland A's in Struggle at the Gate," *Chicago Tribune,* May 11, 1968, 2. See also Ron Bergman, "A's Anchored in Oakland—But What about Seals?" *Sporting News,* January 30, 1971, 35.

6. Wells Twombly, "It's Show Time at Finley Funhouse," *Sporting News,* May 2, 1970, 13.

7. See Ron Bergman, "Service Rotten in A's Stadium, Finley Bellows," *Sporting News,* June 1, 1968, 17; George Ross, "Winning Record," *Oakland Tribune,* September 30, 1968, 38; Ron Bergman, "Finley Hits Roof When Nash Mutters about Moving," *Sporting News,* May 31, 1969, 10. See also Roy Blount Jr., "Out! Short to Yellow to Red," *Sports Illustrated,* March 30, 1970, available at http://www.si.com/vault; Shirley Povich, "Charlie O. Finley Always Has the Last Word," *Washington Post,* May 28, 1984, C1, C7.

8. Bowie Kuhn, *Hardball: The Education of a Baseball Commissioner* (New York: TimesBooks, 1987), 226. See also Alan T. Demaree, "Ewing Kauffman Sold Himself Rich in Kansas City," *Fortune,* October 1972, 98–103; "M as in Money," *Time,* December 1, 1967, 110, 113.

9. Tom Leathers, "The Kauffmans," *Kansas City Town Squire,* May 1971, 16. See also Frank Deford, "It Ain't Necessarily So, and Never Was," *Sports Illustrated,* March 6, 1972, available at https://www.si.com/vault; Joe McGuff, "Fast-Moving Royals Junk Timetable," *Sporting News,* September 25, 1971, 11, 16; Steve Cameron, *Moments, Memories, Miracles: A Quarter Century with the Kansas City Royals* (Dallas: Taylor, 1992), 90.

10. "Angels' Tallis May Be K.C.'s Vice President," *Chicago Tribune,* January 17, 1968, C2; Joe McGuff, "Sporting Comment," *Kansas City Star,* April 9, 1969, 6C.

See also Sid Bordman, "Royals Set A.L. Season-Ducat Mark," *Sporting News,* November 2, 1968, 45; Joe McGuff, "$3 Million Air Pact to Bolster Royals in Their '69 A.L. Debut," *Sporting News,* June 1, 1968, 17; Denny Matthews and Fred White with Matt Fulks, *Play by Play: 25 Years of Royals on Radio* (Kansas City, Mo.: Addax, 1999), 59–61.

11. *Rebels of Oakland,* HBO Sports, 2003, Paley Center for Media, New York City; Bob Oates, *60 Years of Winners* (Fairfield, Iowa: Granger, 1996), 124.

12. Reggie Jackson with Mike Lupica, *Reggie: The Autobiography* (New York: Villard, 1984), 64, 74; Mark Mulvoy, "Maris and the Babe, Move Over!" *Sports Illustrated,* July 7, 1969, available at https://www.si.com/vault; Dayn Perry, *Reggie Jackson: The Life and Thunderous Career of Baseball's Mr. October* (New York: William Morrow, 2010), 59, 110. See also "The Fence-Busters," *Time,* July 25, 1969, 48; "The Big A," *Newsweek,* July 7, 1969, 84; "Home Run King Reggie Jackson," *Ebony,* October 1969, 92–100.

13. Ron Bergman, "Jackson to Minors? 'No,' Storms Reggie," *Sporting News,* June 6, 1970, 20. See also Ron Bergman, "Finley vs. Reggie: A Hot Duel It Was!" *Sporting News,* April 11, 1970, 40.

14. Ron Bergman, "Dick Williams on Finley's Firing Line; McNamara Axing Blamed on Duncan," *Sporting News,* October 17, 1970, 25. See also Bill Richardson, "Finley Sees Stars on A's," *Kansas City Times,* April 8, 1970, 1A, 17A; Ron Bergman, "Jackson's Added Blast," *Oakland Tribune,* September 6, 1970, 17–18; Ron Bergman, "Reggie and Charlie Kiss and Make Up, or Do They?" *Sporting News,* September 26, 1970, 19.

15. Joe McGuff, "Gordon Tells Why He Quit Kaycee Post," *Sporting News,* October 25, 1969, 23; Joe McGuff, "Royals' Gate Plunges by 200,000," *Sporting News,* October 17, 1970, 32. See also Roy Blount Jr., "Tale of the Derailed Metro," *Sports Illustrated,* June 22, 1970, available at https://www.si.com/vault; Charlie Metro with Tom Altherr, *Safe by a Mile* (Lincoln: University of Nebraska Press, 2002), 337.

16. McGuff, "Royals' Gate Plunges," 32.

17. See "The Kansas City Labor History Tour," Worker Education and Labor Studies (WELS) Program, Institute for Labor Studies, University of Missouri–Kansas City, available at http://cas2.umkc.edu/labor-ed/history.htm.

18. See Albert Vetere Lannon, *Fight or Be Slaves: The History of the Oakland–East Bay Labor Movement* (Lanham, Md.: University Press of America, 2000), 65–68, 106–14; Chris Rhomberg, *No There There: Race, Class, and Political Community in Oakland* (Berkeley: University of California Press, 2004), Kindle edition, chap. 5.

19. Lannon, *Fight or Be Slaves,* 141. See also Rhomberg, *No There There,* chap. 5; Charles P. Larrowe, *Harry Bridges: The Rise and Fall of Radical Labor in the United States* (New York: Lawrence Hill, 1972).

20. Bill Bancroft and Bill Eaton, "S.F. Port Dilemma: Years of Decline; a Sudden Crisis," *Oakland Tribune*, September 29, 1974, 3C; John Dengel, "S.F. Port Overshadowed," *Oakland Tribune*, September 26, 1976, 8–P.

21. Melvyn Dubofsky and Foster Rhea Dulles, *Labor in America: A History*, 6th ed. (Wheeling, Ill.: Harlan Davidson, 1999), 374–75.

22. Grace Palladino, *Skilled Hands, Strong Spirits: A Century of Building Trades History* (Ithaca, N.Y.: Cornell University Press, 2005), 171.

23. "One City's Ordeal by Strike," *U.S. News and World Report*, September 14, 1970, 64–65; "Keep Greater Kansas City on the Move," *Kansas City Star*, April 3, 1969, 1.

24. "One City's Ordeal by Strike," 65. See also Rivian Bell, "The Strike That Nearly Killed K.C.," *Columbia Daily Spectator Connection*, December 17, 1970, C2-C3; "Kansas City Hurt by 196-Day Strike," *New York Times*, October 18, 1970, 82.

25. "Complex Plan Judge Target," *Kansas City Times*, April 10, 1968, 3A. See also Robert W. Lewis, *The Harry S. Truman Sports Complex: Rocky Road to the Big Leagues*, June 1977, Missouri Valley Special Collections, Kansas City Public Library.

26. *Skylines*, c. June 1970, Missouri Valley Special Collections, Kansas City Public Library, 6; "A Long and Costly Construction Strike Drags to an End," *Kansas City Times*, October 15, 1970, 14D; Gilbert Burck, "The Building Trades Versus the People," *Fortune*, October 1970, 95.

27. Richard Boyden, "Why the ILWU Strike Failed," *New Politics*, Fall 1972, 65, 68. See also Larrowe, *Harry Bridges*, 382–88.

28. See Lannon, *Fight or Be Slaves*, 140–41.

29. "The Port of No Returns," *Black Panther Intercommunal News Service*, January 13, 1973, A; Jim Miller and Kelly Mayhew, *Better to Reign in Hell: Inside the Raiders Fan Empire* (New York: New Press, 2005), Kindle edition, chap. 8.

30. Palladino, *Skilled Hands*, 176, 181–82; Nicholas von Hoffman, "The Last Days of the Labor Movement," *Harper's*, December 1978, 22.

31. See Krister Swanson, *Baseball's Power Shift: How the Players Union, the Fans, and the Media Changed American Sports Culture* (Lincoln: University of Nebraska Press, 2016), ix–xvii.

32. Jim Bouton, *I'm Glad You Didn't Take It Personally* (New York: Dell, 1972), 74, 79. See also Bouton, *Ball Four*.

33. Curt Flood with Richard Carter, *The Way It Is* (New York: Trident, 1971), 155; Abraham I. Khan, *Curt Flood in the Media* (Jackson: University Press of Mississippi, 2012), 11. See also Leonard Koppett, "Baseball's Exempt Status Upheld by Supreme Court," *New York Times*, June 20, 1972, 1, 45.

34. Most notably, sportswriter Dick Young called Jim Bouton a "social leper"

in the *New York Daily News*. See Bouton, *I'm Glad You Didn't Take It Personally*, 1.

35. Khan, *Curt Flood in the Media*, 89; Flood with Carter, *The Way It Is*, 51–52; Marvin Miller, *A Whole Different Ball Game* (New York: Birch Lane, 1991), 206.

36. Sam Lacy, "Cheers for Flood and His Compatriots," *Baltimore Afro-American*, January 10, 1970, 8; Red Smith, "Lively Times in the Slave Trade," *New York Times*, April 21, 1972, 29. See also Khan, *Curt Flood in the Media*; Swanson, *Baseball's Power Shift*, 158–88.

37. Glenn Dickey, *The Jock Empire* (Radnor, Penn.: Chilton, 1974), 58; Ron Bergman, "A's Harmony and Unity to Depend on Finley," *Sporting News*, October 24, 1970, 25. For more about changes in sportswriting during this era, see "Time of the Chipmunks," *Newsweek*, July 1, 1968, 62; Randall Poe, "The Writing of Sports," *Esquire*, October 1974, 173–76, 373–79.

38. Dick Williams and Bill Plaschke, *No More Mr. Nice Guy* (San Diego: Harcourt Brace Jovanovich, 1990), 120; Roy Blount Jr., "Humming a Rhapsody in Blue," *Sports Illustrated*, July 12, 1971, available at https://www.si.com/vault.

39. Bill Libby and Vida Blue, *Vida: His Own Story* (Englewood Cliffs, N.J.: Prentice-Hall, 1972), 3, 12, 75–76. See also Ron Bergman, "Finley Repeats His Marriage Vows to Oakland," *Sporting News*, December 25, 1971, 34, 38.

40. Gene Fox, *Sports Guys* (Lenexa, Kan.: Addax, 1999), 67–68.

41. Jim Murray, "Mighty Mouse," *Los Angeles Times*, September 26, 1971, C1. See also "Royals' Rojas Lives Baseball," *Abilene (Tex.) Reporter-News*, June 8, 1971, 10A.

42. Bill Lamberty, "Amos Otis," *Society for American Baseball Research*, available at https://sabr.org/bioproj/person/588ccedb; Joe McGuff, "Otis Showing Elated Royals New Zing," *Sporting News*, May 1, 1976, 10.

43. Dick Young, "Royals Will Rate with Royalty," *Sporting News*, October 23, 1971, 14. See also McGuff, "Fast-Moving Royals Junk Timetable"; Joe McGuff, "Tallis' Work with Royals Earns Executive Accolade," *Sporting News*, December 4, 1971, 33, 38; John Swagerty, "Knowing—and Wondering—Keep Mayberry at O. City," *Sporting News*, May 29, 1971, 41.

44. Ed Levitt, "Charley the Salesman Scores Big in Haberdashery," *Sporting News*, March 11, 1972, 46. See also Williams and Plaschke, *No More Mr. Nice Guy*, 132–33.

45. Joe McGuff, "Big Heart Chief Ingredient in Tiny Patek's Comeback," *Sporting News*, May 20, 1972, 4. See also Joe McGuff, "Royals Chafing Over Likely Delay in New Park," *Sporting News*, February 5, 1972, 34; Steve Cameron, "Candid Cameron," *Maryville (Mo.) Daily Forum*, June 9, 1972, 6.

46. Libby and Blue, *Vida*, 87, 123, 169; Ron Bergman, "Bitter Vida Unloads a Tirade at Finley," *Sporting News*, May 20, 1972, 21.

47. Robert F. Burk, *Marvin Miller: Baseball Revolutionary* (Urbana: University of Illinois Press, 2015), 100, 155–57.

48. Ibid., 158. See also Charles P. Korr, *The End of Baseball as We Knew It* (Urbana: University of Illinois Press, 2002), 102–20; Swanson, *Baseball's Power Shift*, 189–217.

49. Ed Levitt, "Strike Three," *Oakland Tribune*, April 2, 1972, 51; "Big League Confusion," *Oakland Tribune*, April 1, 1972, 13E; Joe McGuff, "'Players Must Learn Facts of Life'—Kauffman," *Sporting News*, April 22, 1972, 15.

50. Joe McGuff, "Sporting Comment," *Kansas City Star*, April 14, 1972, 15. See also Ron Bergman, "Finley Plays Leading Role in the Great Compromise," *Sporting News*, April 29, 1972, 21; Korr, *End of Baseball*, 118.

51. "Bergman Bounced by Finley," *Sporting News*, September 23, 1972, 7. See also Jason Turbow, *Dynastic, Bombastic, Fantastic: Reggie, Rollie, Catfish, and Charlie Finley's Swingin' A's* (Boston: Houghton Mifflin Harcourt, 2017), Kindle edition, chap. 4.

52. John Krich, *Bump City: Winners and Losers in Oakland* (Berkeley, Calif.: City Miner Books, 1979), 103. See also Greg Erion, "Blue Moon Odom," in *Mustaches and Mayhem: Charlie O's Three-Time Champions*, ed. Chip Greene (Phoenix: Society for American Baseball Research, 2015), Kindle edition; Ron Fimrite, "Of Taters and Bristles," *Sports Illustrated*, June 18, 1972, available at https://www.si.com/vault.

53. Gib Twyman, "Otis, Patek Sit It Out," *Kansas City Times*, August 15, 1972, 18; Gib Twyman, "Lemon Keeps Door Open for Return of Otis, Patek," *Kansas City Star*, August 15, 1972, 14. See also Ron Bergman, "Catfish Joins Shutout Act," *Oakland Tribune*, August 3, 1972, F39–F40.

54. John Hall, "Talk of the Town," *Los Angeles Times*, August 2, 1972, E3; Joe McGuff, "'Blame Me for Lemon's Exit,' Says Kauffman," *Sporting News*, October 21, 1972, 23.

55. Turbow, *Dynastic, Bombastic, Fantastic*, chap. 5; Williams and Plaschke, *No More Mr. Nice Guy*, 144–45.

56. "A's vs. the Establishment," *Oakland Tribune*, October 14, 1972, 13E; Krich, *Bump City*, 100; Turbow, *Dynastic, Bombastic, Fantastic*, chap. 6. See also Ed Gruver, *Hairs vs. Squares* (Lincoln: University of Nebraska Press, 2017).

57. Krich, *Bump City*, 96–97, 101–2.

58. Ron Bergman, "No Kidding—Oakland's Crazy about the A's," *Sporting News*, November 11, 1972, 44; Krich, *Bump City*, 103; Jan Silverman, "150,000 Fans Cheer Champ A's," *Oakland Tribune*, October 24, 1972, 1; Ron Bergman, "Williams' Reward: Third Raise," *Oakland Tribune*, October 24, 1972, 34. See also Bill and Nancy Boyarsky, *Backroom Politics* (Los Angeles: J.P. Tarcher, 1974), 201–2.

Chapter 4. Chiefs vs. Raiders, Part II

1. Michael Oriard, *Brand NFL* (Chapel Hill: University of North Carolina Press, 2007), 59.

2. Tom Leathers, "'Hair' May Be Hot on the Broadway Stage, But It's Not on the Football Field," *Kansas City Town Squire,* October 1969, 5.

3. Hank Stram with Dave Anderson, "Pro Football's Dazzling New Look," *Look,* September 8, 1970, 34. See also Bill Richardson, "Stram Steady Airport Visitor, Cashing in on Chiefs' Crown," *Sporting News,* May 23, 1970, 60; Tex Maule, "New Decade Setup Game," *Sports Illustrated,* September 21, 1970, available at https://www.si.com/vault.

4. *World Champion Kansas City Chiefs 1970 Yearbook* (Kansas City, Mo.: Kansas City Chiefs, 1970), 5. See also "Two Sides of Eight Chiefs," *Kansas City Town Squire,* November 1970, 36–41; Jim Scott, "Need a Mouthpiece? See Raiders' Conners," *Sporting News,* August 22, 1970, 51; "Hawkins Says He's Retiring," *The Times* (San Mateo, Calif.), January 26, 1971, 17; Tom LaMarre, "Three Raiders Who Make Life Better for Those in Need," *Oakland Tribune,* October 21, 1976, 3-GAME; Monte Poole, "'70s Raiders a Huge Part of Oakland," *Oakland Tribune,* December 10, 2003.

5. "Two Sides of Eight Chiefs," 41; Chip Oliver, *High for the Game* (New York: William Morrow, 1971), 71.

6. Jim Scott, "Ex-Toughie Quits Raiders to Be a Flower Child," *Sporting News,* May 30, 1970, 55; Dave Meggyesy, *Out of Their League* (Berkeley, Calif.: Ramparts, 1970), 6, 147; "Jeremiah of Jock Liberation," *Time,* May 24, 1971, 88–89. See also Oliver, *High for the Game;* Jack Scott, *The Athletic Revolution* (New York: Free Press, 1971).

7. See Harry Edwards, *The Revolt of the Black Athlete,* 50th anniversary ed. (Urbana: University of Illinois Press, 2017).

8. Scott, "Ex-Toughie Quits Raiders," 55; Creative Staff of National Football League Properties, *The First Fifty Years* (New York: Ridge Press/Benjamin, 1969), 23–30. See also Marc Gunther and Bill Carter, *Monday Night Mayhem* (New York: Beech Tree Books, 1988); Jesse Berrett, *Pigskin Nation: How the NFL Remade American Politics* (Urbana: University of Illinois Press, 2018), 11–29, 159–80.

9. See Glenn Dickey, *Just Win, Baby* (Orlando, Fla.: Harcourt Brace Jovanovich, 1991), 85–86.

10. Bill Bruns, "A Tale of Two Quarterbacks," *Life,* December 4, 1970, 44; "Challenge of the '70s," NFL Films, 1971, available at https://www.youtube.com/watch?v=Fulo9heRpZQ. See also George Blanda with Jack Olsen, "A Decade of Revenge," *Sports Illustrated,* July 26, 1971, 44–45. For details concerning the Raiders-Chiefs 1970 tie game, see the introduction.

11. Wells Twombly, *Blanda* (Los Angeles: Nash, 1972), 76–77; Bruns, "Tale of Two Quarterbacks," 46.

12. Blaine Newnham, "Bully Boys Beaten in Hubbard's Alley," *Oakland Tribune,* December 13, 1970, 53–54. See also Peter Richmond, *Badasses: The Legend of Snake, Foo, Dr. Death, and John Madden's Oakland Raiders* (New York: Harper, 2010), 176–80; "Ancient Warrior Blanda Chosen Player of Year," *Sporting News,* February 6, 1971, 24.

13. Robert Moore, "Hank Stram Is Still Fuming about Chiefs' 1970 Collapse," *Southern Illinoisan,* August 31, 1971, 10; Rick Smith, "All's Well with the Chargers; Garrett, Alworth Back in Fold," *Sporting News,* February 27, 1971, 63; Bill Finley, "Father of End-Zone Dance Explains His Happy Feet," *New York Times,* November 13, 2005, available at https://nyti.ms/2NJE6OP; Bob Franklin, "You Gotta Have a Gimmick," *Delaware County Daily Times* (Chester, Pa.), November 2, 1971, 15.

14. Robert H. Boyle, "Call It Catch-As-Catch-Can," *Sports Illustrated,* November 15, 1971, available at https://www.si.com/vault.

15. See Havelock Hunter, "Wells Lost for Season, Has Probation Revoked," *Oakland Tribune,* September 4, 1971, 1; Dave Newhouse, "Forgotten Warren Wells Remains in a Texas Prison," *Reno Gazette-Journal,* December 20, 1979, 85; Dickey, *Just Win, Baby,* 93–98; Richmond, *Badasses,* 124–25, 131–37, 204–11.

16. Bob Valli, "Old George Saves the Raiders," *Oakland Tribune,* November 1, 1971, E39.

17. Gary D. Warner, "Taylor Knew Big-Play Pressure," *Kansas City Times,* December 13, 1971, 1D–2D; Otis Taylor with Mark Stallard, *Otis Taylor: The Need to Win* (Champaign, Ill.: Sports Publishing, 2003), 141.

18. See Gib Twyman, "'71 Playoffs Still Ring Painfully," *Kansas City Star,* December 25, 1991, D1; Harry Jones Jr., "Chiefs' Fans Hear the Hush of Defeat," *Kansas City Star,* December 26, 1971, 7A.

19. Vahe Gregorian, "Fifty Years After Arriving in KC, Jan Stenerud's Extraordinary Story Should Eclipse One Bad Day," *Kansas City Star,* May 13, 2017, available at http://www.kansascity.com; Jones Jr., "Chiefs' Fans Hear the Hush of Defeat," 1A.

20. Gary D. Warner, ". . . And the Chiefs Season Ends," *Kansas City Star,* December 26, 1971, 2S; Joe McGuff, "Sporting Comment," *Kansas City Star,* December 26, 1971, 2S.

21. "Posh Touch at New Stadium," *Kansas City Star,* November 5, 1970, 1–2.

22. Ibid.; Robert W. Lewis, *The Harry S. Truman Sports Complex: Rocky Road to the Big Leagues,* June 1977, Missouri Valley Special Collections, Kansas City Public Library, 95–106; Michael McKenzie, *Arrowhead: Home of the Chiefs* (Kansas City, Mo.: Andrews and McMeel, 1997), 22.

23. "Officials Speak out on County Sports Complex," *Kansas City Times,* December 8, 1970, 26–29, 34.

24. Joe McGuff, "Kansas City Growing Up—And Out," *Kansas City Star,* June 9, 1972, 12; Robert M. Dye, "Wheeler Arena Plan: Link to American Royal," *Kansas City Times,* July 16, 1971, 1A, 6A; David Redmon, "Elation over Arena Bill," *Kansas City Times,* March 1, 1972, 5.

25. McGuff, "Kansas City Growing Up," 15; "Generous Kemper Gift Revives Royal Arena Plan," *Kansas City Star,* October 31, 1972, 24; "Petition Drive Planned Against Meal, Hotel Tax," *Kansas City Times,* March 3, 1972, 4. See also Jon C. Teaford, *The 20th-Century American City: Problem, Promise, and Reality,* 3rd ed. (Baltimore: Johns Hopkins University Press, 2016), chap. 5–6.

26. Robert W. Butler, "Arena in Peril: Bonds Refused," *Kansas City Times,* January 20, 1973, 14A; Thomas J. Bogdon, "Forum for Arena Views," *Kansas City Times,* April 25, 1972, 8; Thomas J. Bogdon, "Six Stand Tough on Arena," *Kansas City Star,* March 17, 1973, 1A. See also Jay Greenberg, "New Arena Caps K.C. Rise to Big-Time Rating," *Sporting News,* January 4, 1975, 19.

27. See Blair Kerkhoff, "It's Been 10 Years. Do You Know Where the Kings Are?" *Kansas City Star,* April 23, 1995, C2.

28. Joe Posnanski, "Scouts Were a Disaster," *Kansas City Star,* July 8, 2007, C1; Steve Cameron, "Hockey: Who Gets the Blame?" *Kansas City,* September 1976, 39. Despite Kansas City's travails in big-league hockey and basketball, the city did benefit from its association with native son Tom Watson, who by the mid-1970s had become one of the world's top professional golfers.

29. George Ross, "The Hockey 'Spinoff' for Oakland," *Oakland Tribune,* February 12, 1966, 13B; Art Spander, "Seals Doomed from the Start," *Sporting News,* July 24, 1976, 46. See also Leo Monahan, "Finley's Follies Fail to Amuse NHL Bigwigs," *Sporting News,* November 7, 1970, 23.

30. John Simmonds, "Cheering Fans Give Warriors Victory Salute," *Oakland Tribune,* May 30, 1975, EE40; Dave Newhouse, "Oakland Deserves Sports Teams That Show It Respect, Loyalty," *Mercury News* (San Jose, Calif.), June 3, 2015, available at http://www.mercurynews.com.

31. Bill and Nancy Boyarsky, *Backroom Politics* (Los Angeles: J.P. Tarcher, 1974), 200.

32. Ibid., 192, 201.

33. Elaine Brown, *A Taste of Power* (New York: Pantheon, 1992), 324–25; Robert O. Self, *American Babylon: Race and the Struggle for Postwar Oakland* (Princeton, N.J.: Princeton University Press, 2003), 300–301.

34. "To Rebuild Our City," *Black Panther Intercommunal News Service,* March 17, 1973, B–C; "The Oakland Coliseum: Fame but No Fortune," *Black Panther Intercommunal News Service,* March 31, 1973, A–B. Three years earlier, the Oak-

land Economic Development Council had published a book that was sharply critical of the city's white establishment (the council was staffed largely by African Americans). Among other things, the book suggested that the electrical cables that had gone into the Coliseum complex could have wired thousands of family homes. See *Discover the Friendly City—Oakland* (Oakland, Calif.: Oakland Economic Development Council, 1970), Oakland History Room, Oakland Public Library. See also Self, *American Babylon,* 203–5, 233–40.

35. See Self, *American Babylon,* 306–8; "The Post Recommends," *Oakland Post,* April 11, 1973, 1; "The Post Recommends," *Oakland Post,* May 9, 1973, 1.

36. McKenzie, *Arrowhead,* 22–23; "Victory for New Stadium," *Kansas City Star,* August 13, 1972, 1A, 20A.

37. "6 NFL Teams Will Be at Home on AstroTurf" (advertisement), *Sporting News,* September 19, 1970, 49. See also Lowell Reidenbaugh, "New Home, Old Grudge, K.C. Gloom," *Sporting News,* September 30, 1972, 35, 54; "Chiefs Seeking 200 Stadium Hostesses," *Kansas City Times,* June 20, 1972, 6A.

38. John Underwood, "New Slant on the Mod Sod," *Sports Illustrated,* November 15, 1971, available at https://www.si.com/vault; Gary D. Warner, "Lame Chiefs Improve," *Kansas City Times,* August 15, 1972, 17. See also Michael MacCambridge, *America's Game: The Epic Story of How Pro Football Captured a Nation* (New York: Random House, 2004), 306–8; Allan Mazur and Jennifer Bretsch, "Looking Back: Synthetic Turf and Football Injuries," *Risk: Health, Safety and Environment* 10.1 (Winter 1999): 1–6.

39. Michael Oriard, *The End of Autumn* (Urbana: University of Illinois Press, 2009), 197–98. See also Kary Booher, "The Longest Wait: Podolak's Next Super Bowl Never Came," *Springfield (Mo.) News-Leader,* February 2, 2014, 1D, 8D.

40. Booher, "The Longest Wait," 8D; Larry Felser, "Beware of Writing Off the Raiders," *Sporting News,* July 15, 1972, 49; Bill Richardson, "$1 Million Pact Makes Stram a Chief Till '81," *Sporting News,* February 12, 1972, 20.

41. See Jean Haley, "Fans Swelter; Chiefs Cold," *Kansas City Times,* September 18, 1972, 1A; "Four Fans Sue Eagles," *Evening Journal* (Wilmington, Del.), November 2, 1972, 27; Bill Richardson, "Eagles Daze Chiefs, 21—20," *Kansas City Times,* October 23, 1972, 1C, 3C.

42. Tom LaMarre, "Hank Rebuts Rap on 'Old' Chiefs," *Oakland Tribune,* November 2, 1972, E37; Baron Wolman and Steve Cassady, *Oakland Raiders: The Good Guys* (Mill Valley, Calif.: Squarebooks, 1975), 14.

43. Bill Richardson, "Chiefs-Raiders Even," *Kansas City Star,* November 5, 1972, 2S; Tom LaMarre, "Raiders, Chiefs Round 1," *Oakland Tribune,* October 31, 1972, E37–E38; Ed Fowler, "Hubbard Does About Face in Mean Talk," *Kansas City Times,* November 6, 1972, 1C.

44. Donald O. Clevenger, "Sorry, Marv" (letter to the editor), *Kansas City Star,* November 8, 1972, 16C; Glenn Dickey, "Keep Those K.C. Fans in Their Cages!"

San Francisco Chronicle, November 7, 1972, 48; Steve Cameron, "Candid Cameron," *Maryville (Mo.) Daily Forum,* November 24, 1972, 4.

45. See Bill Richardson, "Chiefs Keep on Crumbling," *Kansas City Times,* November 20, 1972, 1D; George Ross, "'We Want Marv'—He Cheers Chester," *Oakland Tribune,* November 27, 1972, E29, E31.

46. Richmond, *Badasses,* 22–23.

47. Mark Ribowsky, *Slick: The Silver and Black Life of Al Davis* (New York: Macmillan, 1991), 113. See also George Ross, "Raider Suit Seeks to Have Al Davis Fired," *Oakland Tribune,* April 2, 1973, 1, 14.

48. Ribowsky, *Slick,* 229–37, 247–49; Frank Deford, "A City of Complexes," *Sports Illustrated,* April 1, 1968, available at https://www.si.com/vault.

49. Oriard, *The End of Autumn,* 198; Angela Woodall, "Oakland's O.Co Old and Gray but Still Beloved," *Mercury News* (San Jose, Calif.), March 31, 2012, available at http://www.mercurynews.com; Ken Stabler and Barry Stainback, *Snake* (Garden City, N.Y.: Doubleday, 1986), 92; *Rebels of Oakland,* HBO Sports, 2003, Paley Center for Media, New York City. See also Richmond, *Badasses,* 47.

50. Bill Richardson, "Looking for a Sure Thing? Raiders Could Fill the Bill," *Sporting News,* September 22, 1973, 37; Kathleen Patterson, "Fans Get Something to Cheer About—Chiefs on Top," *Kansas City Times,* October 1, 1973, 1. See also Stabler and Stainback, *Snake,* 84–85.

51. Bob Valli, "Never Beaten So Badly, Says Hank," *Oakland Tribune,* December 9, 1973, 55; Richmond, *Badasses,* 180–81.

52. Ed Levitt, "Madden Zonked," *Oakland Tribune,* December 31, 1973, 5. See also Joe McGuff, "Sporting Comment," *Kansas City Star,* December 17, 1973, 15.

53. William Oscar Johnson, "The Day the Money Ran Out," *Sports Illustrated,* December 1, 1975, available at https://www.si.com/vault. See also Tom LaMarre, "Stabler's Exit Just the Start of Raids on the Raiders," *Sporting News,* April 20, 1974, 42; Bill Richardson, "Hunt Hasn't Changed Mind," *Kansas City Star,* May 20, 1974, 13.

54. Oriard, *Brand NFL,* 65–66.

55. Ibid., 87, 89.

56. Jay Sharbutt, "Karras Scores in Football Bow," *Oakland Tribune,* September 18, 1974, 17; "Oakland Raiders: The Autumn Wind," available at https://www .youtube.com/watch?v=VPLmxtiVOe0; *Rebels of Oakland.* See also Jim Miller and Kelly Mayhew, *Better to Reign in Hell: Inside the Raiders Fan Empire* (New York: New Press, 2005); Travis Vogan, *Keepers of the Flame: NFL Films and the Rise of Sports Media* (Urbana: University of Illinois Press, 2014); Dickey, *Just Win, Baby.*

57. Dickey, "Keep Those K.C. Fans," 48; Joe McGuff, "Sporting Comment," *Kansas City Star,* December 16, 1974, 17.

58. Tom Leathers, "What Really Made Stram Scram," *Kansas City Town Squire,*

February 1975, 24–25; Hank Stram with Lou Sahadi, *They're Playing My Game* (New York: William Morrow, 1986), 153. See also Joe McGuff, "Stram's Exit Called Means to Changing Chiefs' Image," *Kansas City Times,* December 28, 1974, 1A, 2D.

59. Richmond, *Badasses,* 221; Tom LaMarre, "When Will It Be in Cards for the Raiders?" *Oakland Tribune,* December 30, 1974, E31.

Chapter 5. A's vs. Royals, Part II

1. See, for example, Neil J. Sullivan, *The Dodgers Move West* (New York: Oxford University Press, 1987); Bruce Kuklick, *To Every Thing A Season: Shibe Park and Urban Philadelphia, 1909–1976* (Princeton, N.J.: Princeton University Press, 1991).

2. See Lloyd Johnson, "Baseball in Kansas City," in *Unions to Royals: The Story of Professional Baseball in Kansas City,* ed. Lloyd Johnson, Steve Garlick, and Jeff Magalif (Manhattan, Kan.: AG Press, 1996); James R. Shortridge, *Kansas City and How It Grew, 1822–2011* (Lawrence: University Press of Kansas, 2012), 85–90.

3. Kevin Fox Gotham, *Race, Real Estate, and Uneven Development: The Kansas City Experience, 1900–2010,* 2nd ed. (Albany, N.Y.: SUNY Press, 2014), 48, 95–126.

4. Robert O. Self, *American Babylon: Race and the Struggle for Postwar Oakland* (Princeton, N.J.: Princeton University Press, 2003), 165; Peggy King, "A Hard Look at OAL Problems," *Oakland Tribune,* October 19, 1969, 12. See also John P. Spencer, *In the Crossfire: Marcus Foster and the Troubled History of American School Reform* (Philadelphia: University of Pennsylvania Press, 2012), 185–96; "250 Negroes Riot and Beat Teachers; Oakland School Shut," *New York Times,* October 20, 1966, 1, 37.

5. Angela Woodall, "Oakland's O.Co Old and Gray but Still Beloved," *Mercury News* (San Jose, Calif.), March 31, 2012, available at http://www.mercurynews.com; Ken Stabler and Barry Stainback, *Snake* (Garden City, N.Y.: Doubleday, 1986), 92; Frank Deford, "A City of Complexes," *Sports Illustrated,* April 1, 1968, available at https://www.si.com/vault. See also Self, *American Babylon,* 256–90.

6. Bruce Clayton, *Praying for Base Hits: An American Boyhood* (Columbia: University of Missouri Press, 1998), 178; Neil J. Sullivan, *The Diamond in the Bronx: Yankee Stadium and the Politics of New York* (New York: Oxford University Press, 2001), 114. See also Jon C. Teaford, *The 20th-Century American City: Problem, Promise, and Reality,* 3rd ed. (Baltimore: Johns Hopkins University Press, 2016), Kindle edition, chap. 5; Shortridge, *Kansas City and How It Grew,* 97–129.

7. Dick Mackey, "Goodbye," *Kansas City Star,* April 8, 1973, 16D; Bill James, *The Bill James Baseball Abstract 1986* (New York: Ballantine, 1986), 45.

8. *Vine Street District Economic Development Plan,* July 1, 2010, available at http://kcmo.gov/wp-content/uploads/2013/07/vinestreetecondevtplan.pdf, 6–7.

9. Shortridge, *Kansas City and How It Grew,* 112; Michael MacCambridge, *America's Game: The Epic Story of How Pro Football Captured a Nation* (New York: Random House, 2004), 305. See also Joe McGuff, "Sporting Comment," *Kansas City Star,* July 16, 1973, 13–14.

10. Lou Piniella with Bill Madden, *Lou* (New York: HarperCollins, 2017), 56; William Leggett, "Now Comes the Big Blue Machine," *Sports Illustrated,* April 23, 1973, available at https://www.si.com/vault. See also Steve Cameron, *Moments, Memories, Miracles: A Quarter Century with the Kansas City Royals* (Dallas: Taylor, 1992), 114–16.

11. Gerald Jordan, "Hal McRae Puts Winning Ahead of Being Nice," *Kansas City Times,* July 1, 1976, 9A. See also Earl Lawson, "Reds' McRae Tires of His Spear-Carrier Role," *Sporting News,* November 4, 1972, 25; Leggett, "Now Comes the Big Blue Machine."

12. Ron Bergman, "Trade for Fosse Cleans Up Three of A's Trouble Spots," *Sporting News,* April 7, 1973, 34; Art Spander, "In Oakland, 'Nobody Cares,'" *Sporting News,* May 26, 1973, 20. See also Bill Conlin, "Series Rings Will Cost Charlie $1,500 Apiece," *Sporting News,* January 6, 1973, 30.

13. Dick Williams and Bill Plaschke, *No More Mr. Nice Guy* (San Diego: Harcourt Brace Jovanovich, 1990), 156; George Ross, "Billy's Wait Ends," *Oakland Tribune,* May 19, 1973, 13.

14. Rosemarie Ross, "Torrid Love Affair Grips McKeon and K.C.," *Sporting News,* May 19, 1973, 9; Piniella with Madden, *Lou,* 56; Ron Bergman, "Reggie Blasts His Bosses—All Receive New Contracts," *Sporting News,* July 28, 1973, 27. See also Joe McGuff, "McKeon Sees Red over Royal Dearth of Deals," *Sporting News,* June 30, 1973, 16.

15. See Joe McGuff, "Sporting Comment," *Kansas City Star,* July 25, 1973, 1C.

16. Gib Twyman, "Royals Win, 6–5, As Rumbles Ebb," *Kansas City Times,* September 3, 1973, 1F; Ron Bergman, "A's Use Blanda Act," *Oakland Tribune,* September 1, 1973, 7E; Joe McGuff, "Sporting Comment," *Kansas City Star,* September 3, 1973, 6. See also Joe McGuff, "An Avalanche of Problems: Too Big for Royals' Taylor," *Sporting News,* May 29, 1971, 23.

17. George Ross, "K.C. Views Catastrophe," *Oakland Tribune,* September 11, 1973, 34E; Wells Twombly, "Vandals in the Driver's Seat," *Sporting News,* October 27, 1973, 14. See also Ron Bergman, "A's Snap at Each Other . . . Team Up to Hoist Pennant," *Sporting News,* October 27, 1973, 4, 14.

18. See Jason Turbow, *Dynastic, Bombastic, Fantastic: Reggie, Rollie, Catfish, and Charlie Finley's Swingin' A's* (Boston: Houghton Mifflin Harcourt, 2017), Kindle edition, chap. 10; "100,000 Cheer the A's," *Oakland Tribune,* October 23, 1973, F13; Ed Levitt, "$100Gs for Reg," *Oakland Tribune,* October 23, 1973, E33.

19. Red Smith, "When Charlie Got His Comeuppance," *New York Times,* October 19, 1973, 29; William Leggett, "Mutiny and a Bounty," *Sports Illustrated,*

October 29, 1973, available at https://www.si.com/vault; Robert Markus, "Finley Made Big Error on Andrews Play," *Chicago Tribune,* October 17, 1973, C3; George Ross, "A's Lament Finley 'Mistake,'" *Oakland Tribune,* October 22, 1973, E31; Ron Bergman, "'That's Strike 2,' Kuhn Tells Finley," *Sporting News,* November 17, 1973, 31. See also Turbow, *Dynastic, Bombastic, Fantastic,* chap. 11.

20. "We've Built a New Kansas City in Kansas City" (advertisement), *Sporting News,* July 28, 1973, 29. See also "A Model for Airport Terminals," *Business Week,* November 11, 1972, 80–82.

21. "We've Built a New Kansas City," 29; "Convention Center: Jobs, Dollars and a Stable Downtown," *Kansas City Times,* December 17, 1973, 10C; Teaford, *The 20th-Century American City,* chap. 8. See also Robert L. Carroll, "Convention Center Clears by 68 Votes," *Kansas City Times,* December 22, 1973, 1A.

22. "We've Built a New Kansas City," 29; "Crown Center Shops" (special section), *Kansas City Star,* September 23, 1973, 6F, 11F, 14F. See also Patrick Regan, *Hallmark: A Century of Caring* (Kansas City, Mo.: Andrews McMeel, 2009), 176–81.

23. Public Relations Society of America, "Prime Time: Chamber of Commerce, Greater Kansas City, C. Byoir and Associates, 1974" (award citation), available at http://apps.prsa.org/awards/silveranvil/Search; Rick Montgomery and Shirl Kasper, *Kansas City: An American Story* (Kansas City, Mo.: Kansas City Star Books, 1999), 315. See also Virginia H. Hein, "The Image of 'A City Too Busy to Hate': Atlanta in the 1960s," *Phylon* 33.3 (1972): 205–21.

24. William S. Johnson, "Private Thoughts about Public Relations," Midcontinent Perspectives Lectures, March 24, 1987, available at https://shsmo.org/about/kansascity/mcp/, 3. See also Regan, *Hallmark,* 184–85; Glen Gendzel, "Competitive Boosterism: How Milwaukee Lost the Braves," *Business History Review* 69 (Winter 1995): 530–66.

25. Richard Rhodes, "Convention Fever in Kansas City," *Harper's,* May 1976, 28; Calvin Trillin, "U.S. Journal: Kansas City, Missouri," *New Yorker,* April 8, 1974, 94.

26. Trillin, "U.S. Journal," 97; George Ehrlich, *Kansas City, Missouri: An Architectural History, 1826–1990,* rev. and enl. ed. (Columbia: University of Missouri Press, 1992), 186. See also Regan, *Hallmark,* 176–81; Robert A. Kipp, "Crown Center: An Emerging Vision for Urban Development," Charles N. Kimball Lecture, April 20, 1995, available at https://shsmo.org/kansascity/kimball/Kipp-04-20-1995.pdf.

27. John F. Lawrence, "Oakland Uses Sports to Give It an Image as a Big League City," *Wall Street Journal,* December 29, 1967, 3.

28. "Civic Leader Says Museum Center Vital to City Growth" and "Experts Back Downtown Museum Site," *Oakland Tribune,* April 12, 1961, 1; Thomas Albright, "The Oakland Dilemma: Who Runs a 'Museum for the People'?" *New York Times,* September 14, 1969, D27.

29. "Oakland City Center," *Oakland Magazine,* Winter 1975, 6; "Is City Center Rolling Again?" *Glimpse Magazine,* c. October 1973, in "Oakland City Center: 1970–1979" folder, Oakland History Room, Oakland Public Library.

30. Albright, "The Oakland Dilemma," D27; John Beyer, "A New Museum for the West," *American West,* November 1969, 37; Barry Schwartz, "Museums: Art for Whose Sake?" *Ramparts,* June 1971, 41.

31. Joseph A. Rodriguez, "Rapid Transit and Community Power: West Oakland Residents Confront BART," *Antipode* 31.2 (1999): 214.

32. "Urban Renewal Means Black Removal," *Black Panther Intercommunal News Service,* November 30, 1972, C. See also Mitchell Schwarzer, "Oakland City Center: The Plan to Reposition Downtown within the Bay Region," *Journal of Planning History* 14.2 (2015): 88–111.

33. Schwarzer, "Oakland City Center": 99, 103.

34. Ron Bergman, "Letter from Finley Helps to Fog A's Future," *Sporting News,* February 9, 1974, 47.

35. Marvin Miller, *A Whole Different Ball Game* (New York: Birch Lane, 1991), 374; Ron Bergman, "'Inner Strength' to Aid Dark Lead Champ A's," *Sporting News,* March 16, 1974, 42. See also Turbow, *Dynastic, Bombastic, Fantastic,* chap. 12.

36. Ron Bergman, "Peace Reigns Briefly, Then A's Blow Stacks," *Sporting News,* April 27, 1974, 5; Ron Bergman, "Finley Blisters A's After Jackson-North Bout," *Sporting News,* June 22, 1974, 13.

37. Dick Young, "Tallis' Mistake: Disagreeing with Kauffman," *Fort Myers (Fla.) News-Press,* June 16, 1974, 10C. See also Joe McGuff, "Key Question: Will Royals Miss Piniella's Bat?" *Sporting News,* December 29, 1973, 32; Sid Bordman, "Royals Close Their Academy," *Sporting News,* May 18, 1974, 10; Richard Dozer, "Royals' Owner Says Kuhn is 'Absolute,'" *Chicago Tribune,* January 8, 1977, 3.

38. See Frank White with Bill Althaus, *One Man's Dream: My Town, My Team, My Time* (Olathe, Kan.: Ascend, 2012); Joe McGuff, "Academy Grad to Join Royal Camp," *Sporting News,* February 3, 1973, 45.

39. "The KC Royals and Kansas City: 1969–1985," c. 2009, available at https://www.youtube.com/watch?v=fEJXW11Pq6M&t=373s; George Brett with Steve Cameron, *George Brett: From Here to Cooperstown* (Lenexa, Kan.: Addax, 1999), 36.

40. "Royals' Owner Gets Tough," *Detroit Free Press,* August 15, 1974, 9D; Gib Twyman, "Royals Show Shabby Side Again," *Kansas City Times,* October 1, 1974, 20. See also Gib Twyman, "Shocked Royals React Bitterly to Firing of Lau," *Kansas City Star,* September 30, 1974, 11.

41. Ron Bergman, "Finley Prospers on A's Poor Crowds," *Sporting News,* October 19, 1974, 31. See also Art Spander, "Maybe A's Gate Problem Is Costly Tickets," *Sporting News,* July 6, 1974, 34; Turbow, *Dynastic, Bombastic, Fantastic,* chap. 8, chap. 12.

42. Wells Twombly, "A's Fisticuffs Is Just Among Pals," *Sporting News,* October

26, 1974, 26; Murray Olderman, "Reggie Jackson: Blood and Guts of the Fighting A's," *Sport,* October 1974, 54. See also Lowell Reidenbaugh, "A's Three-Ring Circus Steals the Show," *Sporting News,* November 2, 1974, 7.

43. Ed Levitt, "The Town Is Roaring," *Oakland Tribune,* October 18, 1974, E37. See also Turbow, *Dynastic, Bombastic, Fantastic,* chap. 13.

44. Wells Twombly, "There's No Limit to Finley's Ego," *Sporting News,* October 19, 1974, 10; Joe McGuff, "Royals Offer King's Ransom for Paw of the Cat," *Sporting News,* January 4, 1975, 43; Ron Bergman, "Wolf Stalks Finley Door as the Cat Departs," *Sporting News,* January 4, 1975, 36.

45. Bowie Kuhn, *Hardball: The Education of a Baseball Commissioner* (New York: TimesBooks, 1987), 190. See also Turbow, *Dynastic, Bombastic, Fantastic,* chap. 15.

46. Wells Twombly, "A's Have Own Motto: Thank God for Arbitration!" *Sporting News,* February 22, 1975, 29. See also Ron Bergman, "Finley Clear-Cut Winner over His Angry A's," *Sporting News,* March 15, 1975, 37; Ron Bergman, "Over-30 Hill Bunch Giving Hypo to A's Victory Pace," *Sporting News,* July 19, 1975, 24; Joe McGuff, "Lack of Popularity McKeon's Downfall," *Kansas City Star,* July 24, 1975, 17.

47. Ron Bergman, "Smokin' Royals Challenge A's," *Oakland Tribune,* September 8, 1975, 29.

48. Ron Bergman, "Do-or-Die Series: That's What A's Like Best," *Sporting News,* September 27, 1975, 3; Cameron, *Moments, Memories, Miracles,* 218.

49. Ron Bergman, "Red Sox End Era, Dynasty in One Sweep," *Oakland Tribune,* October 8, 1975, EE 39; Ed Levitt, "Fun While It Lasted," *Oakland Tribune,* October 8, 1975, EE 39.

50. Levitt, "Fun While It Lasted," EE 41. See also Ron Bergman, "We'll Be Back—Bando," *Oakland Tribune,* October 8, 1975, EE 41.

Chapter 6. "Triumph and Tragedy"

1. Ron Reid, "American West," *Sports Illustrated,* September 22, 1975, available at https://www.si.com/vault. See also Bob Oates, "Raiders Picked as Super Bowl Kings," *Sporting News,* September 27, 1975, 36; Peter Richmond, *Badasses: The Legend of Snake, Foo, Dr. Death, and John Madden's Oakland Raiders* (New York: Harper, 2010), 230–63.

2. Larry Felser, "Lanier Return Changes Chief Grief to Relief," *Sporting News,* May 24, 1975, 53; Paul Wiggin, "The Long Road Back," *Saturday Evening Post,* October 1975, 64.

3. "Warpaint (mascot)," available at https://en.wikipedia.org. See also See John Clay, "UK's Nightmare Season Evokes Memories of 'Surreal' 1975," *Lexington Herald-Leader,* October 9, 1994, C1; Bob Gretz, *Tales from the Kansas City Chiefs Sideline* (New York: Sports Publishing, 2015), Kindle edition, chap. 8.

4. Ed Levitt, "Old Wrinkle for the Playoffs," *Oakland Tribune,* December 22, 1975, EE 37.

5. See Tom LaMarre, "Raider Dreams in Deep Freeze," *Oakland Tribune,* January 5, 1976, EE35–36; Bob Valli, "Davis Denies Madden Rap," *Oakland Tribune,* January 5, 1976, EE37; "1976 Oakland Raiders," *America's Game: The Super Bowl Champions,* NFL Films, 2007.

6. "Triumph and Tragedy," NFL Films, 1976, available at https://www.youtube .com/watch?v=IU4QJVo-p9w&t=183s.

7. See Charles P. Korr, *The End of Baseball as We Knew It* (Urbana: University of Illinois Press, 2002), 147–67.

8. Ibid., 159, 161.

9. Marvin Miller, *A Whole Different Ball Game* (New York: Birch Lane, 1991), 370–71. See also Robert F. Burk, *Marvin Miller: Baseball Revolutionary* (Urbana: University of Illinois Press, 2015), 182–90.

10. Ron Bergman, "Don't Trade Me, I'm Part of Scene, Begs Reggie," *Sporting News,* February 28, 1976, 46. See also Ron Bergman, "Alvin Praises Lord and Finley on Getting Walking Papers," *Sporting News,* November 1, 1975, 21; Ron Bergman, "Finley Buries All Rumors of A's Departure," *Sporting News,* February 14, 1976, 34.

11. Gib Twyman, "Otis Still Rides Own Style," *Kansas City Star,* June 22, 1991, D1. See also Joe McGuff, "Otis Showing Elated Royals New Zing," *Sporting News,* May 1, 1976, 10.

12. Sid Bordman, "Future Is Now for Super Third Sacker Brett," *Sporting News,* June 5, 1976, 3.

13. Ron Bergman, "Diary of Defeat—A's Were Losers Even in Bus League," *Sporting News,* June 12, 1976, 10; Ron Bergman, "Bay Waters Never Placid with Charlie at the Oars," *Sporting News,* July 3, 1976, 8. See also Bowie Kuhn, *Hardball: The Education of a Baseball Commissioner* (New York: TimesBooks, 1987), 173–82; Ron Bergman, "Finley Bends and A's Strike Threat Breaks," *Sporting News,* July 10, 1976, 7.

14. Ron Bergman, "'Royals Will Choke,' Chortles Charlie," *Sporting News,* August 28, 1976, 16, 30.

15. Joe McGuff, "Royals Plug Ears to Charges of Choke, Panic," *Sporting News,* September 25, 1976, 16, 18; Ron Bergman, "Bitter A's Yearn for One More Taste of Honey," *Sporting News,* September 25, 1976, 13.

16. See Sid Bordman, "For Openers—Royals 3, A's 1," *Kansas City Times,* September 22, 1976, 1A, 1C; Ron Bergman, "A's Near Death, but Royal Rivalry Lives On," *Oakland Tribune,* September 22, 1976, EE37, EE40; Denny Matthews with Matt Fulks, *Tales from the Royals Dugout* (Champaign, Ill.: Sports Publishing, 2004), 40–47.

17. Sid Bordman, "Royals Fall as Pressure Builds," *Kansas City Times,* September 24, 1976, 1A.

18. Del Black, "Royals Still Looking for a Knockout," *Kansas City Star,* September 28, 1976, 17; Ed Schoenfeld, "A's Stretch Drive in High Gear," *Oakland Tribune,* September 29, 1976, EE39.

19. Steve Cameron, *Moments, Memories, Miracles: A Quarter Century with the Kansas City Royals* (Dallas: Taylor, 1992), 139–40. See also Sid Bordman, "A Plunge, An Unveiling, A Soaking," *Kansas City Star,* October 3, 1976, 1S–2S.

20. Ron Bergman, "The A's Sad Finish," *Oakland Tribune,* October 4, 1976, EE19; Dave Newhouse, "A's Lose, Hand KC Flag," *Oakland Tribune,* October 2, 1976, 31E. See also "Last Time in A's Uniform?" *Oakland Tribune,* October 4, 1976, EE1.

21. George Koppe, "Baseball Town Turns into Heartbreak City," *Kansas City Times,* October 15, 1976, 6C.

22. Joe McGuff, "It's Good-by Forever to 22nd and Brooklyn," *Kansas City Star,* October 5, 1972, 33; Joe McGuff, "Royals Are Best in West," in *Official Baseball Guide for 1977* (St. Louis, Mo.: Sporting News, 1977), 159.

23. Rick Montgomery and Shirl Kasper, *Kansas City: An American Story* (Kansas City, Mo.: Kansas City Star Books, 1999), 310; Nancy Parks, "What's Doing in Kansas City, Missouri," *New York Times,* May 16, 1976, sec. 10, 11; Horace Sutton, "Kansas City: Better Than a Magic Lantern Show," *Saturday Review,* June 26, 1976, 14; "Kansas City: Shedding Its 'Cow Town' Image," *U.S. News and World Report,* April 5, 1976, 63; Rowe Findley, "Kansas City, Heartland U.S.A.," *National Geographic,* July 1976, 139.

24. "Down by the River Quay," *Kansas City Town Squire,* July 1972, 37. See also Charles Gray, "Blown Away," *Kansas City Star Magazine,* February 17, 2002, 11–16.

25. Jim Bouton, *Ball Four* (New York: Dell, 1971), 226. See also Frank R. Hayde, *The Mafia and the Machine: The Story of the Kansas City Mob* (Fort Lee, N.J.: Barricade, 2007), 148–61; Brian Tuohy, *Larceny Games: Sports Gambling, Game Fixing and the FBI* (Port Townsend, Wash.: Feral House, 2013), 312–23.

26. James R. Shortridge, *Kansas City and How it Grew, 1822–2011* (Lawrence: University Press of Kansas, 2012), 117. See also Montgomery and Kasper, *Kansas City.*

27. Joe McGuff, "The Bad Ending Just Won't Go Away," *Kansas City Star,* October 5, 1976, 17.

28. Blair Kerkhoff, "In 1973, George Brett Arrived at a Championship Clubhouse in the Making," *Kansas City Star,* July 30, 2013. See also Bob Fowler, "One Misplay . . . Could It Wreck Brye's Career?" *Sporting News,* October 23, 1976, 34.

29. Del Black, "Bitterness at the End," *Kansas City Times,* October 4, 1976, 1D.

30. John Matuszak with Steve Delsohn, *Cruisin' with the Tooz* (New York: Charter, 1988), 139; Wells Twombly, "For Blanda, It's on to the Hall of Fame," *San Francisco Examiner,* August 25, 1976, 51, 53. Although John Matuszak thrived with the Raiders, he never would be able to shake his demons entirely; he died in

1989 at age thirty-eight of an accidental drug overdose. See Richmond, *Badasses,* 279–87.

31. Richmond, *Badasses,* 288; "1976 Oakland Raiders," *America's Game.*

32. Peter Clark, "Raiders Play Santa Claus for Ecstatic Fans," *Oakland Tribune,* December 27, 1976, EE36; Peter Clark, "Raiders' Atkinson Man of Hour," *Oakland Tribune,* December 27, 1976, EE3. After the Raiders won the Super Bowl, Al Davis complained that the NFL had not allocated enough tickets for Oakland fans; it was part of Davis's long-running grudge against the league and commissioner Pete Rozelle. See Mark Ribowsky, *Slick: The Silver and Black Life of Al Davis* (New York: Macmillan, 1991), 264–65.

33. Jim Murray, "The Hip and the Square," *Los Angeles Times,* January 7, 1977, pt. III, p. 1; "A Crowning Glory," NFL Films, 1977, available at https://www.youtube .com/watch?v=6IZisq8q2mE. See also "1976 Oakland Raiders," *America's Game.*

34. Lowell Reidenbaugh, "Big-Victory Raiders Muzzle Their Critics," *Sporting News,* January 22, 1977, 20. See also Ken Stabler and Barry Stainback, *Snake* (Garden City, N.Y.: Doubleday, 1986), 132–33; Bill Richardson, "Misfortune Dogs Unlucky Chiefs," *Sporting News,* September 4, 1976, 60; Richmond, *Badasses,* 321–36.

35. Joseph W. Knowland, "Tribune Editorial," *Oakland Tribune,* January 10, 1977, 1.

36. Jonathan Friendly, "Red Ink Plagues Revamped Coast Newspaper," *New York Times,* July 18, 1982, 14. See also Gayle B. Montgomery and James W. Johnson, *One Step from the White House: The Rise and Fall of Senator William F. Knowland* (Berkeley: University of California Press, 1998), 278–307; Wallace Turner, "Editor Purchases Oakland Tribune," *New York Times,* May 1, 1983, A33.

37. Ishmael Reed, *Blues City: A Walk in Oakland* (New York: Crown Journeys, 2003), 19. See also Wallace Turner, "Blacks Come to Power in Oakland and Whites' Fears Fade," *New York Times,* November 10, 1979, 9; "Hundreds at City Center Plaza Rites," *Oakland Tribune,* October 16, 1976, 2E; "Waterfront Shop Complex Affords Special Environment," *Architectural Record,* April 1976, 126–28; Elaine Brown, *A Taste of Power* (New York: Pantheon, 1992), 417–36.

38. "Black Educator's Angry Message," *San Francisco Chronicle,* March 21, 1973, 4; John P. Spencer, *In the Crossfire: Marcus Foster and the Troubled History of American School Reform* (Philadelphia: University of Pennsylvania Press, 2012), 199.

39. Marcus A. Foster, "Schools Are Improving" (letter to the editor), *Oakland Tribune,* April 3, 1973, 16. See also Spencer, *In the Crossfire,* 217–19.

40. Spencer, *In the Crossfire,* 220–22. Over the next year and a half, Hearst declared allegiance to her kidnappers and became a fugitive. At one point, she was surreptitiously assisted by Jack Scott, the founder of the Bay Area's Institute for the Study of Sport and Society, where former football player Dave Meggyesy

had written his exposé of the NFL. As something of a radical in his views toward sports, Scott also was sympathetic toward the radical left; in addition, he saw himself as a journalist and believed that Hearst would make for a marketable story. In the end, Hearst was arrested, with most of the rest of the SLA ending up either jailed or killed, while Scott avoided prosecution. See Jeffrey Toobin, *American Heiress: The Wild Saga of the Kidnapping, Crimes and Trial of Patty Hearst* (New York: Doubleday, 2016).

41. Spencer, *In the Crossfire*, 15, 224.

42. "1976 Oakland Raiders," *America's Game;* Stabler and Stainback, *Snake,* 2. See also Bryan Burwell, *Madden: A Biography* (Chicago: Triumph Books, 2011), 148–52.

43. "1976 Oakland Raiders," *America's Game;* Baron Wolman and Steve Cassady, *Oakland Raiders: The Good Guys* (Mill Valley, Calif.: Squarebooks, 1975), 34; Jack Tatum with Bill Kushner, *Final Confessions of NFL Assassin Jack Tatum* (Coal Valley, Ill.: Quality Sports, 1996), 17.

44. Bob Valli, "Steelers Talk About Hard-Hitting Game," *Oakland Tribune,* January 5, 1976, EE37; Bob Valli, "Swann Fears for His Life," *Oakland Tribune,* September 13, 1976, EE23, EE26; "Noll Wants Headhunting Review," *Oakland Tribune,* September 14, 1976, EE31.

45. Tom LaMarre, "Atkinson Feels No Remorse for Swann," *Oakland Tribune,* September 15, 1976, EE 39; William Oscar Johnson, "A Walk on the Sordid Side," *Sports Illustrated,* August 1, 1977, available at https://www.si.com/vault. See also Richmond, *Badasses,* 275–79.

46. Frank Deford, "Champagne, Roses and Donuts," *Sports Illustrated,* December 10, 1979, available at https://www.si.com/vault. See also Johnson, "A Walk on the Sordid Side"; Richmond, *Badasses,* 189–211, 275–79.

47. Tatum with Kushner, *Final Confessions,* 327; Ed Levitt, "Accent on Sports," *Oakland Tribune,* September 15, 1976, EE39.

48. Jim Otto and Dave Newhouse, *Jim Otto: The Pain of Glory* (Champaign, Ill.: Sports Publishing, 1999), 3; Terence Moore, "Former Raiders Face Dark Days," *Sports on Earth,* August 17, 2017, available at http://www.sportsonearth.com/article/249001682/oakland-raiders-henry-lawrence-nfl-health.

49. Mark Fainaru-Wada and Steve Fainaru, *League of Denial: The NFL, Concussions, and the Battle for Truth* (New York: Crown Archetype, 2013), 6.

50. Michael Oriard, *The End of Autumn* (Urbana: University of Illinois Press, 2009), 275; Dave Anderson, "The Tragedy of Jim Tyrer," *New York Times,* September 18, 1980, B17; Ken Denlinger, "Tyrer Tragedy: No Coping with Mortality," *Washington Post,* September 21, 1980, F1. See also Aimee Ortiz, "Learn the Symptoms in the Four Stages of CTE," *Boston Globe,* September 21, 2017, available at https://www.bostonglobe.com.

51. Mike Garrett, "Oh, Lord, Deliver Me—for Ceasar Belser's Near," *Kansas City*

Town Squire, December 1969, 10; Terez A. Paylor, "Former Chiefs Safety Ceasar Belser Dies, Will Have Brain Donated to Science," *Kansas City Star*, March 7, 2016, available at http://www.kansascity.com; Otis Taylor with Mark Stallard, *Otis Taylor: The Need to Win* (Champaign, Ill.: Sports Publishing, 2003), 154; Vahe Gregorian, "Bedridden and on Feeding Tube, Former Chiefs Great Otis Taylor Is Cared for by Loving Sister," *Kansas City Star*, February 12, 2016, available at http://www.kansascity.com. At least one former Chief seemed to escape the worst effects of long-term head trauma. After suffering a near-fatal concussion during his rookie season, linebacker Willie Lanier perfected tackling without risking his head. See William C. Rhoden, "Choosing Bearhugs over Big Hits," *New York Times*, October 23, 2010, available at https://nyti.ms/2s0PtHm.

52. Stabler and Stainback, *Snake*, 229; Moore, "Former Raiders Face Dark Days"; Elliott Almond, "Former Raiders All-Pro George Atkinson Struggles for Normalcy as His Mind Deteriorates," *Mercury News* (San Jose, Calif.), April 16, 2016, available at https://www.mercurynews.com. See also John Branch, "Ken Stabler, a Magnetic N.F.L. Star, Was Sapped of Spirit by C.T.E.," *New York Times*, February 3, 2016, available at https://nyti.ms/1KWOr1G.

53. Almond, "Former Raiders All-Pro George Atkinson"; Ken Belson, "Football's True Believers Circle the Wagons and Insist the Sport Is Just Fine," *New York Times*, January 30, 2018, available at https://nyti.ms/2GsPeN4. See also Joe Ward, Josh Williams, and Sam Manchester, "110 N.F.L. Brains," *New York Times*, July 25, 2017, available at https://nyti.ms/2tGP9To; Fainaru-Wada and Fainaru, *League of Denial*.

Conclusion

1. See Bowie Kuhn, *Hardball: The Education of a Baseball Commissioner* (New York: TimesBooks, 1987), 244–52; G. Michael Green and Roger D. Launius, *Charlie Finley: The Outrageous Story of Baseball's Super Showman* (New York: Walker and Company, 2010), Kindle edition, chap. 11.

2. "New Group Seeks to Purchase A's," *Indianapolis Star*, March 9, 1979, 42. See also Tom Weir, "A's Sale Talks Termed 'Amicable'," *Sporting News*, October 7, 1978, 30.

3. Ron Fimrite, "They're Just Mad about Charlie," *Sports Illustrated*, May 21, 1979, available at https://www.si.com/vault. See also Green and Launius, *Charlie Finley*, chap. 12; Jason Turbow, *Dynastic, Bombastic, Fantastic: Reggie, Rollie, Catfish, and Charlie Finley's Swingin' A's* (Boston: Houghton Mifflin Harcourt, 2017), Kindle edition, chap. 17.

4. Green and Launius, *Charlie Finley*, chap. 12. See also Kuhn, *Hardball*, 252–58.

5. Kuhn, *Hardball*, 254.

6. Mark Ribowsky, *Slick: The Silver and Black Life of Al Davis* (New York:

Macmillan, 1991), 279. See also Frank Deford, "A City of Complexes," *Sports Illustrated,* April 1, 1968, available at http://www.si.com/vault.

7. Michael MacCambridge, *America's Game: The Epic Story of How Pro Football Captured a Nation* (New York: Random House, 2004), 345.

8. Ribowsky, *Slick,* 283–85. See also MacCambridge, *America's Game,* 343–47; Charles C. Euchner, *Playing the Field: Why Sports Teams Move and Cities Fight to Keep Them* (Baltimore: Johns Hopkins University Press, 1993), 79–101.

9. Maria J. Veri, "Sons of Oakland: The Raiders and the Raz/Rais(ing) of a City," in *San Francisco Bay Area Sports: Golden Gate Athletics, Recreation, and Community,* ed. Rita Liberti and Maureen M. Smith (Fayetteville: University of Arkansas Press, 2017), 218; Peter Clark, "Raiders' Atkinson Man of Hour," *Oakland Tribune,* December 27, 1976, EE3. See also Euchner, *Playing the Field,* 92–96.

10. See Ribowsky, *Slick,* 284–85, 294–300; MacCambridge, *America's Game,* 345–47.

11. Ribowsky, *Slick,* 307. See also William Oscar Johnson, "A Walk on the Sordid Side," *Sports Illustrated,* August 1, 1977, available at https://www.si.com/vault.

12. Euchner, *Playing the Field,* 80. See also MacCambridge, *America's Game,* 347.

13. See Jim Miller and Kelly Mayhew, *Better to Reign in Hell: Inside the Raiders Fan Empire* (New York: New Press, 2005), Kindle edition, introduction.

14. For an overview of the Royals-Yankees rivalry, see Filip Bondy, *The Pine Tar Game: The Kansas City Royals, the New York Yankees, and Baseball's Most Absurd and Entertaining Controversy* (New York: Scribner, 2015).

15. "Marty's Crusade: Chiefs vs. Raiders in the 1990s," *Chiefs.com,* December 29, 2015, available at https://www.youtube.com/watch?v=AI0sU90HAh8.

16. See Michael Lewis, *Moneyball: The Art of Winning an Unfair Game* (New York: W.W. Norton, 2003). The A's' use of sabermetrics had begun in earnest under Sandy Alderson, Beane's predecessor as general manager.

17. Daniel Rosensweig, *Retro Ball Parks: Instant History, Baseball, and the New American City* (Knoxville: University of Tennessee Press, 2005), xi, 4, 9.

18. See Kevin Collison, "Stadium Proposal Backed—Former Champion of Downtown Park Endorses Measure," *Kansas City Star,* March 3, 2006, C1; Deann Smith and Jeffrey Spivak, "Safe at Home—Rolling Roof Rejected—At Least for Now," *Kansas City Star,* April 5, 2006, A1. The idea of a building a downtown baseball park in Kansas City would be revived in 2017, although no definite plans were in place. See Steve Vockrodt, "Are Royals Headed to Downtown KC? City Starts Talks, Studies Four Sites," *Kansas City Star,* October 4, 2017, available at http://www.kansascity.com.

19. Randy Covitz, "A Storied History Amid Hoopla—Kemper 'Had Its Ups and Downs,'" *Kansas City Star,* March 13, 2005, A1.

20. Lynn Horsley, "New Downtown Arena on the Way: 'A Turning Point' for KC, Barnes Says," *Kansas City Star,* August 4, 2004, A1. See also Keith Schneider, "Welcome to the Neighborhood: America's Sports Stadiums Are Moving Downtown," *New York Times,* January 19, 2018, available at https://nyti.ms/2FSHOT8; Lisa Rodriguez, "Kansas City to Sell Kemper Arena to Foutch Brothers for $1," *KCUR.org,* February 16, 2017, available at http://kcur.org. Kansas City also became home to a Major League Soccer franchise in the 1990s. The team—known by 2011 as Sporting Kansas City—would win two MLS championships by 2018. The team also would play in a new stadium called Children's Mercy Park in Kansas City, Kansas; the stadium was located across the state line after plans fell through to build it on the site of a demolished shopping mall in Kansas City, Missouri. See James R. Shortridge, *Kansas City and How it Grew, 1822–2011* (Lawrence: University Press of Kansas, 2012), 162–63.

21. See Robert Gammon, "Coliseum Arena Finds No Sponsor—Firms Unwilling to Pay for Naming Rights," *Oakland Tribune,* July 26, 2002; Matthew Artz and Chris De Benedetti, "Mayor Libby Schaaf Says Warriors Departure Wouldn't Doom Oracle Arena," *Oakland Tribune,* March 13, 2015.

22. Angela Woodall, "Oakland's O.Co Old and Gray but Still Beloved," *Mercury News* (San Jose, Calif.), March 31, 2012, available at http://www.mercury news.com. See also "New Ballpark Key to Keeping A's in Oakland," *Oakland Tribune,* February 6, 2005; "Oakland Ballpark," *Wikipedia.org,* available at https://en.wikipedia.org.

23. Ashley A. Smith, "Saying No to the Majors," *InsideHigherEd.com,* December 7, 2017, available at https://www.insidehighered.com/news/2017/12/07/peralta-community-college-rejects-oakland-offer-new-ballpark; "Oakland Ballpark"; Kevin Draper, "The Oakland A's Are Trying to Solve Their Stadium Problem. Still," *New York Times,* September 12, 2017, available at https://www.nytimes.com.

24. See "Oakland Raiders Relocation to Las Vegas," *Wikipedia.org,* available at https://en.wikipedia.org; Phil Matier and Andy Ross, "Outline Emerges of Oakland Stadium Deal to Keep Raiders," *San Francisco Chronicle,* November 30, 2016, available at https://www.sfgate.com; Ken Belson and Victor Mather, "Raiders Leaving Oakland Again, This Time for Las Vegas," *New York Times,* March 27, 2017, available at https://nyti.ms/2nFrhLL.

25. Belson and Mather, "Raiders Leaving Oakland Again"; Ken Belson, "With Raiders' Move, N.F.L. Owners Go Where the Money Is," *New York Times,* March 28, 2017, available at https://nyti.ms/2nK9cft.

26. "The Origin of the Chiefs-Raiders Rivalry," *Chiefs.com,* 2016, available at https://www.youtube.com/watch?v=jcKy7nLzURc.

27. As of 2019, the Hall of Famers included Fred Biletnikoff, George Blanda, Willie Brown, Dave Casper, Ray Guy, Ted Hendricks, Jim Otto, Art Shell, Ken Stabler, and Gene Upshaw of the Raiders; Bobby Bell, Buck Buchanan, Curley

Culp, Len Dawson, Willie Lanier, Johnny Robinson, Jan Stenerud, and Emmitt Thomas of the Chiefs; Rollie Fingers, Catfish Hunter, and Reggie Jackson of the A's; and George Brett of the Royals. Additional Hall of Famers included owners Al Davis and Lamar Hunt, coaches John Madden and Hank Stram, and managers Whitey Herzog and Dick Williams.

28. Jon C. Teaford, *The Metropolitan Revolution: The Rise of Post-Urban America* (New York: Columbia University Press, 2006), 91. See also Gene Burd, "The Selling of the Sunbelt: Civic Boosterism in the Media," in *The Rise of the Sunbelt Cities,* ed. David C. Perry and Alfred J. Watkins (Beverly Hills, Calif.: Sage, 1977), 129–49.

29. Michael N. Danielson, *Home Team: Professional Sports and the American Metropolis* (Princeton, N.J.: Princeton University Press, 1997), 8.

30. Ken Stabler and Barry Stainback, *Snake* (Garden City, N.Y.: Doubleday, 1986), 229.

31. Michael Oriard, *Brand NFL* (Chapel Hill: University of North Carolina Press, 2007), 88, 94.

32. Ernest Mehl, "A's Ills Linked to Front Office Interference," *Kansas City Star,* August 17, 1961, 2; Robert A. Baade and Richard F. Dye, "The Impact of Stadiums and Professional Sports on Metropolitan Area Development," *Growth and Change* 21.2 (1990): 10, 12; Veri, "Sons of Oakland," 219.

33. John Krich, *Bump City: Winners and Losers in Oakland* (Berkeley, Calif.: City Miner Books, 1979), 103.

34. Thomas J. Bogdon, "Forum for Arena Views," *Kansas City Times,* April 25, 1972, 8; Belson and Mather, "Raiders Leaving Oakland Again."

35. Glen Gendzel, "Competitive Boosterism: How Milwaukee Lost the Braves," *Business History Review* 69 (Winter 1995): 531; Ray Brewer, "With Move Approved, It's Time to Welcome Raiders with Open Arms," *Las Vegas Sun,* March 28, 2017.

36. Harry Edwards, *The Revolt of the Black Athlete,* 50th anniversary ed. (Urbana: University of Illinois Press, 2017), 161. See also Etan Thomas, *We Matter: Athletes and Activism* (Brooklyn, N.Y.: Edge of Sports/Akashic Books, 2018); Matthew Futterman and Victor Mather, "Trump Supports N.F.L.'s New National Anthem Policy," *New York Times,* May 23, 2018, available at https://nyti .ms/2GMnT7O; Ken Belson, "Football's True Believers Circle the Wagons and Insist the Sport Is Just Fine," *New York Times,* January 30, 2018, available at https://nyti.ms/2GsPeN4.

37. Mark S. Rosentraub, *Reversing Urban Decline: Why and How Sports, Entertainment, and Culture Turns Cities into Major League Winners,* 2nd ed. (Boca Raton, Fla.: CRC Press, 2014), xv–xvi, 335; Bill Turque, "KC Sits on $1.5 Billion in Debt. How Will It Pay for Services, Meet Pension Promises?" *Kansas City Star,* January 26, 2018.

38. Smith, "Saying No to the Majors"; Michael Powell, "The N.F.L. and the Business of Ripping Out the Heart of Oakland," *New York Times,* March 27, 2017, available at https://nyti.ms/2nGqMkB; Marcus Thompson II, "Could This Deal Be Better for Oakland in the Long Run?" *East Bay Times,* March 28, 2017, 1A. See also David DeBolt, "Oakland: Downtown Grows Up with New Residential Towers, But Who Will Afford Them?" *Mercury News* (San Jose, Calif.), March 16, 2017, available at http://www.mercurynews.com; Sam Levin, "Oakland Jogger Caught on Video Tossing Homeless Man's Belongings in Lake," *The Guardian,* June 11, 2018, available at https://www.theguardian.com; Matier and Ross, "Outline Emerges of Oakland Stadium Deal."

39. MacCambridge, *America's Game,* 342.

40. "1969 Kansas City Chiefs," *America's Game: The Super Bowl Champions,* NFL Films, 2006; Joseph W. Knowland, "Tribune Editorial," *Oakland Tribune,* January 10, 1977, 1; "A City United," *Kansas City Star,* November 4, 2015, 1. See also Krich, *Bump City,* 98–103.

41. Boyarsky, *Backroom Politics,* 196. See also Warren Hinckle, "Metropoly: The Story of Oakland, California," *Ramparts,* February 1966, available at http://www.cwmorse.org/metropoly-the-story-of-oakland-california/.

42. See Blair Kerkhoff, "Kansas City Got a Second Chance at the Majors, and Made It Work," *Kansas City Star,* February 15, 2018, available at http://www.kansascity.com.

43. *Rebels of Oakland,* HBO Sports, 2003, Paley Center for Media, New York City; Sid Bordman, "Title of Mr. Baseball Fits Ewing Kauffman," *Kansas City Times,* January 26, 1976, 1C.

44. Joe Posnanski, "The Good Fight—Newspaper Legend Battled Hard to Make KC a Major-League City," *Kansas City Star,* February 6, 2006, C1. In Oakland, sports editor George Ross played a role similar to McGuff's. See Dave Newhouse, "George Ross, Storied Tribune Editor, Oakland Sports Booster, Dies at 98," *Oakland Tribune,* October 7, 2015.

Index

Page numbers in *italics* refer to photographs.

Wells, Warren, 58, 99, 110
West Oakland, 49, 51, 60, 73, 83, 131
Wheeler, Charles, 80–81, 102–4, 108
white flight, 118–21, 175. *See also* suburbanization
White, Frank, 134, 135, 166
White, Gladys, 134
Wiggin, Paul, 139, 149–50
Williams, Dick, 84–85, 86, 90, 123–27, 219–20n27
Williams, John, 130
Williamson, Fred, 56–57, 58, 61
Wilson, Jerrel, 50

Wilson, Lionel, 153, 164, 165
Wilson, Nemiah, 8
Wolf, Ron, 58
Wolfpack (Kansas City fan group), 7, 56
World Football League (WFL), 114, 116
Wright, Elmo, 98–99

Yankee Stadium (New York), 24, 39
Yawkey, Tom, 45–46
Youell, Frank, 36–37. *See also* Frank Youell Field (Oakland)
Young, Dick, 86, 133–34, 200–201n34

MATTHEW C. EHRLICH is a professor emeritus of journalism at the University of Illinois at Urbana-Champaign. His books include *Heroes and Scoundrels: The Image of the Journalist in Popular Culture* and *Radio Utopia: Postwar Audio Documentary in the Public Interest*.

Sport and Society

Cold War Games: Propaganda, the Olympics, and U.S. Foreign Policy
    Toby C. Rider
Game Faces: Sport Celebrity and the Laws of Reputation   *Sarah K. Fields*
The Rise and Fall of Olympic Amateurism   *Matthew P. Llewellyn and
    John Gleaves*
Bloomer Girls: Women Baseball Pioneers   *Debra A. Shattuck*
I Fight for a Living: Boxing and the Battle for Black Manhood, 1880–1915
    Louis Moore
The Revolt of the Black Athlete: 50th Anniversary Edition   *Harry Edwards*
Pigskin Nation: How the NFL Remade American Politics   *Jesse Berrett*
Hockey: A Global History   *Stephen Hardy and Andrew C. Holman*
Baseball: A History of America's Game   *Benjamin G. Rader*
Kansas City vs. Oakland: The Bitter Sports Rivalry That Defined an Era
    Matthew C. Ehrlich

REPRINT EDITIONS

The Nazi Olympics   *Richard D. Mandell*
Sports in the Western World (2d ed.)   *William J. Baker*
Jesse Owens: An American Life   *William J. Baker*

The University of Illinois Press
is a founding member of the
Association of University Presses.

———————————————

Designed by Jim Proefrock
Composed in 11.25/14 Adobe Minion Pro
with DIN 1451 display
at the University of Illinois Press
Manufactured by Sheridan Books, Inc.

University of Illinois Press
1325 South Oak Street
Champaign, IL 61820-6903
www.press.uillinois.edu